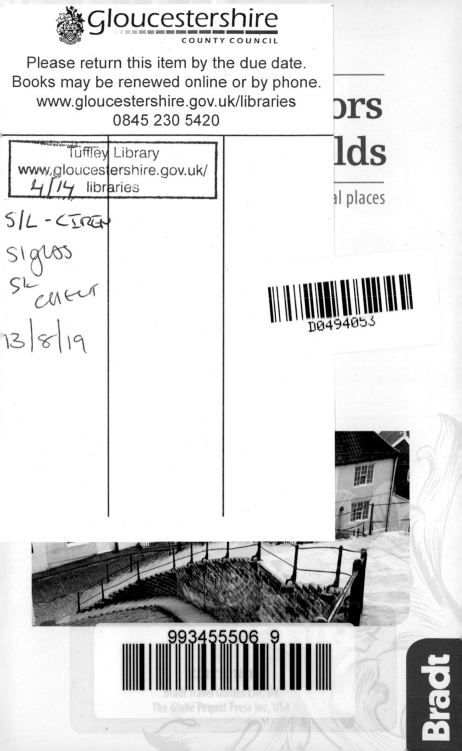

ors
lds

al places

D0494053

993455506 9

Bradt

Bradt Travel Guides Ltd, UK
The Globe Pequot Press Inc, USA

North York Moors & Yorkshire Wolds

*Taking 'the road less travelled' is simple here.
Leave the road altogether and visit the hidden corners
of northeast Yorkshire by train, bike, boat or on foot,
and you will be sure to see the best of the region.*

1 The White Horse of Kilburn, a symbol of the Hambleton Hills. (MKP/A) **2** Sightseers prepare to view Flamborough Head from the deck of a traditional wooden coble. (VHEY) **3** Mountain biking on one of Dalby Forest's many purpose-built tracks. (JS/A) **4** One of the region's farmers' markets: no middle men here, just local food straight from the producer. (VHEY) **5** Canoeing on the River Esk near Whitby: travel doesn't get any more sustainable than this. (MB) **6** The North Yorkshire Moors Railway snakes through the forests of Newtondale. (NYMR)

NATURAL ATTRACTIONS

North and East Yorkshire are very rural counties with more than their fair share of space, peace and quiet. Lack of industrial development has resulted in clean air and rivers, as well as a rich array of wildlife.

1 One of many wooded valleys tucked into the folds of the North York Moors. (NYMNPA/CP)
2 The Cleveland Way long-distance footpath. (SS) 3 Sundew, a rare insectivorous plant found in moorland bogs. (MB) 4 Cotton grass carpets the Moors in high summer. (MB) 5 Eller Beck leaps over a rock ledge near Beck Hole, forming Thomason Foss waterfall. (NYMNPA/MN)
6 The Bridestones near Dalby Forest, a series of weathered sandstone pinnacles. (NYMNPA/RJBP)
7 Salmon have made a recent return to the River Ouse. (S/V) 8 A red grouse hides among the heather, its main source of food. (AP/FLPA) 9 A Wolds barn owl with artist and conservationist Robert Fuller. (YP) 10 The North York Moors is one of the strongholds of the adder. (DO/FLPA)

People have lived in northeast Yorkshire since the last ice age. Their legacies remain in the region's rich archaeological remains, works of art and scattering of magnificent old buildings.

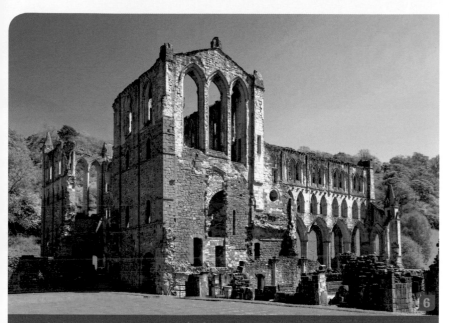

1 Castle Howard in all its Georgian splendour. (s/sh) 2 John Bunting's haunting sculptures in his old workshop at Scotch Corner chapel. (mb) 3 Modern artisans still carve Robert 'Mouseman' Thompson's signature beastie in his home village of Kilburn. (rtc) 4 The World of James Herriot in Thirsk remembers the life and times of that famous vet. (wjh) 5 Simpler days are celebrated at the Ryedale Folk Museum. (nymnpa/tp) 6 Cistercian monks left their legacy in the stones of Rievaulx Abbey near Helmsley. (s/jw) 7 Reflected in its own monastery fish pond, Whitby Abbey teeters on the cliff edge and looks over the town. (mb) 8 At 25ft high, the Rudston Monolith is the tallest standing stone in Britain. (ss/a)

We're 40...
how did that happen?

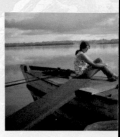

How did it all happen? George (my then husband) and I wrote the first Bradt guide – about hiking in Peru and Bolivia – on an Amazon river barge, and typed it up on a borrowed typewriter. We had no money for the next two books so George went to work for a printer and was paid in books rather than money.

Forty years on, Bradt publishes over 200 titles that sell all over the world. I still suffer from Imposter Syndrome – how did it all happen? I hadn't even worked in an office before! Well, I've been extraordinarily lucky with the people around me. George provided the belief to get us started (and the mother to run our US office). Then, in 1977, I recruited a helper, Janet Mears, who is still working for us. She and the many dedicated staff who followed have been the foundations on which the company is built. But the bricks and mortar have been our authors and readers. Without them there would be no Bradt Travel Guides. Thank you all for making it happen.

Hilary Bradt

AUTHOR

Mike Bagshaw is a Lancastrian by birth and a zoologist by training. After four years as a student in Sheffield he qualified as a biology teacher and has taught full-time ever since. Initially this took place indoors in school classrooms, but since 1987 he has worked in outdoor education centres, introducing children and adults to the delights of water-sports, mountaineering, forest education and how to understand and appreciate the natural world.

In his spare time he has travelled the wild places of the world as a naturalist and explorer, often in a canoe or kayak, and written about his experiences for outdoor magazines. He contributes monthly nature columns to local newspapers and has had a book of poetry published.

CONTRIBUTING AUTHOR

Caroline Mills, author of the York chapter, is a freelance writer of travel guides including the Bradt guide *Slow Cotswolds*, and contributes to various national magazines on travel, food and gardens. Though not officially of Yorkshire stock, she has many family connections with the county she classes as her second 'home'. Having lived in York, she returns to North Yorkshire regularly. Caroline writes, 'It has been great to return "home" for this guide. When you live in an area, it's easy to take your surroundings for granted and stop exploring. Returning to Yorkshire, I've visited with a fresh pair of eyes and have been able to talk with residents about places they didn't know were on their doorstep.'

First edition published March 2014
Bradt Travel Guides Ltd
IDC House, The Vale, Chalfont St Peter, Bucks SL9 9RZ, England
www.bradtguides.com
Print edition published in the USA by The Globe Pequot Press Inc,
PO Box 480, Guilford, Connecticut 06437-0480

Text copyright © 2014 Bradt Travel Guides Ltd
Maps copyright © 2014 Bradt Travel Guides Ltd
Photographs copyright © 2014 Individual photographers (see page 197)
Series Editor: Tim Locke
Project Managers: Anna Moores, Maisie Fitzpatrick & Laura Pidgley
Series Design: Pepi Bluck, Perfect Picture
Cover research: Pepi Bluck, Perfect Picture

ISBN: 978 1 84162 548 5 (print)
e-ISBN: 978 1 84162 851 6 (e-pub)
e-ISBN: 978 1 84162 847 9 (mobi)

British Library Cataloguing in Publication Data
A catalogue record for this book is available from the British Library

Front cover image Fryup Dale moor, North York Moors National Park (F/AF)
Back cover image Robin Hood's Bay (J/D)
Title page image 199 steps, Whitby (SS)

Photographers
See page 197 for details.

Maps Pepi Bluck, Perfect Picture & David McCutcheon FBCart.S
Typeset from the author's disc by Chris Lane, Artinfusion
Production managed by Jellyfish Print Solutions; printed in the UK
Digital conversion by the Firsty Group

ACKNOWLEDGEMENTS

A big thank you goes to all those people that have helped me with this book. All those Yorkshire contributors who shared a little of their lives and passions and allowed me to quote them; Caroline Mills for contributing a chapter of writing; and everyone in the Bradt team, especially Tim Locke for being so professional and patient.

DEDICATION

To my Dad, Harry (1928–2013) who first brought me to Whitby all those years ago.

Mike Bagshaw

AUTHOR'S STORY

On the face of it, a Lancastrian 'townie' writing about rural Yorkshire is an unusual phenomenon, but the truth is that I have spent more of my life in this adopted county than in the one of my birth.

My first experience of Yorkshire, a seaside holiday to Whitby in the late 1960s, was a shocking one; for a ten-year-old boy used to the Gulf Stream waters of Wales, swimming in the North Sea came as a very rude awakening.

Fast forward three or four years and I am back over the border again, this time on the other side of the county in Dentdale, where we teenagers enjoyed many residential stays in the school's country cottage. With hindsight, those first exposures to real country life – windswept hills, clean rivers and undisturbed wildlife – were life-changing experiences, for which I am eternally grateful.

Following that initial love affair with the Yorkshire Dales, I have revisited every

Easter since, accompanied by a handful of like-minded school friends, and during that time we reckon to have visited just about every hill-top and decent pub available. That, coupled with my 25 years living and working in the North York Moors, led me to believe that I knew pretty much all there was to know about North Yorkshire. How wrong I was.

The very welcome opportunity to write this guide has allowed me to see familiar places in a new light, and discover corners that for years I had unwittingly missed. It also gave me the incentive to go and do some of those things that I'd always promised myself, like kayaking under the bird cliffs at Flamborough or walking a long-distance trail like the Yorkshire Wolds Way. Best of all, it's rekindled my desire to go out exploring again, and see what else I might have missed in this wonderfully varied county.

Suggested places to base yourself

These bases make ideal starting points for exploring localities the Slow way.

Durham

MIDDLESBOROUGH

Loftus

GREAT AYTON page 20
Childhood home of Captain James Cook, with great moorland walking from the doorstep. Linked by a scenic railway to the Esk Valley and Whitby.

Guisborough

Great Ayton

CHAPTER 2

Tees

A172

NORTH YORK MOORS

CHAPTER 1

A167

Swale

Northallerton

A168

A19

HAMBLETON HILLS

A170

Helmsley

THIRSK page 27
A bustling market town 15 minutes by train from York and in the shadow of the Hambleton Hills.

A167

Thirsk

A1

Ure

Skipton-on-Swale

North Yorkshire

CHAPTER 4

Ripon

A1(M)

A19

HELMSLEY page 31
A small, genteel town nestled between the North York Moors and Howardian Hills. Perfectly placed to visit nearby castles, stately homes and abbeys.

Boroughbridge

A61

A168

Nidd

Knaresborough

A59

A59

HARROGATE

YORK

Wetherby

CHAPTER 6

BRADFORD

LEEDS

Selby

West Yorkshire

Wharfe

A19

M62

A1

A1(M)

CASTLEFORD

Don

M18

YORK page 173
History and culture at every turn. The home base of choice for the Slow urbanite.

POCKLINGTON page 155
Slow market town that specialises in relaxing watersides — along the canal and by the lily ponds of Burnham Hall. The best of the Yorkshire Wolds is right on the doorstep.

WHITBY page 60
Cliffs, beaches and history – a mini York by the sea with easy access to the wilds of the North York Moors National Park.

N

0   10 miles
0   10 km

NORTH SEA

A174

Whitby

A171

North Yorkshire
Moors Railway

CHAPTER 3

Scalby

SCARBOROUGH

A169

ickering

Derwent

Filey

A64

alton

**East Riding
of Yorkshire**

A165

A164

Bridlington

Bridlington
Bay

A166

CHAPTER 5

Driffield

ocklington

A1079

Hornsea

Market Weighton

A165

Beverley

Cottingham

**KINGSTON
UPON HULL**

A62

A63

Hessle

A1033

Barton-upon
-Humber

Humber

A15

Lincolnshire

GRIMSBY

PICKERING page 81
William the Conqueror's own personal castle lords it over this friendly market town. The North Yorkshire Moors steam railway links it to the moors and coast and Dalby Forest is just a short cycle ride away.

FILEY page 107
A peaceful seaside resort with the bright lights of Scarborough 20 minutes away by train – who needs it though when you have the longest beach in North Yorkshire. A stone's throw from Flamborough Head and the rest of the Yorkshire Wolds.

MALTON page 138
A proud and traditional riverside market town at the foot of the Wolds and in sight of the North York Moors and Howardian Hills. Good train and bus links to almost everywhere in this book.

BEVERLEY page 150
The Wolds are on the doorstep of this genteel, quiet and civilized little town but so is the bustling city of Hull (a mere 15 minutes away by train). If you want the history and culture of York but without the crowds then Beverley is for you.

CONTENTS

THE NORTH YORK MOORS & WOLDS

North Yorkshire is England's largest county, and an astonishingly diverse region. Over 100 miles separate the lofty peaks of the Pennine west from the sea-cliffs and sandy strands of the east, with pastoral limestone dales, rich farmland and rolling heather moors nestled in between. In the first edition of this book, which appeared as *Slow North Yorkshire*, I attempted to cover most of the county in one volume. A Slow appraisal of a place shouldn't skim, but needs to look at the detail, so inevitably some very deserving places didn't make it in.

For this new, more focused guide, the western side of the county has been dealt with separately in *Slow Yorkshire Dales*. There is no such place as northeast Yorkshire, but if it did exist it would be the subject of this book, comprising the North York Moors, the Howardian Hills and York itself. I could hardly leave out the county town, especially as it is also one of the most fascinating, historic and 'Slow' cities in the country.

Covering a smaller area has consequently allowed some new places to sneak into this volume. Last time, I couldn't resist including Flamborough Head, part of East Yorkshire, with the excuse that it was a very visible from North Yorkshire, and I like it. Geologically, Flamborough Head is part of the Yorkshire Wolds, so this time I have put it where it belongs and added a new chapter featuring the rest of the Wolds.

My old neighbour Frank, God rest his soul, led an extraordinary life, that many of us in this day and age could not imagine, not because of what he did, but for what he didn't do. During all of his 70-odd years, Frank never left Yorkshire, not a single step over the border for one minute. He was born on a farm in Goldsborough, near Whitby, worked there all his life and brought his family up in the house next door. In his spare time he played football and cricket for the village, and occasionally took exotic holidays – to a caravan on another farm in the Yorkshire Dales. When I asked Frank why he hadn't travelled more, his reply was that he had no need to, that Yorkshire was as good as anywhere else, and gave him all he wanted for a happy and contented life.

Frank and his beloved Goldsborough are not unique, and that's what makes North Yorkshire so special in the Slow stakes. While many places are rediscovering the value of the traditional, real and genuine, and renewing connections with their history and landscape, many corners of rural North Yorkshire never lost them in the first place. This old-fashionedness has attracted some good-natured humour, and not a little malicious ridicule in its time but, as far as I'm concerned (all the more so the older I get), it's an attribute rather than a fault.

So-called progress has brought us cheap, mass-produced goods sold in supermarkets the size of villages and even bigger shopping malls. Thankfully, a backlash is taking place, and rural North Yorkshire is at the forefront of the push to preserve those things that make places different, interesting and … well, real. Folk are fighting hard to keep their village shops open, promote locally produced, high-quality food and drink, and encourage their own artists and artisans. These are the special people – the brewers, potters, shop-keepers, fishermen, farmers, wood-carvers, butchers, bakers and candlestick makers – that have managed to capture a little of the essence of their corner of this singular county, and enable you to feel it, smell it, taste it or even take a little of it away with you.

I hope this book inspires you, not just to read about this corner of North Yorkshire, but to live it – to come and meet these people, spend some Slow time where they live and get to know it as they do.

Climb a few hills, stroll through the woods and meditate in a ruined abbey, eat a pork pie by the river from the village butchers and finish the day in an old stone pub, with a glass of your favourite tipple and a crackling fire to toast your feet on – I can think of worse ways of passing time. Maybe Frank had it right – why go anywhere else?

THE NORTH YORK MOORS NATIONAL PARK

When William Smith produced the first geological map of England, he was particularly fascinated by outcroppings of Jurassic rocks that run in a broad band from the Dorset coast, diagonally up the country to meet the sea again in North Yorkshire. Just before they disappear beneath the cold, grey waves of the North Sea, these rocks bulge up in a range of rolling, flat-topped hills.

The sandstone that capped these uplands produced a thin, acid soil that could only support sparse forest, which Bronze Age people found relatively easy to clear. This natural woodland has never returned, but

THE SLOW MINDSET

Hilary Bradt, Founder, Bradt Travel Guides

> We shall not cease from exploration
> And the end of all our exploring
> Will be to arrive where we started
> And know the place for the first time.
>
> T S Eliot 'Little Gidding', *Four Quartets*

This series evolved, slowly, from a Bradt editorial meeting when we started to explore ideas for guides to our favourite country – Great Britain. We wanted to get away from the usual 'top sights' formula and encourage our authors to bring out the nuances and local differences that make up a sense of place – such things as food, history, nature, geology, or local people and what makes them tick. So without our realising it at the time, we had defined 'Slow Travel', or at least our concept of it. For the beauty of the Slow movement is that there is no fixed definition; we adapt the philosophy to fit our individual needs and aspirations. Thus Carl Honoré, author of *In Praise of Slow*, writes: 'The Slow Movement is a cultural revolution against the notion that faster is always better. It's not about doing everything at a snail's pace, it's about seeking to do everything at the right speed. Savouring the hours and minutes rather than just counting them. Doing everything as well as possible, instead of as fast as possible. It's about quality over quantity in everything from work to food to parenting.' And travel.

So take time to explore. Don't rush it, get to know an area – and the people who live there – and you'll be as delighted as the authors by what you find.

hundreds of square miles of alien coniferous forest were planted in the 1930s. Although not popular with many naturalists and landscape purists, these woods are now maturing into a certain Scandinavian-style beauty, which I feel adds more to than it detracts from the character of the region. Certainly the Forestry Commission now comes across as a much more enlightened, visitor-friendly and Slow organisation than it has done in the past.

Across the rest of the hill tops, acid-tolerant **heather** has taken over, resulting in the largest uninterrupted expanse of heather moorland in England, with an abundance of Bronze Age settlement remains. The North York Moors (as in, moors north of the city of York, not moors in North Yorkshire) were designated as a national park in 1952, primarily to preserve this internationally important habitat (Britain has 70% of the world's heather moorland), its wildlife, and rich archaeology, both ancient and industrial, and the dramatic Heritage Coast, where the hills abruptly meet the sea.

The **National Park Authority** has a delicate balancing act to perform, working with the big grouse-shooting estates that actually own and maintain most of the moors, whilst opening up these glorious acres for visitors to enjoy. On the whole they do a magnificent job, especially in educating visitors about what you can see and do here, and giving practical help to get you out experiencing it.

They produce leaflets detailing a variety of **cycle** routes around the park, and similar help for **horseriding**, with a *Horse Riders' Guide to the North York Moors* and *Newtondale Horse Trail*, a guidebook to a 35-mile circular route specifically for horses.

If **walking** is your thing, then you will be very well looked after; the park provides free, downloadable walk leaflets, details of 15 routes accessible to wheelchair users and invaluable information regarding access to wild country. The right of access to open land, which became law in 2005, has been a welcome arrival for those of us that enjoy exploring our country's uplands; for lovers of the North York Moors it has been a revelation. This right means that you can walk just about wherever you wish, across swathes of spectacular moorland, once jealously guarded by the shooting estates and out of bounds to the public. The national park gives detailed advice for responsible use of this privilege, online and at moorland access points marked on OS maps.

For more **information** about what the North York Moors National Park has to offer to Slow visitors, log on to their website (⌖ www.northyorkmoors.org.uk) or get hold of a copy of their annual guide/newspaper, *Out and About in the North York Moors*.

HEATHER, GROUSE & HONEY

The existence of the North York Moors as a national park depends almost solely on one plant. It is also responsible for a significant proportion of the economy of this region; it's not a timber tree or a farmer's crop, but a wild, woody perennial called *Calluna vulgaris*, or ling – the humble, common heather. It dominates the Moors to a staggering degree, but ironically only because we let it. Without human management, by controlled burning or mowing, and sheep grazing, these upland heaths would soon revert to their natural vegetation of oak forest.

An awful lot of landowners' time, effort and money goes into keeping these vast acres covered in heather, not for us to ooh and aah over their colour in August, or have long, uninterrupted views on our walks, but to encourage the populations of one species of wild bird – the red grouse.

Grouse are very specific in their habitat requirements, needing young heather shoots to eat, and old heather bushes to nest in, so a moorland gamekeeper's job is to maintain a mosaic of different-aged patches of heather on the land. 'Most estates do this by burning old heather, small areas at a time, and then allowing it to regenerate,' explained Simon Bassindale, one of the national park's rangers. 'We depend on the gamekeepers doing this well, to maintain the national park landscape, and it's quite a skill of theirs, choosing the right day to do it. If the ground is too dry, or the wind too strong, the fire can burn out of control which can be disastrous.' A good population of grouse means a healthy income from the autumn and winter shoots, with customers paying upwards of £1,000 a day for the privilege of bagging a brace. Love it or hate it, without grouse shooting, the North York Moors would not exist as we know it.

What's good for grouse is fortunately also attractive to lots of other unique wildlife, and this area is a real stronghold for adders, lizards, curlews, golden plover, short-eared owls and, my favourite of all, a dashing little falcon called the merlin.

One other harvest that can be taken from the heather is that of nectar, which bees can transform into what is widely regarded as the best-quality honey available. Rows of hives, moved up on to the edge of the moor for the mass purple-flowering, are a common sight in August. Sadly, honeybees have been hit hard by disease in recent years, so you may find getting hold of locally produced honey difficult, but your best bet are specialist food shops in the villages, and farmers' markets.

HOW THIS BOOK IS ARRANGED

MAPS

The colour map at the front of this book shows the area of land that falls within each chapter. The chapters themselves begin with a more detailed map bearing numbered points which correspond to numbered headings in the text. Featured walks have an even larger scale map accompanying them.

By far the most complete and useful maps for walking, cycling, horseriding and general sightseeing are the OS 1:25,000 Explorer series. Those covering the region described in this book are as follows:

- OL26 North York Moors – Western area
- OL27 North York Moors – Eastern area
- 290 York
- 294 Market Weighton & Yorkshire Wolds Central
- 300 Howardian Hills & Malton
- 301 Scarborough, Bridlington & Flamborough Head

ACCOMMODATION

Accommodation has been recommended on the basis of location and because it embraces a Slow approach either in its 'green' ethos or its overall feel.

Hotels, B&Bs and self-catering options are indicated by the symbol ♠ after town and village headings, and campsites by ⩕, with a cross-reference to the full listing under Accommodation, pages 198–203.

CAR-FREE TRAVEL

TRAINS

York is the hub of the rail network hereabouts. From York Station, you can travel north on the East Coast Main Line for **Thirsk** (*Chapter 1*) or east on the Trans-Pennine Express to **Malton** (*Chapters 4* and *5*) and **Scarborough** (*Chapter 3*). From Scarborough the Yorkshire Coast Line, visits **Filey** (*Chapter 3*) then skirts the **Wolds** (*Chapter 5*), with stations at Hunmanby, Bempton, Bridlington, Driffield and **Beverley**. A circular route can be completed back to York via Hull and Selby.

The only other 'Network' rail line in the region is the wonderful **Esk Valley Line** which runs between Middlesbrough and Whitby, calling at Great Ayton (*Chapter 1*) and of the many places featured in *Chapter 2*.

Not counting the miniature North Bay Railway in Scarborough, only one private train line operates in the region and that is the **North Yorkshire Moors Railway**, running from Pickering to Grosmont. On its 18 mile route it calls at Levisham and Goathland and at peak times a steam service continues along the last six miles of the Esk Valley line to Whitby.

BUSES & COACHES

A cheaper (but slower) way of **getting here** is by the excellent Yorkshire Coastliner bus. This service runs every day from Leeds to York (every 15 minutes) and then on to Malton (every 30 minutes). Here the service splits, with buses travelling to Scarborough (every hour), Whitby via Pickering and Goathland (three times a day) and Filey and Bridlington (three times a day).

Once you have got here, **getting around** by bus is not quite so simple. As is the way with bus services, the smaller and more isolated the place the poorer the service, especially in the less mainstream tourist venues. Buses around the quieter corners of the Howardian Hills and Wolds are particularly sparse.

Below is a list of bus hub-towns, the relevant bus numbers and the villages with no better access. Check before you use them because some are very infrequent, summer and/or weekends only.

Beverley X4, X46, 746 The Hull–York bus that calls in on Market Weighton and Pocklington.
Great Ayton 29 and 81 to Stokesley, then 80 and 89 for Great Broughton, Carlton, Faceby, Swainby and Osmotherley.
Malton 194 to Helmsley via all the 'Street' villages plus Nunnington and Hovingham; 182 and 183 to Castle Howard via Welburn and Bulmer; 133 for Wharram le Street, Thixendale, Fridaythorpe, Sledmere, Wetwang and Garton *en route* to Driffield.
Scarborough 93 for Burniston, Cloughton, Robin Hoods Bay and Whitby; 128 to Helmsley via Pickering, Sinnington and Kirbymoorside; 121 for Cayton.
Thirsk 59 serves Kilburn and Coxwold.

Whitby 93 for Ugthorpe and Scaling Dam; 5 for Sandsend, Lythe, East Barnby, Runswick Bay and Staithes; X40 for Goathland.

Vintage buses

Open-top buses operate in three of the region's towns. York has two companies running tours, Scarborough likewise and Whitby has just the one. Whitby also has a 1960s heritage bus that runs out to Goathland on Heartbeat Country Tours (www. coastalandcountry.co.uk) and two vintage vehicles touring the town itself. Charlotte is a 1920s charabanc and Elizabeth a fantastic 1930s steam-powered bus (www.whitbysteambusandcharabanc. co.uk).

PARK-&-RIDE

Parking can be a headache, especially in popular destinations at busy times. At the time of writing there are two towns featured in the book with successful park-and-ride schemes; York has five alternatives dotted around its ring road (www. york.gov.uk) and Scarborough two (www.northyorks.gov.uk/ scarboroughparkandride). The place that needs one most, Whitby, has one in the pipeline but in the meantime you can always leave your car at a village on either the Esk Valley or North Yorkshire Moors rail lines and catch a train into town.

BOAT TRIPS

The harbour towns of the North Yorkshire coast have no ferries to take you from A to B but lots of opportunities exist for trips out and back in the summer months (weather permitting). Scarborough and Whitby offer the most options. All of Scarborough's vessels operate out of the harbour. Numerous boats advertise angling trips, usually with a sandwich board on the harbourside; just turn up and take your pick of the most reputable-looking one. Three enterprises offer pleasure cruises, **Queensferry Coastal Cruises**, **Scarborough Pleasure Steamers** and the *Hispaniola* (a mock sailing ship).

Details of the 19 sea-angling charter boats that operate from Whitby harbour can be found on www.wcsa.whitbyseaanglers. co.uk or contact Whitby Tourist Office. As for cruises here, the company **Whitby Coastal Cruises** has three boats of various sizes (and exposures to the elements!) running trips up the coast, out to sea for whale-watching and up the river when the tide is in. The *Bark Endeavour* is a scale replica of Captain Cook's famous sailing ship that also does short sea trips. One of the town's historic, retired lifeboats, the *Mary Ann Hepworth*, runs trips of a similar distance to the Endeavour.

The two small harbours of Staithes in the north of the region and Flamborough in the south, have one charter boat each – **All my Sons** in Staithes and **Emmerson's** in North Bay at Flamborough.

It is also possible to get afloat on inland waterways, of course. River Ouse boat trips are available in York (see page 186) or you could indulge in a gentle chug on the Pocklington canal (see page 156).

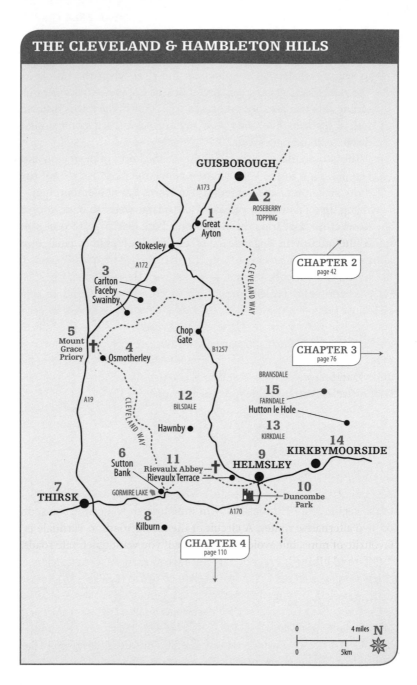

GUISBOROUGH

A173

▲ **2**
ROSEBERRY
TOPPING

1
Great
Ayton

Stokesley

A172

CLEVELAND WAY

CHAPTER 2
page 42

3
Carlton
Faceby
Swainby

Chop
Gate

B1257

5
Mount
Grace
Priory

4
Osmotherley

CHAPTER 3
page 76

BRANSDALE

15

FARNDALE
Hutton le Hole

A19

CLEVELAND WAY

12
BILSDALE

Hawnby

13
KIRKDALE

14
KIRKBYMOORSIDE

6
Sutton
Bank

11
Rievaulx Abbey
Rievaulx Terrace

9
HELMSLEY

7
THIRSK

GORMIRE LAKE

10
Duncombe
Park

A170

8
Kilburn

CHAPTER 4
page 110

0   4 miles   **N**
0   5km

1

THE CLEVELAND &
HAMBLETON HILLS

Travelling up or down the Vale of York you are likely to be moving at speed, whether in a car on the A19 or on a train on the East Coast main line. Either way, to the east of you will see a range of hills stretching in an almost unbroken escarpment from Thirsk in the south up to Teesside in the north. Occasional crags stand proud from the slopes, tree-muffled valleys bend teasingly out of sight, and ruined castles and priories poke just their heads into view. You may be sorely tempted to break your speedy journey, turn off the fast route and go-slow in the hills for a while. Succumb to temptation, because this is low-gear territory par excellence, from the limestone country of **Kirkbymoorside**, **Helmsley** and **Hambleton** to the brooding sandstone giants overlooking **Osmotherley**, **Great Ayton** and **Guisborough**.

SELF-POWERED TRAVEL

CYCLING

If you are OK with testing hills then **road biking** here is good, particularly on the National Route No 65 which traverses a good chunk of the region from Hutton Rudby in the north to Kilburn in the south, on two alternative routes. A circuit of the minor roads in Farndale is a favourite of mine, but avoid daffodil time if you want quiet, safe roads.

Off-road biking is exceptional. Testing routes for fit and experienced riders are easy to find; just spread out a copy of the 1:25,000 OS Explorer map OL26 and link together bridleways and green lanes across the moor tops. Some particularly good, but deserted, routes head out of the heads of Farndale and Bransdale. For flatter and easier riding, **Farndale's** high-level disused ironstone railway is a fabulous five miles from Blakey Ridge, that can be extended to a ten-mile horseshoe using the Westside

Road green lane. A steep descent will bring you to the pub at Church Houses, a mile from the start point but unfortunately over 1,000 feet lower. Another flattish high-level route is the Cleveland Way north of **Sutton Bank**. The first half a mile is footpath so you need to detour to Dialstone Farm or walk the bike, but from Whitestone Cliff there are three loops of four, six and eight miles, easy enough for families and returning along the tarmac Hambleton Road. This last route takes you close to the best forest track riding in the region, in **Boltby Forest**.

CYCLE REPAIRS

Bike Scene Park Lane, Guisborough ✆ 01642 610735 ✍ www.bikescene.co.uk. No bike hire is available anywhere in the region, but this is the place for mountain bike parts, repairs and maintenance.

HORSERIDING

You will find lots of scope to ride here, with or without your own horse, on hundreds of miles of bridleway, green lane and permitted forest track. If you bring your own horse, places offering horse accommodation can be found in the booklet *Horse Riders' Guide to the North York Moors*, produced by the national park.

RIDING CENTRES

The following riding centres provide trekking or hacking:

Bilsdale Riding Centre Hawnby ✆ 01439 798225 ✍ www.horseholiday.co.uk.

Boltby Pony Trekking and Trail Riding Centre Boltby ✆ 01845 537392 ✍ www. boltbytrekking.co.uk.

Helmsley Riding School Helmsley ✆ 01439 770355 ✍ www.helmsleyridingschool.co.uk.

WALKING

The one official National Trail in the region is the **Cleveland Way** (110 miles) with one end (whether it's the start or the finish is your choice) at Helmsley. It follows the whole length of the Hambleton and Cleveland hills before heading to the coast near Skinningrove. Much of the cream of the walking in the area is along this route, taking in as it does the high edges and getting huge views; two of the best areas to head for are Sutton Bank (extremely easy, level strolling along the top from the visitor centre) and in either direction from the B1257 north of Chop Gate (circular walks work particularly well here, joining Chop

---

i TOURIST INFORMATION

Great Ayton High Green Car Park ✆ 01642 722835
Helmsley Castlegate ✆ 01439 770173
Sutton Bank National Park Visitor Centre ✆ 01439 770657
Thirsk Market Pl ✆ 01845 522755

Gate with the Cleveland Way). Other less official but still very popular long-distance routes are the **Tabular Hills Way** (48 miles), heading east from Helmsley to join the two loose ends of the Cleveland Way together; the **Lyke Wake Walk** (40 miles), a very old traditional route from Osmotherley to Robin Hood's Bay; and the **Hambleton Hillside Mosaic Walk** (36 miles), a circular trail from Sutton Bank.

Shorter sections of all these trails make good day or half-day walks, the perennial problem being transport, as they are not circular routes. Some sections that can use public transport one way are **Kildale to Great Ayton via Captain Cook's Monument** (a pleasant, mainly woodland walk of three miles using the Esk Valley Railway as a shuttle); **Carlton to Swainby via Carlton Bank** (an airy five-mile moorland traverse with extensive views of the Vale of Mowbray; bus 89 gets you back); and **Sutton Bank to Rievaulx or Helmsley** (five or seven miles, along the lovely valleys of Nettle Dale and Ryedale – best done this way as it is downhill; use buses 128, M71, M91 for the return leg). In **Farndale** and **Rosedale** some of the best walking takes in the valleys themselves and the high moors just above, though the route-finding through fields can be very intricate; once you're up on the Moors, however, it's a different world.

"Shorter sections of all these trails make good day or half-day walks."

THE CLEVELAND HILLS

The gradually rising land of the North York Moors has its precipitous swansong in its northwestern corner; a final celebration of altitude in a series of buttresses, overlooking the Cleveland plain. Clustered around the ankles of these hills are a string of old villages, the largest being **Great Ayton** and **Osmotherley**.

1 GREAT AYTON

🏠 **Shepherd's Rest** Low Easby (see page 199)

Soon after your arrival in Great Ayton you may begin to suspect the existence of a famous old boy, one James Cook, whose former presence is writ large, though he only spent nine years of his youth living here. Born in 1728 in Marton (now a suburb of Middlesbrough), James Cook was one of the great explorers, and his sea voyages charted much of New Zealand and Australia. The Cooks moved to Great Ayton when he was a child, and his father worked nearby at Aireyholme Farm on the slopes of Roseberry Topping where the family lived; the Cooks also had a cottage in the village, dismantled in 1933 stone by stone and re-erected in Melbourne, Australia. The **Captain Cook Schoolroom Museum** (✆ 01642 724296 🖰 www.captaincookschoolroommuseum.co.uk; open afternoons Apr–Oct, all day Jul and Aug) is in the very school the young James attended for four years, and has displays about his life and the village's past.

The main street running parallel with the river has a village green at either end, Upper and Lower, and is overlooked by a Quaker school, the Great Ayton Friends' School, founded in 1841, but sadly closed in 1997. The railway line here doubles as the boundary of the national park, with Great Ayton outside and this spectacular branch of the Cleveland Hills most definitely in. Two summits stand out, **Easby Moor** with its tall memorial pillar and the unmistakable outline of **Roseberry Topping**.

🍴 FOOD & DRINK

For **shopping** head three miles south to the market town of Stokesley which has two excellent pubs and a Friday market, or four miles north to the much bigger town of Guisborough. This former capital of Cleveland also has a market (Tuesday, Thursday and Saturday).

Mill Riggs Organic Farm Store Stokesley TS9 5HQ ✆ 01642 715784. A farm shop on the A174, selling mainly meat and eggs.

Spread Eagle High St, Stokesley ✆ 01642 710278. A small and unspoiled market town pub with good-value, home-cooked food and a range of real ales including guests from micro-breweries. The beer garden backs on to the River Leven and has duck-feeding potential.

Suggits Café and Shop High St, Great Ayton ✆ 01642 722522. An ice cream shop since the 1920s, old-fashioned sweet shop and very popular cyclists' café – very much a local institution. Waterfall Park opposite is a pleasant place to sit and enjoy your ice cream.

The White Swan West End, Stokesley ✆ 01642 710263 🖰 www.captaincookbrewery.

A walk to the Captain Cook Memorial

OS Explorer map OL26; start: Great Ayton Station, grid reference NZ574108.

C aptain Cook's Memorial stands proud a short walk southeast of Great Ayton. Thank goodness common sense prevailed in 1827 when sites for a memorial to Captain Cook were discussed, and Roseberry Topping was rejected in favour of Easby Moor. This flat-topped hill is enhanced by the 51-foot tower whereas the Topping needs no help in catching the eye. Ringed with old sandstone quarries, capped with heather and a healthy population of red grouse, this is good walking country, though rarely quiet, as the Cleveland Way crosses the top. My preference is to link it with Roseberry Topping to create a five-mile walk from Great Ayton to Kildale, returning by train. This strategy has the added advantage of calling in on the excellent café near Kildale Station to re-fuel while you wait for your train.

The walk starts at Great Ayton Station, heads north on a minor road then a bridleway or footpath beyond Aireyholme Farm to the summit of Roseberry Topping. The return trip follows the Cleveland Way south to Captain Cook's Monument, followed by another choice of paths through Mill Bank Wood to finish at Kildale.

co.uk. A typical 18th-century, one-room pub with an interesting 'J'-shaped bar, and excellent beer from the Captain Cook Brewery next door. The pub does not do food with the exception of the Beer and Cheese Festival around Easter time and a similar beer and pie celebration in the autumn. Brewery tours next door by arrangement.

2 ROSEBERRY TOPPING

Some high mountains disguise their altitude with a humble show of rounded slopes and flat, grassy tops. Roseberry Topping is the opposite, a hill with delusions of grandeur, sometimes even referred to as the Matterhorn of Yorkshire. Such is its prominence, with an abrupt conical shape and rocky summit, that it is possibly the most recognised, best-loved and most often climbed peak in Yorkshire, probably deserving the title of 'Little Mountain' despite not even managing the altitude title for the Cleveland Hills, as nearby Round Hill on Urra Moor is over 300 feet higher.

"Roseberry Topping provides a fine venue for a walk, inviting from every angle, and with a panoramic view from the top, hard to beat anywhere else in the country."

A history of reverence is hinted at in the name, which probably derives from Odin's Berg, the Vikings associating it with their chief god, but later generations treated it with far less respect. One local historian commented that Roseberry Topping is an industrial summary of the North York Moors ... almost everything that has been taken from the ground in Cleveland has been pillaged from its slopes – jet, coal, alum, sandstone, fossils, ironstone and basalt. This last surprising mineral product was quarried up until the 1980s from the

A DEATH FORETOLD

Many local stories have Roseberry Topping as a backdrop but probably the oldest is the tragic tale of the death of Prince Oswy. It had been prophesied that King Osmund's beloved only son would drown before his second year was out.

In a desperate attempt to thwart the prediction the King sent his infant son, with his mother, as far from water as he could find in his Kingdom of Northumbria – the summit of Roseberry Topping. On Oswy's second birthday, the queen dozed in the sun on the hillside and the boy wandered off. Her frantic search for him on waking ended with the tragic discovery of his body, lying face down in a shallow pool of spring water. Roseberry Well, now merely a marshy patch of ground, is marked on the OS map.

Whinstone Ridge, a ruler-straight igneous intrusion crossing the Moors and breaking the surface here, and also at Egton Bridge, Goathland Moor and Sneaton Forest.

Despite its human ravages, Roseberry Topping provides a fine venue for a walk, inviting from every angle, especially the Cleveland Way extension from the east, and with a panoramic view from the top, hard to beat anywhere else in the country. The most direct route of ascent is from the hamlet of Newton under Roseberry, just north of Great Ayton, and if you happen to be here on the first Sunday of the month, then after your walk call in on the farmers' market at Pinchinthorpe Hall, another mile up the road.

¶¶ FOOD & DRINK

Glebe Cottage Tea Room Station Rd, Kildale YO21 2RH ☎ 01642 724470
🖰 www.glebecottagekildale.co.uk. An excellent little licensed café. Closed Thursday.

3 CARLTON IN CLEVELAND, FACEBY & SWAINBY

Both Carlton and Swainby, and the smaller **Faceby** in between, are close enough to the A19 to cater mainly for the commuters of Teesside, but each has attractions for visitors. All three have a pub, **Carlton**'s being the pick of the bunch, and old churches with unusual dedications; St Botolph's in Carlton is the most northerly in the country to be named after this Lincolnshire monk, while **Faceby**'s St Mary Magdalen's Church has a fine collection of 'Mouseman' carvings (see page 30). Carlton has an outdoor activity centre if you fancy exerting yourself.

"Being a no-through valley, this is a haven of peace and quiet."

Swainby is one of those settlements that moved sites after the ravages of the Black Death. All that is left of the old village of Whorlton are ruins of the 11th-century castle, and nearby, probably even older, church of the Holy Cross. Modern Swainby is an attractive collection of stone buildings lining the banks of Scugdale Beck, including a bustling village shop that had its post office counter taken away recently, so converted the space into a small coffee shop.

Two roads lead uphill out of the moors end of Swainby, one the scenic back lane already mentioned to Osmotherley, and the other, the winding, dead-end road up Scugdale. Being a no-through valley, this is a haven of peace and quiet, the only visitors being walkers, and climbers coming to play on its crags.

¶¶ FOOD & DRINK

The Blackwell Ox Carlton in Cleveland 📞 01642 712287 🖰 www.theblackwellox.co.uk. A typical village local pub with caravan site attached. The extensive menu is predominantly Thai, and the permanent Hambleton beer fronts a range of cask ales.

Potto Grange Organics Potto DL6 3HH 📞 01642 700646 🖰 www.pottograngeorganics. co.uk. Organic beef, lamb and pork, direct from the farm or via Stokesley farmers' market.

ACTIVITIES

Carlton Outdoor Education Centre Carlton in Cleveland 📞 01642 712229 🖰 www. carltonoutdoors.org. A wide variety of half- and full-day activities, like climbing, canoeing, bushcraft, caving and archery, is available at weekends and school holidays. Small groups can book an instructor for the activity of their choice.

4 OSMOTHERLEY

The most satisfying mode of arrival into this village is on foot from the south along the Cleveland Way. This route treats you to tempting glimpses, from high up on Black Hambleton Hill, of the village tucked into a fold of the valley-bottom fields, and descends through the verdant woods of Oak Dale.

Even using wheeled transport, it is possible to visit Osmotherley avoiding the nearby A19 dual carriageway, by approaching via the spectacular moor road over from Bilsdale, or the minor back road from Swainby. This latter route could well have been the one followed by the Queen of Northumbria and her dead child (see box, page 22). According to legend, she buried Oswy at the church in Tivotdale, and joined him soon afterwards when she died herself, of grief and guilt. Tivotdale's name changed to commemorate Oswy-by-his-mother-lay – a rather far-fetched, but poignant story.

However you arrive, you will find yourself at the village green, decorated by an ornately carved market cross and stone barter table, where goods were exchanged. The table is more famous now for one of Osmotherley's many religious connections, as it was used as a preaching pulpit by John Wesley in 1745. He obviously made an impression, as one of the oldest Methodist chapels in the world is hidden away down a cobbled alley across the road.

¶¶ FOOD & DRINK

Coffee Pot North End ✆ 01609 883536. The only café in the village – a good one, fortunately.

Golden Lion West End ✆ 01609 883526 🖰 www.goldenlionosmotherley.co.uk. A dark-stone inn overlooking the village green. Inside, wood is the theme in the bar, and the beer is sourced from Timothy Taylors, Hambleton and the continent. The menu is refreshingly simple with an excellent range of gluten-free meals, and the wine list is extensive.

5 MOUNT GRACE PRIORY

Two miles north of Osmotherley, DL6 3JG ✆ 01609 883494; open Apr–Sep, Thu–Mon; Oct–Mar, Thu–Sun. English Heritage.

Of the bewildering array of orders of monks and nuns to have lived in Yorkshire, the Carthusians, the last to arrive from the continent, are perhaps the least known. There have only ever been ten Carthusian priories, or Charterhouses, in England and Mount Grace is the best preserved of them all. Its position displays the usual monastic good taste for beautiful locations, tucked as it is beneath the steep wooded slope of Swinestye Hill. What struck me was how different Mount Grace was to more traditional sites like Fountains and Rievaulx; no one, big, dominating abbey church here, but smaller, homely buildings. This reflects the Carthusian philosophy of solitary hermitage, with each monk or nun living silently in their own cell, meeting only for chapel services and one long, communal walk, the only time they could speak – I bet that was a noisy affair.

Mount Grace Priory is owned by the National Trust but, oddly, administered by English Heritage. Areas of interest include a reconstructed cell, an exhibition upstairs in the attached manor house, a shop and activities for children. The gardens are full of wildlife, notably a family of famous stoats that have featured in various BBC wildlife documentaries.

THE HAMBLETON HILLS

When the heathery tops of the Cleveland Hills give way to grass, you will know that you have arrived in the limestone country of Hambleton. The most public face of these hills is its steep, scarp slope, often refered to as **Whitestonecliffe**, that stretches ten miles south from Thimbleby, and looks out west over **Sutton-under-Whitestonecliffe**, to **Thirsk** town and the rest of the Vale of York. At its more hidden, southern end, it tumbles down to **Kilburn**, to then merge imperceptibly with the Howardian Hills.

6 SUTTON BANK

The village of Sutton-under-Whitestonecliffe has two claims to fame, the longest place name in England, and the cliff itself that provides the label. The busy road that passes through Sutton is one of the main routes into the North York Moors, but as the many warning signs insist, it is not recommended for lorries or towed caravans. Sutton Bank, the hair-pin section up Whitestonecliffe, is blocked by stranded vehicles with monotonous regularity. At the top of Sutton Bank you will find the **national park visitor centre** of the same name (℡ 01845 597426 🖰 www.northyorkmoors.org.uk), with a shop, exhibition centre and tea rooms inside. A very entertaining half-hour can be spent with a cup of tea or coffee, gazing out of the window at one of the busiest bird feeding stations that I've ever seen.

From the centre, six waymarked **walking trails** can lead you between two and nine miles astray, the best to my mind being a five-mile circuit taking in Gormire Lake; or just for a blast of air and the sublime views, head across the A170 on the dead-level, dead-easy stretch of the Cleveland Way, which heads along the top of the great cliff that is Sutton Bank for a very easy mile or so towards the **White Horse of Kilburn**.

"Don't just gaze down to the lake, woods and Vale of York, but glance upwards and you may be treated to the sight of a glider drifting silently overhead."

On your walk, don't just gaze down to the lake, woods and Vale of York, but glance upwards every now and again, and you may be treated to the sight of a glider drifting silently overhead. If it seems like an idyllically peaceful way to travel, and you fancy having a go – the good news is that you can! The **Yorkshire Gliding Club**'s base is hidden away in the trees less than a mile from Sutton Bank, and they offer trial lessons where, under the expert guidance of an instructor, you can actually fly the glider with no previous experience. My wife bought me one for my birthday and it was the most exciting hour's experience I've had for a long time, especially the take-off.

A map detailing six circular bike routes from the centre, between 11 and 23 miles, is also available.

Gormire Lake

Beneath the Hambleton Hills scarp and one of the few natural lakes in North Yorkshire, this is also one of its most beautiful. With the pale cliff above and surrounding lush forest reflected in its crystal-clear limestone spring waters, the name hardly seems deserving, as it literally means 'filthy swamp'. Gormire is not only a haunting and evocative place, it's a prized haven for wildlife. The rich limestone woodland surrounding it is managed by the Woodland Trust, mainly for its flora, and the lake itself supports important numbers of winter waterfowl, like goosanders, tufted duck, pochard and kingfishers. The whole area is designated as a Site of Special Scientific Interest (SSSI).

Probably because lakes are such a rarity in this part of the world, many legends have grown up around Gormire Lake, some involving it being bottomless, or telling of it swallowing witches or geese and spitting them out in wells miles away (Gormire has no in- or out flow river). The most common theme though, a white mare leaping off the cliff and into the water, complete with doomed rider, possibly derives from White Mare Crag, the alternative name for Whitestonecliffe. This refers to the shape of a horse that used to be visible in the rock face, not the White Horse at nearby Kilburn.

¶¶ FOOD & DRINK

The Hare Scawton ☎ 01845 597769 ⌂ www.thehareinn.co.uk. An inn reputedly once used as a brewhouse by the monks of Rievaulx Abbey in the 13th century, and now a dining pub with traditional English menus, Yorkshire ales from Timothy Taylors and Black Sheep, and an extensive wine menu.

Yorkshire Gliding Club Low Town Bank Rd, Sutton Bank ☎ 01845 597237 ⌂ www.ygc. co.uk. The clubhouse has a restaurant and bar open to the public, an ideal vantage point to watch the gliders come and go. Gliding courses and lessons are available, and the club also operates a campsite.

7 THIRSK

This small town has ticked along, minding its own business, for over a thousand years. Nothing momentous has ever happened here, no battles or royal visits to the castle (because there's no castle), just a lower-league manor house and an old, but fairly average, church. For me, it is a celebration of ordinary Yorkshire life through the centuries, centred on trade in its busy market square and surrounding shops and inns. **Market days** are still the high points of the week (Mondays and Saturdays), with the cattle market moved to a purpose-built venue on the trading estate (Thursday) and a farmers' market there on the first Saturday of each month.

How apt then, that the town should earn some outside fame from the venue of a favourite local pastime, its racecourse, and the reminiscences of an ordinary working man, who just happened to write about his experiences particularly well.

Alf Wight was the local vet in the 1940s, but the world knows him better under his pen-name of **James Herriot**. His entertaining stories appeared in print in the 'vet' series of books of the 1970s, but it was when they were televised as *All Creatures Great and Small* that a legend was born, and Thirsk became Herriot country.

His original surgery, in Kirkgate, the real-life Skeldale House, has been restored to its 1940s state and opened to the public as the **World of James Herriot** (✆ 01845 524234 ☞ www.worldofjamesherriot.org).

Another museum faces this one in Kirkgate. **Thirsk Museum** (✆ 01845 527707 ☞ www.thirskmuseum.org) celebrates life in the town from Saxon times to the present day, and famous pre-Herriot old boys, like Thomas Lord (of Lord's cricket ground) whose house this was.

¶¶ FOOD & DRINK

Arabica Market Pl ✆ 01845 523869. A small modern coffee shop with a good range of coffees, and free Wi-Fi.

Yorks Tea Rooms Market Pl ✆ 01845 526776. A traditional café serving quality Taylors teas and coffees, and substantial snacks – not cheap but very good.

Pubs

As you would expect of an active market town, Thirsk's eight pubs rub shoulders with each other around the marketplace and Kirkgate. Unfortunately, in this case, competition hasn't pushed up standards, but travelling out of town you will find the following:

Crab and Lobster Dishforth Rd, Asenby YO7 3QL ✆ 01845 577286 ☞ www. crabandlobster.co.uk. A 17th-century thatched pub with a formidable reputation for gourmet food in its restaurant. Seafood is the speciality and influences are French and Italian.

The Nags Head Pickhill YO7 4JG ✆ 01845 567391 ☞ www.nagsheadpickhill.co.uk. Out of town to the west, this 200-year-old coaching inn has got the balance just right; a cosy pub tap-room, comfy lounge bar and sumptuous restaurant, with good food and drink served in all three rooms. B&B available.

Pick-your-own

Spilman Farming Church Farm, Sessay YO7 3NB ✆ 01845 501623 🖰 www.
spilmanfarming.co.uk. Soft fruits for sale in Jun and Jul; including strawberries, raspberries,
gooseberries, redcurrants and blackcurrants – all grown on the farm.

ART

Zillah Bell Gallery Kirkgate ✆ 01845 522479 🖰 www.zillahbellgallery.co.uk. A nationally
renowned gallery featuring mainly Yorkshire artists. Regularly changing exhibitions.

8 KILBURN & OLDSTEAD

The unofficial emblem of the Hambleton Hills, logo of a local brewery
and name of numerous local pubs, is carved into the side of Roulston
Hill above this village, and consequently bears the name, the **White
Horse of Kilburn**. Impressively large and visible for many miles (from
York Minster tower for instance) it was created in 1857 by a local
schoolmaster with the aid of his pupils.

The village itself has something of a Cotswoldy charm, with a beck
gurgling down the side of the main street (in a deep unfenced trench
– so beware), but is very small, and would be relatively unknown
except for a famous former resident, Robert 'Mouseman' Thompson,
woodcarver. The **Mouseman Visitor Centre** (✆ 01347 869102 🖰 www.
robertthompsons.co.uk) has outgrown his old workshop and is now in
the old blacksmith's buildings over the road. Kilburn also has a busy pub
and village store.

The Hambleton escarpment takes a sharp turn to the east above
Kilburn, and at this corner an ancient drover's road descends to
the valley, where **Oldstead** village nestles. The name Scotch Corner
commemorates the nationality of many of the drovers and in times gone
by an old farm-cum-pub sat here. Now the only building to be seen is
a chapel – an amazing place created single-handedly and almost from
scratch in 1957, by the sculptor John Bunting whose artwork adorns the
walls and grounds. Its story is told brilliantly by his daughter Madeline,
in her book *The Plot*.

🍴 FOOD & DRINK

Black Swan Oldstead YO61 4BL ✆ 01347 868387 🖰 www.blackswanoldstead.co.uk. It's
well worth the mile stroll, or cycle, over from Kilburn to this 400-year-old gem. A Michelin
star tells you all you need to know about the food, and the beer is good too. Low beams,

THE MOUSEMAN OF KILBURN

There's no doubt that Robert Thompson was an extremely talented woodcarver, whose skills alone may well have earned his fortune, but from the moment he came up with the inspired idea of carving a mouse on to every item he produced, his international fame was well and truely assured.

He was born in 1876 and, as a young man, took over his father's joinery business in Kilburn. His early work was mouse-less but his reputation grew, and Thompson carvings began to appear in many local churches and Ampleforth Abbey. The idea for the emblem apparently came when his carving companion, while working on a church screen, commented that their jobs left them as 'poor as church mice'. Robert had a light-bulb moment and carved his first mouse there and then.

By the time of his death in 1955 'Mousey' Thompson's work was to be found all over the country, including York Minster and Westminster Abbey. Such is his fame that a letter sent from Australia with just a picture of a mouse and the word 'woodcarver' on the envelope, was delivered safely to his workshop. The Mouseman Visitor Centre is still an operating workshop employing 30 craftsmen, but also a shop and café. Some of the furniture isn't cheap, but they produce smaller items such as napkin rings that make excellent souvenirs.

Robert's other legacy has been an upsurge of interest in quality, hand-carved furniture in the area. Ten workshops are included in the Thirsk Furniture Trail (www.thirskfurnituretrail.co.uk), each of which has its own motif carved on to every item, of course. You will have fun finding the hidden unicorn, fox, wren or beaver, but I suspect none will ever have the impact of that original humble church mouse.

roaring fires and wooden floors make this a comfortable space in which to enjoy superb food and quality tipple.

Forresters Arms Kilburn 01347 868386 www.forrestersarms.com The food can't quite compete with the Black Swan's on quality, but then it is half the price. The beer however is in a different league with three cask Yorkshire ales, including White Horse Pale Ale brewed by Wharfebank.

THE WESTERN DALES

Three valleys bite into the southern slopes of the Cleveland Hills, and channel their rivers and becks to the Vale of Pickering. The upper reaches of Farndale, Bransdale, Bilsdale and Ryedale are rural in the extreme, with some of the most inaccessible acres in the whole of the national park. Where these hills meet the Vale's rich farmland, is where you'll find most of the villages as well as the area's two small towns, **Helmsley** and **Kirkbymoorside**.

9 HELMSLEY

🏠 **Black Swan Hotel** (see page 198).

Helmsley possibly attracts more visitors in relation to its size than anywhere else in the North York Moors. It has achieved this pulling-power without resorting to anything 'fast' or tacky, having unconsciously carved itself a niche as an upmarket resort and, perhaps incongruously, a destination for touring motorbike clubs, who almost fill the market-square car park some weekends. Families will not find a huge amount here to entertain young and active children, but it has a wealth of historic buildings, serene walled gardens, aristocratic connections and quality, speciality shops.

When Helmsley is at its busiest the crowds spoil the experience for me, so I try to visit on off peak days. My favourite is on Friday when the street market is held, and the town is bustling and vibrant without being heaving. This is a very small town so almost all the interest is around the market square or, in the case of the outrageously ornate **Feversham monument**, smack bang in the middle of it. Here is where all four of Helmsley's old coaching inns are, along with most of its ten cafés and two exceptional **food shops**: Hunters and Perns (run by the Star at Harome).

Behind the library you will find yourself in Castlegate; carry on around the castle walls to the **tourist office**, which doubles as the entrance to **Helmsley Castle**. Signs here will direct you to **Helmsley Walled Garden**, once part of the **Duncombe Park Estate**, supplying the big house with a large variety of seasonal fruit and vegetables, and now hiding away behind the castle.

Two more venues away from the centre are worth seeking out; one for daytime entertainment and the other evenings. **Helmsley Arts Centre** (🖰 www.helmsleyarts.co.uk) lies a short walk away up an alley off Bridge Street. This old Quaker meeting house is the town's very active theatre, putting on a wide variety of plays, films, concerts and readings. The volunteers that run it are never less than really welcoming and the place always seems full. Slightly further afield is a welcome rarity for outdoor swimmers. The River Rye is not quite big enough for wild swimming but **Helmsley open-air swimming pool** (✆ 07772 395368 www.helmsleysports.org), in Baxton Road, opens afternoons and early evenings, late June to early September.

Helmsley Castle
 01439 771580; English Heritage.

This jagged ruin merits a brief peep, but does not have the spectacular position of Scarborough, the royal connections of Pickering or the level of preservation of Bolton in Wensleydale. It was however, founded by a character with one of my all-time favourite names from English history – Walter the Woodpecker, or Walter l'Espec as he was known to his Norman compatriots. He was succeeded by Robert de Roos who was responsible for most of the fortifications, and later the Manners family built the Elizabethan mansion which is still partly intact. English Heritage now maintains it and has provided complete wheelchair access at ground level with some good hands-on exhibitions in the mansion range.

Helmsley Walled Garden
 01439 771427 www.helmsleywalledgarden.org.uk.

My first visit to this place was during a 'Green Day', a festival of sorts to celebrate all things environmental and earthy. The place was cluttered with information desks about recycling and nature reserves, stalls selling local honey, cheese and pickles and everywhere the sounds of folk music, sizzling sausages and happy people. It was great, but it was busy, busy, busy.

"The place was cluttered with stalls selling local honey, cheese and pickles and everywhere the sounds of folk music, sizzling sausages and happy people."

The second time I went was an altogether different experience, and what walled gardens are all about. I sat on a bench in a quiet, sunny corner – it's easy to find solitude in a five-acre space. The only sounds were the buzzing of the bees on the nearby roses and a wren trilling within the wall ivy. In the baking heat I could actually smell the apples on the branch hanging over my head, just before I dozed off. To think this lovely garden nearly disappeared, but for the efforts of a concerned group of mainly volunteers, who in 1994 started the long job of restoring the orchards, vine house and orchid house. The gardens are now back in full production and almost everything is available for you to buy.

Its demise up until recent years is a sad and poignant story. From its construction in 1758 until 1914 it supported 19 full-time gardeners and supplied produce to Duncombe Park House. At the start of World War I, all the gardeners went to serve their country, but not a single one returned. This peaceful place is a fitting memorial to their sacrifice.

¶¶ FOOD & DRINK

Beadlam Grange Farm Shop and Tearoom Pockley YO62 7TD ✆ 01439 770303 ⌂ www.beadlamgrange.co.uk. A resident butcher serves locally produced beef, lamb, pork, poultry and game, with fruit and veg and Yorkshire cheeses on the deli counter. The café is in the upstairs granary.

Black Swan Tea Room Market Pl ✆ 01423 770466 ⌂ www.blackswan-helmsley.co.uk. If you thrive on extreme sophistication then this is for you. Pure hedonism at ridiculous prices.

Feathers Hotel Market Pl ✆ 01439 770275 ⌂ www.feathershotelhelmsley.co.uk. Although Helmsley has more select hotels, this is by far the most welcoming and comfortable as a pub.

Scotts Fish and Chips Café Bridge St ✆ 01439 772465 ⌂ www.scottsofhelmsley.co.uk. Not cheap, but very good fish and chips to eat in or take away.

Vinehouse Vegetarian Café Helmsley Walled Garden ✆ 01439 771427 ⌂ www. helmsleywalledgarden.org.uk. Within the walled garden, the newly restored Victorian vinery houses an atmospheric café beneath the climbing vegetation. Most of the produce is organic, home produced, vegetarian or fair trade.

SHOPPING

The Stickman Cleveland Way ✆ 01439 771450 ⌂ www.thestickman.co.uk. Keith Pickering is a walking-stick maker operating from a workshop just outside the Walled Gardens. He has impressive credentials: he made the Archbishop of Canterbury's crook.

10 DUNCOMBE PARK

YO62 5EB ✆ 01439 770213 ⌂ www.duncombepark.com; open Easter Sun–late Oct (closed Fri and Sat); house tours during the afternoon; good-value family and season tickets.

Lord and Lady Feversham probably wouldn't thank me for saying this, but Duncombe Park is, in essence, a second division Castle Howard. I don't mean that as an insult, because I actually prefer the Duncombe experience, but just as a measure of scale. They are both massive, opulent, privately owned and run 18th-century houses with surrounding parklands to match, but the Feversham estate is slightly lower key, the house and gardens smaller and, in terms of visitors, much quieter.

The origins of the house are unusual in that it was built from scratch by a commoner. Sir Charles Duncombe was a London goldsmith who made his fortune with more than a whiff of suspicion of insider dealing. He bought the whole Helmsley estate from the Villiers family after the death of the infamous Charles, Duke of Buckingham. Helmsley Castle he declared 'un-liveable' and built The Great House on a green-field site further up the hill finishing it in 1713, three years after Castle Howard. Since then the two major events in the life of the house were a catastrophic fire in 1879 and a 60-year spell on let as a girls' boarding school. This chapter ended in 1986 when the Feversham family decided to return the house to its former glory and open it to the public.

"You may want to time your visit to coincide with point-to-point racing, or a brass band concert, or a steam fair ..."

The house has an astonishing 200 rooms, around ten of which you can visit if you choose to go inside, but you can find more than enough to do here for half a day without going in the house, or even the gardens for that matter.

The parklands cover nearly 3,000 acres, a large chunk of which is a National Nature Reserve, primarily to protect some of the oldest and biggest hardwood trees in the country, and the rare invertebrates and birds which depend on them. Two waymarked walks will take you through the best of the wild areas; the **Country Walk** and **River Walk** are both about three miles long but can be easily combined to create a five-miler for those who fancy a decent stride out. The hub of the garden landscape design is a half-mile-long terrace adorned at each end by two classical 'temples' – strikingly similar in conception to Rievaulx Terrace, three miles up the valley above Rievaulx Abbey.

At the end of your walk, or instead of it, refreshments are available at **Fountain Tea Room** in what was originally the estate's fox-hound kennels (01439 771115). It sells the usual hot and cold snacks and drinks (including beer and wine), fresh and locally sourced or fair trade, and not overly priced.

Next door to the café is a new venture for the estate – the Northern branch of the International Centre for Birds of Prey. A large collection of raptors are on show with flying demonstrations three times a day. Ring 08447 422035 to find out when.

Like Castle Howard, many outdoor special events are held here throughout the year, but mainly in the summer. You may want to time your visit to coincide with point-to-point racing, or a brass band concert, or a steam fair … or avoid them altogether for a quiet day away from the crowds.

11 RIEVAULX ABBEY & RIEVAULX TERRACE

Rievaulx Abbey Rievaulx ✆ 01439 798228; closed weekdays in winter; English Heritage.
Rievaulx Terrace and Temples Rievaulx ✆ 01439 798340; closed in winter; National Trust.
With a name like that, there has to be a French influence. It was 12th-century Cistercian monks who brought themselves, and the name, over from the continent to settle in this breathtakingly beautiful bend of the valley of the River Rye and found **Rievaulx Abbey**. They were granted vast areas of land by the then Lord of Helmsley, Walter l'Espec, and quickly became very rich and powerful landowners. The monastery's influence peaked in the early 1400s when the community numbered more than 200, and then went into steady decline, with the Black Death hitting particularly hard. By the time Henry VIII spoilt the party completely, numbers were down to 23. Even though the abbey was significantly dismantled during the Reformation, it remains a stunning building – 'the most beautiful monastic site in Europe', according to the landscape painter, Turner. English Heritage also obviously rates it highly as it scores £1 more than Helmsley Castle on its strange sliding scale of entrance fees.

Traffic can be unpleasant on the narrow lanes around Rievaulx but a bus does call here regularly in summer, from Helmsley or Sutton Bank. By far the nicest way to get here, though, is to walk or bike the three miles from either Helmsley, Scawton or Old Byland.

Arguably the best views of the abbey are from a landscaped grassy walkway on the hillside above, called **Rievaulx Terrace**, although no access exists from one to the other, except via the road. Ownership here is a confusing issue; both the abbey and the terraces were the possession of Duncombe Park Estate, but they sold the former to English Heritage and the latter to the National Trust, along with the two **neoclassical temples** that grace either end of the walk: a rotunda called the Tuscan Temple and a lavish banqueting hall called the Ionic Temple and resplendent with painted ceiling and wood carving. The Trust keep the main part of the terraces mown as per its original design, but manage the verges as flower meadows. They are a rich riot of spring and summer colour:

A walk around Bilsdale Head

✳ OS Explorer map OL26; start: Chop Gate, grid reference NZ559998.

The best of Bilsdale Head can be taken in during a six-mile circular walk, including Urra Moor, the Wainstones climbing crag and Cold Moor. Being circular, this walk could be started anywhere and done in either direction. I have described it clockwise starting at the hamlet of Chop Gate, although Clay Bank car park (✳ grid reference NZ573035, near where the B1257 crosses the Cleveland Way) is a good alternative starting point. Head north on the bridleway by the Methodist Chapel, to the top of Cold Moor then along the ridge to where it ends with panoramic views over Teesside. From here follow the Cleveland Way eastwards, down and up a couple of big dips, to the top of the steep slope above Clay Bank. Here a bridleway branches off from the Cleveland Way and follows an ancient earthwork as it contours around Urra Moor. Take this route for 1½ miles until it meets another bridleway which plunges down the hill to your starting point. The highest point on this route, the top of Chop Gate pass, is quite a geographical landmark, as it marks the watershed between two major river systems; to the north all waters flow into the River Tees, while southwards, it's a much longer journey to the Humber estuary.

The views throughout this breezy moorland route are glorious and constantly changing, although its finest section is undoubtedly along the Cleveland Way.

cowslips, yellow rattle and early purple orchids in May with spotted orchids, betony and cranesbills later in the year. The obvious similarity to the terrace at Duncombe Park is not coincidental; it was once all part of the Duncombe estate and was laid out in 1758 by Thomas Duncombe III, the grandson of the creator of the Duncombe Park version.

12 BILSDALE

🏠 **Laskill Country House** near Hawnby (see page 198).

Too few motorists bother to stop and explore here, which is a shame, because walking on both sides of the valley, and neighbouring upper Ryedale, is as good as anywhere else in the moors. In particular you might revel in exploring the remains of **jet mines** here. In my ignorance I always assumed that the jet industry was confined to the coast around Whitby, so was staggered at the number of jet mine spoil heaps I found lining the side of Tripsdale (❀ grid reference NZ5897).

Hawnby is the largest village hereabouts, with a very pleasant pub, a bridge which replaced one lost in the flash floods of 2003, and a horse trekking centre. Woodland walking just to the north of the village, along the banks of the infant Rye, is tremendous.

⑂ FOOD & DRINK

Hawnby Stores and Tea Room Hawnby YO62 5QR ℡ 01439 798723. This is one of those cornucopia places: a general store with lots of local information and a café that does particularly good cream teas and breakfasts.

The Inn at Hawnby Hawnby YO62 5QS ℡ 01439 798202 🖱 www.innathawnby.co.uk. A light and airy bar, usually serving three Yorkshire ales, which can also be enjoyed in the beautiful beer garden, weather permitting. The menu features local game, often cooked in a continental style.

13 KIRKDALE

In its infancy, Hodge Beck flows through the very isolated fields of Bransdale, which in its lower reaches does something very unusual for a valley – it changes its name, twice. It becomes Sleightholmedale for a while, but lower down still, between Kirkbymoorside and Helmsley, it takes on its most widely-known label of Kirkdale, and is visited most for its minster and a cave.

St Gregory's Minster is a tiny church with no village to accompany it, but the fact that it qualifies as a minister, and has a valley named after it, hints at its historical importance. Its south wall carries its most remarkable feature, a **Saxon sundial**, carved into a single block of sandstone seven feet in diameter, and set above an outside doorway. It is the most complete one of its kind in the world and its creator also left us a very informative inscription detailing his name (Hawarth), the owner of the church (Orm) and the priest (Brand).

JET-SETTERS, WHITBY-STYLE

A chat-up line that I would love to try out is 'Did you know that your dangly, black ear-rings were once part of a log, floating down a river 180 million years ago?' I'm not sure how successful that would be though.

Jet is fossil wood, but from one particular species of tree only, the *Araucaria* or monkey-puzzle tree. This very particular specification makes it beautifully carveable and polishable but also rare – the only place in Britain where it can be found is under the North York Moors.

A common misconception is that the Victorians invented jet jewellery in Whitby. They were certainly the first to mechanise the process, and Queen Victorian's morbid obsession with all things black popularised it, but jet artefacts have been found in Bronze Age tombs and at almost all Roman excavations. As for its presence at the coast, these are merely the most visible exposures of the seams; more than half the jet that ended up in the Whitby workshops was dug from beneath the western moors. Wherever river valleys had cut down far enough through the rock strata to expose the jet series, miners would tunnel 'drifts' into the hillsides, leaving a telltale line of spoil heaps today, in Bilsdale, Scugdale, Farndale and along the Cleveland escarpment. A happy

geological accident resulted in a thin band of hard limestone being laid down just above the jet, and this Top Jet Dogger made a very convenient strong mine roof, allowing the drifts to penetrate deep underground. Working so far underground by candlelight, miners could not distinguish the black jet from dark-grey shale, so the whole lot was wheeled out in a barrow and sorted in the daylight.

Jet is still collected from the coastal cliffs to supply the small-scale workshops in Whitby, mainly by professional fossillers like Mike Marshall (see page 70) and storm-bound fishermen, but on nowhere near the scale of the Victorian boom-time, when 1,500 jet workers were employed in the town. Over in the Cleveland Hills, the only evidence of this 150-year-old industry are those lines of collapsed tunnels on the valley sides and pub names like the Jet Miners Arms in Great Broughton.

If you do find any black pebbles on the beach or hillside that you suspect may be jet, here's the test; scratch it on to a piece of pale sandstone and examine the colour of the mark. If it's black, bad luck, you have a piece of coal; if it's chocolate brown you have maybe struck it rich!

Fascinating and charming as it is, don't restrict your Kirkdale visit just to the church; a mere 200 yards from St Gregory's you will find a small hole, part-way up a quarry wall. This is the entrance to **Kirkdale Cave**, which, although the longest cave in the North York Moors, is far more famous for what was found in it. In 1821 when quarry workers exposed the entrance, they found it full of the bones of prehistoric, and largely extinct, mammals from around 70,000 years ago. It turns out that this cave was a hyena lair, and the bones were the remains of their many meals, including hippo, lion, elephant and rhino – Yorkshire was obviously a warmer place back then. The cave is not open to the public, and a deep exploration is not recommended, but a short scramble up, to crouch in the entrance and peer into the blackness, is an atmospheric experience. Kirkdale valley upstream from the cave and minster makes an excellent walking objective. You can follow **Hodge Beck**, one of those disappearing and reappearing limestone watercourses, and enjoy rich woodland, full of flowers in spring-time. A maze of paths on both sides of the beck gives you a range of options for return loops.

14 KIRKBYMOORSIDE

'Kirby', as it is known to local folk, is a small but busy market town, leaning on the southern slopes of the North York Moors – hence the name. It has many similarities to Helmsley seven miles down the road; it is roughly the same size with a castle, a market square surrounded by old coaching inns, and a nearby stately home and estate. Are the two places friendly, co-operative neighbours then? Not a bit of it. A traditional rivalry exists between the towns that poor old Kirby always seems to lose out on. The castle is a feeble bit of wall built into a younger building, and the pubs, although busy, aren't quite as genteel as those of the 'posh' place. Even the National Park Authority seems to have been deliberately insulting; their headquarters are in Helmsley, whereas the park boundary takes a deliberate detour to completely exclude Kirby. None of this bad press is warranted of course because this is an agreeable little town, especially around the marketplace, and a start point for some pleasant walks in the hills behind – and a particular favourite bike ride of mine.

Take either of the tiny but cycleable routes of Park Lane or Swineherd Lane from Kirby, and you will find yourself joining Back of Parks Road to Gillamoor (re-hydrate in the Royal Oak), thence to Fadmoor and back to Kirby by a choice of minor roads (five or six miles in total).

¶¶ FOOD & DRINK

Newfields Organics The Green, Fadmoor YO62 7HD ☎ 01751 431558 ⊕ www.newfields organics.com. A wide variety of organically grown vegetables for sale direct from the farm.

Penny Bank Café Market Pl, Kirbymoorside ☎ 01751 432606 🖱 www.pennybankcafe.
co.uk. Friendly and very popular Mediterranean-style bistro/café.
Summit Bakery and Café Market Pl, Kirbymoorside ☎ 01751 430033 Formerly a
bookshop, now an organic bakery and a very pleasant café.

Pubs

The four pubs on the marketplace have had mixed fortunes in the last few years but they are
all open and selling good beer as I write. Even so, you may feel that it's worth a journey of a
couple of miles up the road to Gillamoor for real quality.
The Royal Oak Gillamoor ☎ 01751 431414 🖱 www.theroyaloakgillamoor.co.uk. A solid
17th-century stone inn on the village green noted for its food, wines and Black Sheep beer.

15 HUTTON LE HOLE & FARNDALE VALLEY

Hutton or 'Hightown' presumably refers to this village's elevated attitude
in relation to nearby Kirkbymoorside and 'le Hole' the pretty hollow it
sits in. This is one of the national park's honeypot villages, with many
visitors drawn here by the excellent Ryedale Folk Museum, but more
than a few just to enjoy strolling around the village green, or calling in
the pub or café for refreshment. The delightful river that tumbles over
the limestone ledges of Ravenswick is the Dove, fresh from its journey
further upstream through Farndale.

As quiet as anywhere in the Moors for 11 months of the year, **Farndale
Valley** bursts at the seams with visitors in late March and early April. The
reason for this popularity is the best display of **wild daffodils**, or lenten

"The delightful river that tumbles over the limestone ledges of Ravenswick is the Dove, fresh from its journey further upstream through Farndale."

lilies, in the country. Most of the valley has
been designated a National Nature Reserve
to protect the millions of blooms; strangely
no-one really knows how they got here and
why there are so many of them, although
one theory has the monks of Rievaulx
introducing them from France. To cope
with the 40,000 admirers that arrive during
the four-week flowering season, paths have
had to be paved, a shuttle-bus service from Hutton le Hole put on and
the seasonal Daffy Café opened.

The official **Daffodil Walk** runs from Low Mill to Church Houses but it
can be extremely crowded; for almost as many daffs all to yourself walk up
the Dove from Lowna Bridge, or catch the bus to Low Mill and walk back.

Ryedale Folk Museum

Keld Lane, Hutton le Hole YO62 6UA 📞 01751 417367 🖰 www.ryedalefolkmuseum.co.uk; open daily except for its winter break during most of Dec and Jan.

The small and unassuming frontage to this museum, on the village main street, gives no clue to the delights hidden behind. Over 20 buildings, strung-out down a long, thin, three-acre site, house recreations of Ryedale country life through the centuries, all the way back to a thatched Iron Age roundhouse. Many of them are genuine historic buildings moved from their original sites, and rebuilt stone by stone, to house the artefacts of many rural craftsmen and craftswomen, like blacksmiths, wheelwrights, coopers, saddlers and dairy-maids. Trails and activities are provided for children, and many hands-on events are put on throughout the year, usually with an old-fashioned theme; the ancient board-game of Merrills, for instance, once had its world championships held here. Recent attractions have included a cottage cooking weekend, harvest festival, dry-stone walling taster, bee-keeping workshop and Maypole dancing. The Ryedale Folk weekend is a regular feature in May.

¶¶ FOOD & DRINK

The Crown Keld Lane 📞 01751 417343. Busy and welcoming village pub serving Black Sheep beer and wholesome traditional food.

Feversham Arms Inn Church Houses, Farndale East YO62 7LF 📞 01751 433206 🖰 www.fevershamarmsinn.co.uk. An archetypal country pub, with stone flag floors and horse-brasses, serving simple but wholesome pub food and Yorkshire cask beer. Hugely popular at daffodil time. Good value, and offers self-catering accommodation.

CRAFTS

The Craft Workshops Keld Lane 🖰 www.hutton le hole-crafts.co.uk. Five small artisans' studios (wood-worker, chocolate factory, candle-maker, felt artist and garden furniture maker) and a café, next to the folk museum.

UPDATES WEBSITE

You can post your comments and recommendations, and read the latest feedback and updates from other readers online at 🖰 www.bradtupdates.com/northyorkmoors.

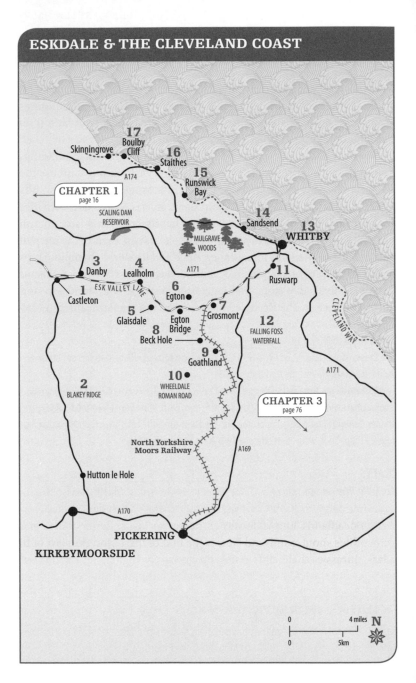

ESKDALE & THE CLEVELAND COAST

17 Boulby Cliff
16 Staithes
15 Runswick Bay
Skinningrove
A174

CHAPTER 1
page 16

SCALING DAM RESERVOIR

14 Sandsend
13 WHITBY

MULGRAVE WOODS

3 Danby
4 Lealholm
ESK VALLEY LINE
1 Castleton
A171
11 Ruswarp

6 Egton
5 Glaisdale
7 Grosmont
8 Beck Hole
Egton Bridge
12 FALLING FOSS WATERFALL

9 Goathland

10 WHEELDALE ROMAN ROAD

2 BLAKEY RIDGE

CHAPTER 3
page 76

North Yorkshire Moors Railway
A169

Hutton le Hole

A170

2

PICKERING

KIRKBYMOORSIDE

CLEVELAND WAY

A171

0   4 miles   N
0   5km

2
ESKDALE & THE CLEVELAND COAST

Eskdale, the 'valley of the winding river', is at the heart of the North York Moors, and the River Esk is the life-blood of the dale. It is only 25 miles long but it punches way above its weight; it has more charm, variety and points of interest than many rivers twice its size. Until recently the Esk was the only salmon-river in Yorkshire, and is the only site in eastern seaboard England with a population of freshwater pearl mussels.

What I love most about the modern River Esk are its moments of wild inaccessibility. Long stretches where it wanders away from civilisation, often plunging into narrow ravines and crag-shadowed gorges where no tarmac road dare follow, and the only way to explore it is by foot or by canoe.

Eskdale ends at the point where the river enters the sea, the entrance to **Whitby** harbour, with this last leg of its journey in a surprising direction. Because of a geographical quirk, this stretch of the Yorkshire seaboard faces due north, so consequently, the coastline to the left, towards Teesside and Scotland, runs away westwards – and what a coastline it is.

The first two miles of it is beach, until the sand ends at a village called simply **Sandsend** – the first of a string of small, former fishing communities, tucked into what little shelter they can find behind rocky headlands, known locally as 'nesses' or 'nabs'. Resembling a giant crocodile's snout, Sandsend Ness is the first of these, and the start of the dark, Jurassic, shale cliffs rising progressively higher the further west you go. **Runswick Bay** is the next haven, hiding behind the heights of High Lingrow, followed by the derelict iron-mining harbour of **Port Mulgrave**. Further west still, at **Staithes** a beck has cut a way through the cliffs to form a spectacular, natural walled harbour. Beyond looms the huge bulk of **Boulby Cliff**, the highest point on the east coast of England, and reputedly the burial place of famed Saxon warrior Beowulf.

SELF-POWERED TRAVEL

CYCLING

If you can cope with occasional very steep hills, **cycling country lanes** in and around Eskdale is great, especially up the quieter side dales. A circuit of Little and Great Fryupdales is my particular favourite, mainly because the slopes are fairly forgiving, but also as the pass between the two dales navigates the delightfully named Fairy Cross Plain.

The picture for the coastal strip is less attractive as few alternatives to the horribly busy A174 exist, except the lane over the top of Boulby Cliff, linking Cowbar and Skinningrove.

Off-road biking is sparse down in the valley bottoms, and tends to be muddy for most of the year anyway, but bridleways and former miners' tracks abound on the moor tops. Danby Beacon and Glaisdale Rigg are two good areas with less challenging routes and are ideal for families. The national park actively promotes biking in the south and west of the Moors but rather neglects this area I think, although their excellent little *Pedal and Puff* guide details routes involving return by train, as both railways in Eskdale allow free bike transport, space permitting.

HORSERIDING

Hundreds of acres of moorland, and mile upon mile of bridleway, bode well for potential horseriders, especially if you have your own horse or pony, as opportunities for hiring are limited.

RIDING CENTRES

Borrowby Equestrian Centre Borrowby TS13 5EH ✆ 01947 840134 ⏚ www.borrowby equestriancentre.co.uk. The only trekking stable in the region. Rides of half an hour or longer for any ability over four years of age. Children's riding parties can be arranged.

WALKING

Walkers are very well served here. For long-distance yompers, the Coast to Coast Walk and the Cleveland Way both skirt the edge of the area, but the **Esk Valley Walk** lies wholly within it. Starting at the Lion Inn on Blakey Ridge above Castleton (the highest pub in the North York Moors) and marked by leaping salmon signs, it follows the complete length of the river from its source to the sea at Whitby. The number of shorter walks, to suit all levels of fitness and enthusiasm, is almost endless. You could for example try a short section of the **Coast to Coast Walk**, like Glaisdale to Grosmont, or vice versa, and take the train back to your start point. As ever, for **information**, the national park website or visitor centre at Danby are the places to pick up details of waymarked walks or walking guidebooks.

One gem of a walk worth a special mention is the **Rail Trail** from Grosmont to Goathland; rich wildlife, safe river access for the children to go paddling, and wheelchair accessible along most of its three-mile length.

ESKDALE

The River Esk flows from west to east, starting at the head of the dale, which the Vikings, not known for their imagination or sense of irony, named Westerdale, and ending gradually by mixing itself with the sea for its last two miles between **Ruswarp** and **Whitby**. In between nestle a string of thoroughly Yorkshire villages; solid but unassuming, chiselled from dark sandstone and growing up the dale-side at each important crossing point. They include rural idylls like **Lealholm** and **Egton Bridge**, the ancient fortified settlements of **Castleton** and **Danby**, and two survivors of a brutal industrial past, **Grosmont** and **Glaisdale**.

The mother river is fed by a series of tributary becks along its length, each with its own mini-dale. The largest of these, the Murk Esk, actually qualifies for 'river' status itself, albeit briefly at only 2½ miles long, and navigates even wilder country than the Esk. This is especially so in its upper reaches, through the moorlands and forests near the village of **Goathland**.

1 CASTLETON

Don't come here expecting turreted ruins: the building that gave this place its name is long gone, with the mound site now occupied by a private manor house. The village is mainly just a service centre for the upper dale, with two pubs, two shops and a petrol station. Visitors do stop here briefly for a café of note and fine art gallery, but Castleton can't really compete in the tourism stakes with neighbouring Danby, which ironically does have a castle.

Most of Castleton village isn't actually in Eskdale bottom, but strung out along a road escaping up the valley side towards Blakey Ridge, arguably the most dramatic moor-top crossing, and a fantastic bus journey to or from Hutton le Hole.

¶| FOOD & DRINK

Castleton Tea Rooms Station Rd ✆ 01287 660135. Cyclists always know the best cafés, and my contacts rave about this one, especially for the cakes.
Eskdale Inn Station Rd ✆ 01287 660333. Both pubs in Castleton are good but this has the edge. An idyllic river- and rail-side position just out of the village. B&B available.
Westerdale Heather Honey The Bungalow, Westerdale YO21 2DE ✆ 01287 660208. Locally produced heather honey sold from the door.

ART & PHOTOGRAPHY

Montage Gallery Church St ✆ 01287 600456. Rambling and many-roomed building with locally sourced artwork and home gallery of superb black-and-white photographer, Graham Lowe.

2 BLAKEY RIDGE

A lonely moorland road from Castleton to Hutton le Hole heads along the exhilarating Blakey Ridge, which wonderfully encapsulates the wildness of the North York Moors. At the top stand a scattered collection of standing stones, guiding travellers across the moor at the head of three valleys – Westerdale, Danbydale and Rosedale. The tallest stone, named Young Ralph Cross, is the symbol of the national park, and along with two others, is said to commemorate the survival of three medieval travellers, lost in a deadly fog – Ralph the guide, and Fat Betty and Margery, two nuns from Rosedale.

Not far from the crosses is **Loose Howe**, a Bronze Age burial mound where a 3,000-year-old body was found, prepared for his voyage into the afterlife, armed, clothed and interred in a dug-out boat. In sight of Loose Howe, and surrounded by even older Neolithic burial mounds, the **Lion Inn** makes a most unexpected sight in an astonishingly inhospitable position and 1,325 feet above sea level; like the similarly remote Tan Hill Inn in the Dales it was built to serve miners – those working in coal and iron in this case.

¶¶ FOOD & DRINK

Lion Inn Blakey Ridge YO62 7LQ ☎ 01751 417320 🖰 www.lionblakey.co.uk. A 16th-century inn in a superb isolated moor-top location. The building, though very large, has low ceilings and open fires which give it a homely feel. Beer is from Theakstons and other guest breweries, and the wholesome meals are very popular. B&B available.

3 DANBY

Five miles from its source, the River Esk is straddled by a pair of Siamese twin villages, joined at a venerable bridge. Both communities sit comfortably in the valley bottom, with old pubs at their centre, the Duke of Wellington on the north bank in Danby, and over the water, the Fox and Hounds in Ainthorpe. The river here is still very young and narrow, and a good running leap could clear it in places, but it carries enough water to power Danby Watermill, whose wheel still turns the internal machinery, but sadly not within public view.

A long history of settlement is evident in the vicinity, with a wealth of Bronze Age earthworks and field systems on adjacent hills (Danby Rigg in particular), a Norman castle, and a medieval packhorse bridge. Despite all this, however, Danby's most influential building today, the Moors Centre, is predominantly Georgian. **Danby Castle** overlooks the village from nearly a mile away, and has its own access road crossing the river via a structure even older than that in the village. Duck Bridge, built in the 1300s as Castle Bridge, was renamed much later after a local stonemason who renovated it.

The minor road beyond Danby Castle leads into the wonderfully named **Little Fryupdale**, which itself is linked to **Great Fryupdale**. Both valleys, named in honour of the Viking goddess Freya, not a plate of bacon and eggs, offer great potential for foot and pedal exploration. Road cycling is quiet and gentle, a superb off-road route follows the Cut Road around the dale heads, and walking is excellent, especially on the central hill of Heads, which separates the two Fryupdales. It boasts a heathery cap and stunningly beautiful forest in Crag Wood at its northern end. Facing Danby Crag on Heads, across Eskdale, is the prominent **Beacon Hill**, complete with modern commemorative beacon, accessible by tarmac road to the summit. This road continues over to **Scaling Dam reservoir**, the largest lake in the Moors, and a good birdwatching venue – breeding greylag geese and little ringed plovers are specialities, with ospreys as regular passage migrants.

The Moors Centre

Lodge Lane, YO21 2NB ✆ 01439 772737; open daily, but weekends only Jan and Feb.

This building originated as the palatial shooting lodge for the Dawnay Estate and is now the flagship visitor centre for the North York Moors National Park. You could easily spend a whole day here, especially in fine weather, as there is just as much to do outside as in. Within the grounds short, wheelchair-accessible walks follow the riverside and delve into Crow Wood, an orienteering course and climbing frame can entertain those energetic children, the artistic will enjoy the sculpture trail and if you just want to sit and picnic, there are acres of lawn space. For those happy to wander further afield, five waymarked walks start at the lodge. Recently revamped, the building contains an indoor climbing wall, a gallery with changing exhibitions of arts and crafts inspired by the local landscape, a shop and a tea room.

Danby Castle

Danby YO21 2NP ✆ 01287 669219 🖰 www.danbycastle.com.

In a long and eventful life since it was built in the 12th century, this petite castle has passed through the hand of many aristocratic owners; Catherine Parr, who married into the Neville family, lived here as a young woman long before her recruitment as Henry VIII's sixth wife. As part of the Danby section of the Dawnay Estate, like the Moors Centre, it is owned by Viscount Downe. After many years of part-ruin, attached to a hillside farm, Danby Castle's latest chapter involves a neat juxtaposition of ancient and modern. Every October the Danby Court Leet, one of the few still in existence, meets in the jury room of the castle, as it has for centuries, to administer the affairs of the local common lands. The same room doubles as a wedding chapel operated by Danby Castle Ltd, a family enterprise comprising Duncan and Carolyn who live in the farmhouse (the southeast tower).

The castle is not officially open to the public, but you can nose around the outside of the ruins, and if you give them a ring they will be happy to let you in.

⑪ FOOD & DRINK

Camphill Village Trust Botton Farm YO21 2NJ ✆01287 661211. Camphill community shop has Botton bread, cakes, milk, yoghurt and cheese.

Duke of Wellington Danby ✆01287 660351 🖰 www.dukeofwellingtondanby.co.uk. A large, rambling but homely village pub on the central crossroads. Cask beer is Tetleys Imperial, Daleside and a guest; there's a selection of pies. River fishing tickets available behind the bar.

Fox and Hounds Brook Lane, Ainthorpe YO21 2LD ✆01287 660218 🖰 www. foxandhounds-ainthorpe.com. A big 16th-century coaching inn with quoits pitch nearby. Cask Yorkshire beers and basic pub grub.

Stonehouse Bakery Briar Hill, Danby ✆01287 660006 🖰 www.stonehousebakery.co.uk. Speciality breads, cakes and confectionery to take away or eat in the café.

4 LEALHOLM

Back in the 1990s I was always baffled as to why Lealholm was not more popular as a place to visit. Granted, the riverbank and quoits pitch would be dotted with picnickers on a sunny weekend, but nothing like the hordes that would descend on Goathland or Grosmont rain or shine. Back then, there was only enough custom to support the pub and one tea shop at the Shepherd's Hall. Now numbers must have perked up, or people are drinking more, because three places supply those wanting to indulge in a cup of tea and a scone, and the pub is busier than ever.

"The farmyard can be a bit 'clarty' – the Yorkshire dialect way of saying that you may find yourself up to the knees in a mixture of mud and cow muck."

I guess the reason for the influx is that more people are using the Esk Valley line and hopping off at the station here, the growing reputation of the revitalised Board Inn, or the fact that word has got out about the excellent walking and cycling routes from the village.

Two circular jaunts from Lealholm I would recommend are a low-level route and another longer one, partly on the moors above the valley. The beauty of them is that, following bridleways and minor roads, they can be done on foot, bike or horseback. The shorter of the two starts along the track just below the car park, and following the river eastwards (downstream). At Underpark Farm, the route heads under the railway and uphill to Rake Lane. The farmyard can be a bit 'clarty' – the Yorkshire dialect understated way of saying that you may find yourself up to the knees in a mixture of mud and cow muck. A left turn at the quiet dead-ended Rake Lane takes you back to Lealholm via Lealholmside. The longer high-level route climbs up Danby Beacon and back via moorland track and Oakley Walls Road.

¶¶ FOOD & DRINK

Board Inn Village Green ☎01947 897279 🖱 www.theboardinn.com. An 18th-century alehouse in a glorious riverside position, with a quoits pitch out front.

Shepherds Hall Tea Rooms Main St ☎01947 897746 🖱 www.shepherdshalltearooms. co.uk. Reopened after a period of closure, with a craft and local produce gallery attached. Beware steep steps to get in!

Stepping Stones Cottage Bakery Village Green ☎01947 897626. Lovely fresh bread and pastries to eat in the sun on the village green opposite.

SHOPPING

Forge House Gallery Main St ☎01947 897901 🖱 www.forgehousegallery.co.uk. Gallery of contemporary, 19th- and 20th-century paintings, and shop with local craft items.

Forge Pottery Main St ☎01947 897457. A small pottery workshop opposite the gallery, selling its products and a few other arts and crafts.

Lealholm Village Store Main St ☎01947 897310. The village's sole shop.

Poets Cottage Shrub Nursery Main St ☎01947 897424 🖱 www.poetscottage.co.uk. A serene hideaway just behind the village store, named after the 19th century, Irish-born poet, John Castillo, who lived here.

5 GLAISDALE

🏠 **Bank House Farm** (see page 199)

A more rural picture would be difficult to imagine, but the Glaisdale of 150 years ago was an altogether different scene: the river polluted, the air full of black industrial smoke, the clank and rattle of heavy machinery and rail carriages, and its erstwhile pub full of ironstone miners and foundry workers. Glaisdale's industrial revolution was short-lived and the scars have healed, but sharp-eyed industrial archaeologists will still have plenty to find.

The history of this long, straggling village goes way back beyond the Victorian iron boom as the graceful 17th-century packhorse bridge over the river testifies. It was constructed on the instruction of one Thomas Ferris, originally a poor farmer's son, who fell in love with the Squire of Glaisdale's daughter, but was refused her hand in marriage unless he went away and made his fortune. When he succeeded in the task he returned, married his love and built 'Beggar's Bridge' to commemorate his wading of the swollen river to see her during their courtship, and to ensure that later needy suitors kept their feet dry.

At the point where Beggar's Bridge reaches gracefully over the river, a small railway viaduct does the same, though not quite so delicately. Glaisdale Beck joins the Esk through one of its arches, having just flowed down through West Arncliffe Wood. Strangely, this beck has been nowhere near Glaisdale village, which actually resides in Eskdale; the valley of Glaisdale, where the beck originates, is a rarely visited corner nearby. Its one minor road loops up one side of the dale, and back down the other, providing an excellent, gentle, family cycling circuit.

¶¶ FOOD & DRINK

Gillbeck Organic Homegrown Low Gill Beck Farm YO21 2QA ☎01947 897363. Seasonal soft fruits for sale.

R H Ford & Son Butchers Main St ☎01947 897235. Beef and lamb from their own farm; other local farms supply pork for bacon, shop-made sausages and shop-salted hams. The black pudding is legendary and, of the numerous kinds of pie available, Monty Don once declared the pork pie to be the best he had ever tasted. All in all, a pretty good butchers.

Padmore's Bank House Farm YO21 2QA ☎01947 897297. Organic beef, lamb and pork straight from the farm. Also sole-use bunkhouse accommodation.

6 EGTON & EGTON BRIDGE

⚑ La Rosa Campsite (see page 200)

The trees that gave 'oak town' its name are gone, but one survivor from the village's past is alive and well. **Egton Show**, on the last Wednesday in August, is the largest of its kind in the North York Moors, and is such an event in the country calendar that for many people it is the one and only time they visit during the year. Others may call in to one of the two pubs here, or the village shop while passing through, but not much else will hold your attention.

A mile down the road, the ancient river crossing at **Egton Bridge** attracts far more visitors. Like its hill-top neighbour, it has two pubs, one on either side of the river, with a delightful stepping-stone and island-hopping potter between them. A steady stream of admirers always seem to find their way to Egton Bridge, some just happy to gaze at the magnificent 18th-century redwood trees by the river, or to saunter along its banks. Downstream, a flat and just-about wheelchair accessible track leads to Grosmont, while the other direction takes you into the spectacular Arncliffe Gorge and a glorious woodland trail to Glaisdale along the Cleveland Way. Other visitors are Roman Catholic pilgrims visiting **St Hedda's Church**, one that seemed to miss the Reformation and large enough to be dubbed the Cathedral of the Moors. Despite these attractions, the only time it really gets crowded here is at gooseberry show-time.

¶ FOOD & DRINK

It's very rarely that I feel I can recommend every pub/hotel in a place for food, drink and accommodation but these five deserve it:

Horseshoe Hotel Egton Bridge ☎01947 895245 🖰 www.egtonbridgehotel.co.uk. Serene rural location by the river. On warm days most folk prefer the large beer garden but the snug bar with fishing memorabilia is the place on wet days or winter evenings.

Ye Horseshoe Inn Main St, Egton ☎01947 895274 🖰 www.yehorseshoe.co.uk. Known locally as the Top Horseshoe to distinguish it from the Horseshoe Hotel down the hill. Dog-friendly bar and B&B.

Postgate Inn Egton Bridge ☎01947 895241 🖰 www.postgateinn.com. Small and cosy pub by the railway station that doubles as the 'Black Dog' in Heartbeat but in real life is named after a local Catholic martyr.

Wheatsheaf Inn Main St, Egton ☎01947 895271 🖰 www.wheatsheafegton.com. A comfortable and traditional village pub. Best on a winter's evening with a roaring fire in the bar corner range. B&B plus dog-friendly self-catering.

White's Restaurant Broom House, Egton Bridge YO21 1XD ☎01947 895279 🖰 www.

GROWING GIANT GOOSEBERRIES

A world record was broken in Egton Bridge in 2009. It wasn't one that made the national news, but among the soft-fruit growing fraternity, the biggest gooseberry ever seen was a major event.

The Egton Bridge Old Gooseberry Society (🖰 www.egtongooseberryshow.org.uk) has been holding an annual show on the first Tuesday in August for over 200 years, making it the oldest in the country. Come along in the afternoon for public viewing of the 600 or so entries and prizes for the winners. You will learn about reds, whites, yellows and greens and the relative merits of the Lord Derby, Lord Kitchener and Montrose varieties but you're not likely to see the like of Bryan Nellist's monster 35-dram (two and a bit ounces) Woodpecker in the foreseeable future.

egton-bridge.co.uk. Unexpected sophistication in the middle of nowhere (half a mile west of Egton Bridge on the Glaisdale road). Tasteful B&B.

7 GROSMONT

⋏ Priory Farm Campsite (see page 200)

In the past two centuries life has almost gone full circle for Grosmont, from rural backwater to industrial centre and back again. Almost but not quite, because, although the ironstone mines and blast furnaces are gone, the railways (two of them) still remain.

The smoke-stained buildings of Grosmont sit at the confluence of two river valleys, the Esk and then the Murk Esk, and are consequently the junction of the two railway lines in those dales. The Esk Valley line is three stations away from Whitby here, and is joined by the **North Yorkshire Moors Railway**, now a very popular private steam and diesel line crossing the moors from Pickering. Up until recently this was the terminus for steam services, but old locomotives puffing their way through Sleights and Ruswarp to Whitby are now regularly seen in summer.

Such was the impact of the railway when it arrived in Grosmont that its common name changed to 'Tunnel', after the line's short underground journey. It was during the digging of the first small tunnel for a horse-drawn tramway, that ironstone was first discovered, and this route has since become a footpath to the **railway engine sheds**. Another footpath, over the top of the tunnels, then follows the rest of the track bed of the old line, planned and built by George Stephenson, the 'railway king'. The Rail Trail crosses the Murk Esk four times on its three-mile journey to Goathland via Beck Hole.

Grosmont Engine Sheds

The public face of the North Yorkshire Moors Railway is the station and level crossing in the village main street, but if you want to see what makes this organisation really tick, stroll over the footbridge across the river and through the Stephenson's Tunnel footpath. This takes you to the Grosmont Engine Sheds where the locomotive restoration, maintenance and servicing takes place, and where hard-core enthusiastic volunteers work; there's probably enough oil under their collective fingernails to keep a small car on the road. A public viewing platform lets you watch the work going on and the shed shop sells enthusiasts bric-a-brac.

¶¶ FOOD & DRINK

The Geall Gallery and Artisan Café Front St ✆ 01947 895007 🖰 www.chrisgeall.com.
A showcase gallery for talented local landscape artist Chris Geall and others. Admire the
artwork from the comfort of the in-house Artisan Café.

8 BECK HOLE

Almost every approach to this tiny hamlet involves a precipitous hill, to
where its dozen or so houses nestle at the bottom of a natural excavation
– no surprises where the name came from. Becks Hole (plural) would
be more accurate, as this is the point where Eller Beck, still visibly and
audibly excited after its recent fall over Thomason Foss, joins West Beck
to create the River Murk Esk. As at Grosmont, ironstone was worked
here, and many old buildings served the miners and furnace workers,
some as alehouses.

Only one pub remains, but the **Birch Hall Inn** is the heart and
soul of the village; that and the quoits pitch, scene of many sepia-
coloured triumphs decorating the walls of the pub. Of all my visits over
the years, the most memorable have been on wet winter nights, with
a fire blazing in the big bar, a wet dog steaming in front of it and just
a handful of locals to share the craic. For
me, the Birch Hall is as near perfection as a
pub can get, and my favourite anywhere in
the country.

*"Of all my visits over
the years, the most
memorable have been
on wet winter nights,
with a fire blazing, a
wet dog steaming in
front of it and just a
handful of locals to
share the craic."*

On a quiet day, the best sort here, you
can hear steam engines pass without
stopping on the 'new' line higher up the
hill but Beck Hole's station is a 'ghost' on
the 1836 route, at the foot of the feature
which caused its closure. The incline up to
Goathland was way too steep for horses
or locomotives to pull carriages up, so ropes and cables did the job,
first using an ingenious water-filled counterweight tank coming
down, then a big, fixed engine at the top. Rope and cable failure
caused mayhem on more than one occasion so, after a crash causing
two deaths and 13 injuries, in 1864 the line was re-routed to bypass
the incline.

Scope for walking around Beck Hole is extensive, especially half-day
rambles that use part of the old railway track at some stage. For a glorious

two-mile woodland and heather circuit, go west to circumnavigate Randy Mere reservoir (✳ grid reference NZ812018). Steam enthusiasts will enjoy following the railway to Darnholm and the incline back (another two miles) or of course the full three-mile **Rail Trail** from Goathland to Grosmont is a classic, following the original route the railway took (including up an inclined plane for its final section into Goathland), and you can travel back on the train.

⑪ FOOD & DRINK

Birch Hall Inn Beck Hole YO22 5LE ✆ 01947 896245 🖰 www.beckhole.info/bhi.htm. This little alehouse is a genuine national treasure, made up of two tiny bar rooms, served by hatches, and a sweet shop sandwiched in between – virtually unchanged for 70 years. Three beers are usually available, Black Sheep, the house brew 'Beckwatter' from the North Yorkshire Brewing Co. and a guest, and food is simple but wholesome; Botham's roll butties and Radford's pies.

9 GOATHLAND

I was always a little surprised at the popularity of Goathland even before *Heartbeat* hit our TV screens, as I don't think it has anywhere near the charm and neatness of Lealholm or the character of Grosmont. Now though, its visitor-pulling power is in a different league since it became Aidensfield, and its railway station starred as 'Hogsmeade' in the first *Harry Potter* film. I prefer to pass through and visit some of the glorious countryside nearby, like **Wheeldale** or the gorges of Eller Beck, towards **Beck Hole**, and West Beck nearer at hand.

A signpost opposite the church (✳ grid reference NZ827007) indicates the direct route down to the surprisingly verdant netherworld of **West Beck**, with a waterside footpath that takes you past the silky tresses of **Mallyan Spout waterfall**, or under it if you're feeling bold or hot, or both. If you are up for a challenge, then the mile of public footpath upstream from here is for you, as it follows a deep, narrow and boulder-strewn ravine up to New Wath Bridge on the Egton road. This can be a serious scramble, especially when wet or icy, and West Beck floods the path after heavy rain. Come here on a warm summer afternoon though, and it shows its other face; wood warblers singing in the tops of the oaks, dippers zipping up the rapids and dragonflies snatching a meal from the clouds of gnats that dance over the chattering waters – a glorious place.

10 WHEELDALE ROMAN ROAD & WHEELDALE MOOR

South of Goathland, a vast tract of land rises as whale-backed hills, pimple-topped with Bronze Age burial mounds and smothered in what is part of England's largest continuous area of **heather moorland**. Two Howes Rigg, Simon Howe and **Wheeldale Moor** are all Access Areas where you can in general walk where you please: for lovers of peace and tranquillity in the natural world it is a slice of heaven. I have spent many a day up here, striding through the heather or squelching across bogs, with the spicy scent of sweet gale in the air and the bubbling of curlews in my ears, and often not seen another human all day.

Hot summer days are best for wildlife, with the air alive with bees and dragonflies, green tiger beetles scurrying across the sandy soil and an excellent chance of seeing lizards or adders. In August add the bonus of the spectacular flowering of the heather; trillions of tiny blooms combining to form a purple blanket across the hill. Take care from the 12th of the month onwards though, as areas of moor may be closed for shooting.

QUOITS

Nothing better reflects the dogged insularity of the Yorkshireman than the game of quoits. It is played virtually nowhere else in the world other than this corner of northeast England, and Eskdale is its heartland.

Norse in origin, as are most things hereabouts, the game involves tossing a metal ring from one end of a pitch to the other, aiming to 'hoopla' a metal pin (a two-point 'ringer'); touch it for one point or at least thunk into the surrounding square of clay nearer than your opponent's quoit.

The tiny hamlet of Beck Hole has had more than its fair share of 'world' champions in its time, so I asked Mike Mendelsohn, a multiple winner of that prestigious title, what made a great quoits player.

'A good strong arm's important. That ring weighs five pound, which is a fair weight to be slinging. You don't want to be straining to reach the pin. It's best to have a bit of distance to spare, which is why me father had us throwing full sized quoits as bairns to build us up. What else do you need? A good eye, a nasty streak and a willingness to go down the pub regularly and practice!'

Almost all the region's quoits pitches are in front of a village pub, and many a visitor has been seen puzzling over the wooden covers and peeping at the mysterious clay beneath. Turn up on a Saturday and all will be revealed; and what better way to spend a summer evening than discussing the day's walk and sipping a beer to the

Wheeldale Moor has a half-mile stretch of the best preserved and excavated **Roman road** in the country. The easiest access is at the Stape Road end where an interpretive board describes the local legend of Wade the giant and his labour of love. Wade lived in Mulgrave Castle near the coast at Sandsend but his wife Bel lived in Pickering castle. To make visiting easier they decided to build a road linking the two, but with only one rock-breaking hammer between them, they had to throw it across the Moors to each other. The road is still known locally as Wade's Causeway, but the less romantic reality is that it linked the Roman garrison town of Malton to a chain of coastal signal stations.

11 RUSWARP

Twice a day the River Esk does something odd: prompted by the rising tide it flows backwards away from the sea and a mile inland to the village of Ruswarp, (pronounced Ruzzup). Its short journey winding under two big viaducts over the estuarine floodplain is a joy, and one that you can follow on foot, by train or, best of all, by boat. Some of the trip boats will venture up the river at high tide and there are possibilities

clink of metal on metal, as local rivalries are settled in an inter-village fixture. You never know, you may even be asked to join in. One of my proudest moments was making up the numbers in a Goldsborough team at home to Fryupdale. I was accosted by my neighbour Alwyn, as I sauntered over to the Fox and Hounds for a swift half one evening. 'Do you fancy a game Mike?' he asked. I laughed and muttered something about leaving it to the experts and having a pint waiting. 'No,' he said. 'I'm serious. Will Lewis is on a coastguard shout and we're down a man.'

So, the upshot was that I was given a quick resumé of the rules, watched what the others were doing and attempted to copy them.

My practice throws were a bit wayward, a couple of under-thrown bouncing bombs and an over corrected heave that cleared the clay and rebounded into the fence behind. By the time the opposition had arrived and the match got under way I had sort of found my distance and, while I never mastered the finer points of throwing 'Frenchman' or laying a 'gater', I didn't let the team down; 'steady away' was the verdict in the bar afterwards. If memory serves me rightly, we came out 21–19 winners.

To find the local quoits venues and match days, go to ☞ www.tradgames.org.uk or to have a go yourself visit one of the many village shows in summer. They often have a come-and-try-it quoits stall.

for paddling or rowing your own boat. You're at the richest section of the whole river for wildlife and on the right day it can be a memorable experience: very rare saltmarsh plants like wild celery and hemlock water dropwort grow on the banks alongside vitamin C-rich scurvy grass, which sailors took as a preventative supplement on voyages. The water teems with tiny opossum shrimps, attracting fish, which in turn bring herons, cormorants, dabchicks and kingfishers. When the sea-trout and salmon are running, seals follow them up the river and otters are here, although dawn and dusk are the only times you are likely to see them, such is their shyness.

"You can get welcome respite from the crowds of Whitby here while still finding things to occupy you."

Up until the 15th century the Esk was tidal all the way to Sleights along what is still known as The Carrs, meaning flooded woodland, but for 600 years a watermill weir has stopped the tide at Ruswarp. You can get welcome respite from the crowds of Whitby here while still finding things to occupy you: a circuit of the miniature steam railway, feeding the ducks on the mill pond or just watching the river go by from the Bridge Inn beer garden or Riverside café. Sadly, no footpath follows the river for its next languid mile upstream, but half-hourly buses or, better still, the train four or five times a day can take you to **Sleights** where a bridleway picks up the Esk Valley Walk route. The River Esk trickles when it's low or roars at high levels, over another weir at Sleights with a fish ladder at the side. In flood conditions the salmon don't bother with their staircase but jump straight up the main wave, and this is the best place on the whole river to watch them do it. The nearby pub, not surprisingly, is called the Salmon Leap.

Rowing & paddling at Ruswarp

Various alternatives exist for you to get afloat at Ruswarp and explore the river using your own muscle power. **Ruswarp Pleasure Boats** (✆01947 604658 ⌁ www.ruswarp-pleasure-boats.co.uk) hire out rowing boats or sit-on-top kayaks to explore the non-tidal mile of flat river upstream to Sleights.

If you have access to your own canoes or kayaks you can arrange launching with Ruswarp Pleasure Boats and stay on the flat water or descend the friendly weir and run the tidal section of river to the public slipway at Whitby marina, returning by train. Alternatively, launch at Whitby an hour or two before high tide, drift up with the flood, spend a relaxing hour in Ruswarp, before coming back down river with the ebb-tide.

If all that sounds tempting but the lack of a boat is stopping you (as boats from the hire company only go upstream) then the whole trip can be arranged by East Barnby Outdoor Education Centre (✆01947 893333 ⊕ www.outdoored.co.uk). You choose the route and do all the paddling but they provide transport, equipment (including possibilities for wheelchair users) and a guide.

ⵜ FOOD & DRINK

The River Gardens Briggswath YO21 1RR ✆07785 573625 ⊕ www.perrysplants.co.uk. Plant nursery and riverside café. The crab sandwiches and local Radford's steak pies are particularly good.

Ruswarp Riverside Café The Carrs, Ruswarp YO21 1RL ✆01947 600109 ⊕ www. chainbridgeriverside.com. The name sums it up – lots of duck-feeding potential while you have a brew. Self-catering accommodation available.

12 FALLING FOSS

Just over three miles south of Ruswarp, May Beck's tumble over a 67-foot shale cliff creates Falling Foss, the highest waterfall in the North York Moors, and the centrepiece of a secretive wooded valley. It is possible to drive and park close to the falls but I find it much more satisfying to arrive here on foot along the beck, with the noise of the cascade gradually developing from a distant hiss to a spray-filled roar as I approach.

Of the two routes in, the northerly upstream one is probably the more trodden, as the final mile joins up with the Coast to Coast Walk. It can be started from Sleights railway station (✽ grid reference NZ868081) and follows a tributary of the River Esk which has a confusing habit of changing its name. It is Iburndale Beck for its first mile, then Little Beck as it passes through the rich rainforest-like woods owned by the Yorkshire Wildlife Trust. Just before you arrive at the falls, look out for The Hermitage, a remarkable hollowed-out boulder shelter, complete with seats.

The southerly downstream approach starts at Sneaton Forest car park (✽ grid reference NZ893024) and follows our stream under its third pseudonym, May Beck, on either bank, along a half-mile nature trail to Midge Hall and its tea rooms on the lip of Falling Foss.

Other very popular Forestry Commission trails head in the opposite direction from May Beck car park, visiting more waterfalls as they enter the vast expanse of Sneaton Forest, a great place to see reptiles and amphibians. Adders and lizards are common in heathery clearings and the plethora of round ponds (World War II bomb craters) boil with frogs, toads and newts in springtime.

¶¶ FOOD & DRINK

Beacon Farm Sneaton YO22 5HS ℡ 01947 605212 ⏚ www.beacon-farm.co.uk. A farm that has diversified into Yorkshire dairy ice-cream production with a café attached.
Falling Foss Tea Garden Midge Hall, Sneaton Forest YO22 5JD ℡ 07723477929 ⏚ www. fallingfossteagarden.co.uk. The former gamekeeper's cottage of Midge Hall houses an Edwardian tea garden in a most idyllic woodland site. Recently renovated and restored to sell drinks and snacks. Provides poohsticks for the nearby bridge and lots of other activities to entertain children.

13 WHITBY

🏠 **The Boathouse** (see page 199) and **La Rosa Hotel** (see page 199).

'If you want a quiet day in Whitby, try a wet Tuesday in February, with the X Factor final on telly,' was Jim the taxi driver's advice, and his reasoning is plain to see. Whitby is an extremely popular destination, bursting at the seams every weekend, and even midweek if the sun appears. The root of the town's pulling power is its possession of a little bit of something for everyone, seeming to combine in a melting pot all the best that Yorkshire has to offer with a dash of Cornish fishing port and more than a drop of Transylvanian blood. The place is dripping in history, it oozes from the pores of every building like a little York-by-the-sea with Tudor halls, gothic ruins, Saxon churches, smugglers' pubs and fishermen's cottages – they all have their stories to tell. And then, cheek by jowl, you will find the other, more modern Whitby of buckets and spades, amusement arcades and fish and chip shops, but even this has a dated and quaintly retro feel to it.

Three figures stand tall in Whitby's past: a woman who famously arrived on a mission, a man who left three times and changed the world, and a character who never even came here, because he didn't really exist. The woman was a Northumbrian princess called **Hild** who came in the year

AD656 and founded a Saxon monastery on East Cliff, the first Whitby Abbey. The seafarer who repeatedly left in the 18th century, along with shiploads of crewmates, was **Captain James Cook**. He returned twice, but never made it back from his third voyage, having been clubbed to death on a Hawaiian beach – the sort of thing that always upsets your travel plans. Ironically, the most well-known of the three characters is a fictitious literary creation of the Victorian novelist **Bram Stoker**, the infamous Count Dracula. The horrifically evocative Chapter 7 of Stoker's novel *Dracula*, where the Count, in the form of a black dog, leaps off a ship grounded in the harbour, and bounds through the alleyways of the town, should be read on a bench in the churchyard overlooking the scene, for full effect. Dracula's link with Whitby has inspired one of the town's most lively and entertaining annual events, the Goth Festival, which takes place on the weekend nearest to Halloween each year (so popular that there's now another one every spring).

Whitby owes its existence to the **River Esk** and the fact that it is a natural sheltered anchorage for ships using the North Sea. This is still what it always was, a working harbour, and going to sea in boats will always be at the heart of the town. In the 18th century fleets of sailing ships left these shores, not just explorers in Cook's *Resolution, Discovery* and *Endeavour* but whalers of world renown like the captains (father and son) Scoresby. In the early 20th century when herring fishing was at its peak, hundreds of boats packed

"Their place on the wharf has been taken by a proliferation of pleasure boats – tourism is king now."

the harbour and it was said you could walk from one side to the other without getting your feet wet. Overfishing and, latterly, European quota-setting have been the death knell for the fishing industry and only four deep-sea trawlers operate from Whitby. Their place on the wharf has been taken by a proliferation of pleasure boats such as yachts, cruisers, scuba-diving inflatables and boat trips – tourism is king now.

The river both unites and divides the town, even more so pre-1767 when no bridge linked the two sides. Separation breeds suspicion and the inhabitants of each bank used to refer to each other as 't'other side o' watter dogs'. Such was the mistrust that when the first bridge was opened, locals celebrated with a pitched battle in the middle. Even today, old-established families say they come from East Whitby or West Whitby, not Whitby. The first bridge lifted to allow boats through but the Victorian replacement that survives today is a swing bridge and is the focal point of the town. Whitby has so much to see that I would recommend splitting it into two trails to visit on foot, both starting here.

Scarborough Borough Council produces two excellent **town trail** books, one for each side of the river and available from the tourist office. The *West Side Trail* takes in Baxtergate's yards, a lifeboat museum, the whalebone arch (recalling the town's former connection with the whaling industry), Captain Cook's statue and the fish quay but it fails to mention what, to me, should always be a compulsory prime objective, weather and phobias permitting – the end of the **pier**. This is as far out to sea as it is possible to get without a boat and an exhilarating experience in rough weather. **Whitby harbour** faces due north and is one of the few places in the country where watching the sunrise and sunset over the sea is possible on the same day – you are allowed to go for a cup of tea in between. On your way out or back, look out for dinosaur 'fossils' carved into the concrete by local stonemason Darren Yeadon, and take a walk up the spiral staircase in the **lighthouse** if it's open (✆01947 601344).

"On your way out or back, look out for dinosaur 'fossils' carved into the concrete by local stonemason Darren Yeadon."

The east side is my favourite; more compact and with fewer new intrusions, this is where I can best let my historical imagination run riot. The *East Side Trail* mentions the jet shops, old inns, lifeboat pier, **Captain Cook Memorial Museum** (with displays about his voyages of discovery that started from Whitby), market square (still operational Tuesdays and Saturdays) and 199 steps up to the church and abbey but stops again at the foot of the pier. Owing to wave damage only half of the east pier is accessible but it's a wild and evocative place and a sanctuary for large numbers of sheltering purple sandpipers in winter.

Off the trail, and around the corner under the cliffs, a short mile's wander along the wave-cut platform to Saltwick Bay makes a tremendous diversion, with the return to the abbey via the cliff-top Cleveland Way. Small boats anchored just offshore here may be carrying sub-aqua divers visiting the wreck of the *Rohilla*, a World War I hospital ship which hit Whitby Rock on a stormy night in 1914 with the loss of 85 lives. One survivor, a nurse, had only ever been on a ship once before – the *Titanic*. I don't suppose she ever went to sea again.

Whitby Abbey
☎ 01947 603568; English Heritage.

If ever a place could be described as having a chequered history, then this is it: founded by Saxons, destroyed by Vikings, rebuilt by Normans, dismantled by Tudors and bombarded by Germans.

When Princess Hild was sent from Hartlepool in AD656 she arrived in the tiny fishing hamlet of Streoneshalh (Whitby was a later Danish name) and became first Abbess of the wooden Columban abbey of St Peter. She later became the patron saint of the town and had many wells and a fossil named after her. *Hildocerous bifrons* is an ammonite common in the cliffs below the abbey and commemorates the legend that St Hilda turned snakes infesting the headland into stone and threw them over the cliff. Medieval monks even carved heads on to them and sold them as 'snake-stones'. During her time a dispute between the Roman and Celtic churches over the date of Easter was settled at the Synod of Whitby and we still use their convoluted formula today, to annual confusion.

After the Vikings razed the original structure, the Normans rebuilt, in local sandstone, the present Benedictine abbey. At the Dissolution much of the abbey stone was used to build the Manor next door which now houses the Abbey Visitor Centre.

In one last twist of fate, during World War I, a flotilla of German battleships bombarded the east coast of England. Scarborough and Hartlepool were also targeted but the abbey was particularly badly damaged during Whitby's shelling. This won't be the final chapter: when the abbey was built it stood half a mile from the sea but in the intervening 900 years that distance has been reduced to 200 yards by the erosional power of the North Sea. In a few more hundred years, the stones of the abbey will be on the beach growing seaweed.

St Mary's Church
I have a soft spot for St Mary's, as it was here my daughter was baptised. That said, I can still safely claim, without being accused of bias, that this is one of the most fascinatingly quirky churches in the country.

Being next door to the abbey, you might expect it to be dedicated to St Hilda instead of St Mary. The reason lies in the church's antiquity – it was already here, complete with name, when the Princess came calling. The fact is that the heart of this building is older than its neighbour but has been added to piecemeal ever since. The outside is full of interest – Norman arches a-plenty and a strange ship's-deck-style roof – but go inside and you could be in a museum. A rare set of 17th-century box pews, a three-decker pulpit with ear trumpets for a deaf vicar's wife, a multi-locked treasure chest, and more, all candle-lit and heated from a central pot boiler.

Don't confine yourself to the building but wander around the graveyard surrounding it. Like a mouthful of loose and rotting teeth, this has to be the perfect horror film set. Those gravestones still legible tell of boat sinkings and drownings, master mariners and lifeboat men. One of the eeriest is the Huntrodds memorial, to a husband and wife born on the same day, married on their birthday and dying within hours of each other on ... you guessed it, their birthday again.

Whitby Museum

Pannett Park ☎ 01947 602908 ⏱ www.whitbymuseum.org.uk; closed Mon.

If you enter this building expecting a high-tech, hands-on multi-sensory modern museum, you will be disappointed. The words hotchpotch and higgledy-piggledy could have been invented for Whitby Museum; it is unashamedly old-fashioned, cramped, politically incorrect, poorly set out, and full of glass cases, but that is what sets it apart and gives it its charm. It is not only a museum of things, but a museum piece of museums.

Themes seem infinitely varied: model ships, stuffed birds, local archaeology, fossils, military clothing, and a brilliant weather-forecasting machine based on leeches called a tempest prognosticator – a little bit of everything but not much of anything. Don't get the impression that it's all junk in here though. One of the model ships made from food-ration chicken bones by Napoleonic prisoners of war is reportedly worth £250,000 and the carved jet collection is the best in the world, and features two wonderful jet chessboards.

What I like best about this place, though, is the chance to explore and discover things for myself. I read elsewhere of a sea kayak in here, the only one of its design in the world, so I searched and eventually found it, on top of a wall cabinet, unlabelled – that's this place to a tee.

¶¶ FOOD & DRINK

Black Horse Inn Church St ☎ 01947 602906 ⏱ www.the-black-horse.com. An unspoiled architectural gem, possibly the oldest pub in town with the original Victorian bar. Traditional in every sense of the word, with up to five cask ales including Whitby Black Dog, Yorkshire cheese or seafood 'tapas' to eat, and snuff to sniff.

Elizabeth Botham and Sons Skinner St ✆01947 602823 🖰 www.botham.co.uk. The nicer of their two long-standing tea rooms; family-run craft bakery since 1865.

Fortunes Smokehouse Henrietta St ✆01947 601659 🖰 www.fortuneskippers.co.uk. Traditional kipper-smoking shed with shop. Kippers sold in pairs wrapped in newspaper.

Greens Bridge St ✆01947 600284 🖰 www.greensofwhitby.co.uk. Restaurant/bistro specialising in exceptional local seafood. Polite and helpful staff.

Magpie Café Pier Rd ✆01947 602058 🖰 www.magpiecafe.co.uk. World-famous café serving superlative seafood, especially fish and chips. Be prepared to queue.

Royal Fisheries Baxtergate ✆01947 604738 🖰 www.fuscowhitby.com. The locals' favourite take-away chippy since 1968 when the Fusco family moved here from Pickering. Known as 'Fuscos' in town.

ART & CRAFTS

Doodlepots Creative Studio Skinner St ✆01947 825824 🖰 www.doodlepots.co.uk. Paint your own plain plate/cup/pot/bowl, etc, and then have it fired to pick up later.

Studio of John Freeman Market Pl ✆01947 602799 🖰 www.johnfreemanstudios.co.uk. Resident artist working in watercolours.

Sutcliffe Gallery Flowergate ✆01947 602239 🖰 www.sutcliffe-gallery.co.uk. Books and black-and-white photographs by the master Victorian photographer.

Wash House Pottery Blackburn Yard ✆01947 604995. Customised tiles, planters, house plaques and plates made on site.

Whitby Jet Heritage Centre Church St ✆01947 821530 🖰 www.whitbyjet.net. An original Victorian jet works with working craftsmen.

THE CLEVELAND COAST: SANDSEND TO SKINNINGROVE

A few years ago from the back of a ferry leaving Newcastle, I saw through binoculars a dark line on the horizon to the southeast. What I was seeing 40 miles away was the great bulge of the northern North York Moors meeting the sea in a line of dark crags. Marauding Vikings approaching from the North Sea over a thousand years ago had the same view, prompting them to name this part of England the Land of Cliffs – Cleveland. This wall of rock stretches seemingly unbroken, from Saltburn southeast to Whitby and beyond. Prehistoric erosion has breached the wall in a handful of places, allowing the coastal communities of **Sandsend**, **Runswick Bay**, **Staithes** and **Skinningrove** to develop. In the past all have relied for their livelihood on the silver harvest of the sea and the mineral wealth from the cliffs themselves, but now to a greater or lesser degree each depends on tourism.

14 SANDSEND

This village is certainly aptly named: two miles of golden beach stops abruptly at the foot of The Ness and this cluster of sandstone cottages, hotels and shops huddle in what little shelter it provides. A closer look reveals two hamlets here; one for each of the small streams that flow into the sea 200 yards apart.

East Row, at the beach end, is older but smaller, and hosts the White Hart pub, two cafés, a restaurant, a very tasteful art and craft shop and the main entrance to **Mulgrave Woods**. At the cliff end, most of Sandsend proper hides up the little valley of Sandsend Beck, with a sleepy hobbit village air to it. Even at the height of summer when the beach is crowded, and boy does it get crowded, all stays serene and peaceful up here, with little to disturb the grazing goats.

"Even at the height of summer when the beach is crowded, all stays serene and peaceful up here, with little to disturb the grazing goats."

What the original valley inhabitants were hiding from was the full force of the North Sea. Houses and shops along the seafront are now protected from the worst by a concrete sea wall, but even this doesn't stop the road being shut at least once a year, when waves from a high spring tide and northeasterly gale combined can send spray over the top of three-storey buildings. The final two buildings at this end of the village are the old railway station and the remains of an alum works, now a café and car park. Beyond lies an industrial archaeologist's wonderland, visited by the **Sandsend Trail**.

The Sandsend Trail

Once you have climbed 30 or so steps up from the car park to join the old railway line, and leant on the station platform to catch your breath, you can relax, because you needn't go uphill again during the rest of this walk.

ESPIONAGE, FIRE WATER & URINE – THE ALUM STORY

Back in the 16th century, the only known chemical able to fix dyes in cloth was alum, but the complex process for extracting it from rock was known only to chemists in the Vatican. In the first ever documented case of industrial espionage, Henry VIII managed to steal the formula and the English alum industry began. The shale of the Cleveland coast contains 2% alum and to get it, the rock had to be quarried by pick and shovel, piled up and roasted by fire for months, treated with an alkali and then dissolved in water and dried, to allow the crystals to form.

Here comes the bit of the process everyone always remembers: the cheapest source of alkali was stale urine, and such volumes were needed that every household in Whitby was required by law to put out all their urine for collection. At the height of the industry demand exceeded supply, so barrels of urine were shipped up from London. Rather than send the barrels back empty they were filled with butter for the rich appetites of the folk in the capital. As the barrels were never rinsed, this is said to account for Southerners' taste for yellow salted butter!

This cindery track bed heads along the cliff edge to what locals call 'The Moon', giving grandstand views of wheeling fulmars and surfers on the famed reef break (known as 'caves' to surfers) below. It weaves its way between vast quarried holes and artificial hills called 'clamps' – remnants of 300 years of the alum industry. Spoil from the works is so disagreeable to plant life that most areas remain completely bare of vegetation, hence the lunar references.

The flat trail ends abruptly at a railway tunnel entrance a mile down the line. You can retrace your steps or continue along the Cleveland Way you have been unwittingly following, and brave the big climb over the tunnel. Roof falls and subsidence have made the underground route unsafe but I did get the chance to traverse its three-quarter-mile length once, while searching for a missing person with the auxiliary coastguard. We didn't find anyone, but had a huge scare when torchlight revealed an old wetsuit that some practical joker had stuffed to look like a headless corpse. The air turned blue with relief when we realised our mistake.

Mulgrave Woods

If you can, arrange your visit to Sandsend for a Wednesday, Saturday or Sunday, because these are the days that access is granted to these private woods. Large-scale pheasant rearing has spoiled some parts but this is a big wood and there are still lush, pristine corners. It boasts three castles, alum quarries, cement stone mines and a wealth of wildlife – easily a full day's worth of exploration. The woods cloak the two parallel ravines of East Row Beck and Sandsend Beck and the Castle Rigg in between, so a circular walk could take you up one valley and back down the other. Alternatively, a taxi drop-off two miles inland, where the East Barnby road crosses the woods, would allow you a linear walk downhill to the sea.

¶¶ FOOD & DRINK

Estbek House East Row ☎ 01947 893424 🖰 www.estbekhouse.co.uk. A quietly elegant

---

ROCK POOLING

No trip to the seaside would be complete without a spot of rock pooling, and it was ever thus. How many of us have vivid childhood memories of mornings splashing in the waves, gritty sandwiches for lunch and then, as the tide recedes, ferreting in warm pools with a net and a bucket?

Without doubt, the prime quarry of most rock-poolers are **crabs**. My day job involves taking schoolchildren on to the seashore to introduce them to the inter-tidal ecosystem, but sooner or later, even with A-level biology groups, proceedings usually degenerate into a 'biggest crab' competition. I have often pondered why we are all fascinated by these creatures, and have come to the conclusion that it is their creepy alien-ness (walking as they do sideways on eight legs) and the thrill of real danger; even a small crab can give a powerful and painful nip.

You will find four common species of crab without much difficulty, and the **shore** or **green crab** is by far the most abundant. Lift up flat rocks among the seaweed and

they will scuttle away, or dangle a piece of meat-baited string into a deep pool and you could tempt them out into the open. These are the characters that are hauled up on crab lines to fill enthusiasts' buckets in Whitby and Scarborough harbours. **Edible** or **brown crabs** can be found lower down the shore, but only small, young specimens. The adults that end up on the fishmonger's slab live in deeper water. Identification is easy – the only crab with a shell the shape of a Cornish pasty and black mittens. **Hermit crabs** are many people's favourite, living as they do in someone else's shell, usually a periwinkle, top-shell or dog whelk. If you want to get a good view of the creature, place its shell upside down underwater and the crab will slide itself almost all the way out when it thinks the coast is clear and turn itself right way up. You will know if you have found a **velvet swimming crab** or, more to the point, you will know by the excited squeals if someone else has found one. They are restaurant next door to the White Hart pub and overlooking East Row Beck, as the name suggests.

Sandside Café East Row ✆ 01947 893916. Fantastic position right on the beach with great views of the surf while you have your drink or snack.

SHOPPING

Sandside Stores The Parade ✆ 01947 893214. Everything in the village revolves round Fraser's shop which doubles as newsagent, post office and delicatessen. He also runs the surf school down on the beach.

Turnstone Gallery East Row ✆ 01947 893289 🖱 www.turnstonegallery.net. A tasteful selection of arts and crafts produced by local artisans. Regularly changing exhibitions.

---

beautiful with velvety backs, electric blue claws and bright red eyes but are without doubt the most aggressive creature on the shore. I have seen one actually jump up off the rocks to attack my approaching hand, and can testify from experience that their pincers are very sharp.

Crabs may be the most extrovert inhabitants of rock pools, but they are by no means the only ones. North Sea rocky shores are incredibly rich habitats, so within an hour or two's searching you could easily find over 30 different species, from deep maroon **sea anemones** and small green sea urchins to translucent **prawns** and big knobbly **lumpsucker fish**. Here are some top-tips for the best results:

- Get as far down the shore as you can. A low spring tide is best of all as you can get in among the exposed kelp forest.
- Take a deep white tray to put your finds in for examination.

- A small aquarium net is the only way you will catch fast or slippery prawns and fish.
- Take an identification guide. The Field Studies Council (🖱 www.field-studies-council.org) produce an excellent waterproof key, and the best field guidebook is *The Seashore*, published by Country Life Books, or you can call in at East Barnby Outdoor Education Centre and they will give you a free simple ID sheet.
- The best accessible sites for rock pools along the North Yorkshire coast are between Staithes and Port Mulgrave, Runswick Bay, Robin Hood's Bay, Scarborough North Bay and Filey Brigg.

One last safety note: take care on wet, slippery rocks and consult tide tables before you stray away from the main beach. Happy searching.

15 RUNSWICK BAY

⚑ Runswick Bay Caravan and Camping Park (see page 200).

Runswick Bay possesses two particularly appealing features, a huddle of pantile-roofed cottages that comprises the village, and the beach. The village resembles a miniature Robin Hood's Bay with its maze of alleys and passageways but the beach is much more attractive than that of the larger near neighbour. Ice creams, buckets and spades, multi-coloured wind-breaks and crowds of bank holiday sunbathers; Runswick Bay beach does all of that, but venture a frisbee-throw away from the car park and slipways and it shows a much wilder side to its nature. Halfway round the sandy bay, and just past the yacht club, low shale cliffs begin and the guttural cackles of nesting fulmars compete with the 'swosh' of the waves. This place is known as **Hob Holes** locally, after the old jet mines at the crag foot. Legend has it that a hobgoblin lived in the darkness with the unexplained ability to cure whooping cough. A chant of 'Hob, Hob, me bairn's got kink cough. Takk it off, takk it off,' was the brief and to-the-point request that was supposed to do the trick.

"Here the only company you can expect are oystercatchers and turnstones ferreting around in the seaweed, and maybe a nosey seal, head bobbing in the water offshore."

The Cleveland Way footpath makes its way to the top of the cliff at Hob Holes, so very few people carry on along the shore beyond this point, but the extra effort is well worth it. Just around the corner is the handkerchief-sized beach of Kettleness Sand, a wonderful secluded corner cowering beneath the battleship-grey walls of **Kettleness** itself. Here the only company you can expect are oystercatchers and turnstones ferreting around in the seaweed, and maybe a nosey seal, head bobbing in the water offshore.

Take care where you lie and sunbathe though; too close to the cliff bottom and you are in danger of being landed on by one of the regular small rock falls. Back in the 1990s one family had a very close call when a huge section of cliff buried half of the beach. Fortunately it came down in instalments so they had time to make their escape down to the water's edge. Apparently their tartan rug and Tupperware are still deep under the rocks – an interesting find for the archaeologists of the future!

Cliff falls are maybe not good news for the average visitor to Kettleness Sand, but they certainly are for Mike Marshall, a professional fossilhunter operating from his workshop at Sandsend (📞01947 893222 🖥 www.yorkshirecoast fossils.co.uk). 'I love going down on the seashore searching,' he said. 'You never know what you're going to find. Mostly it's ammonites of course; there are hundreds of different types in the rocks around here and they are my bread-and-butter – what I make my day-to-day living from. They don't take too long to prepare and polish, then I'll sell them to shops in Whitby, or on my website at £10–£30 or so. The really exciting moments are when big, important specimens turn up. I'm still working on an Ichthyosaur (giant fish-like reptile) that I found 15 years ago, which will probably sell for £15,000 when it is finished; that is my pension fund.'

While Mike's sale-quality ammonites and belemnites make great souvenirs, hundreds more lie waiting to be found for free among the beach pebbles here. Half the fun is in the searching and children can be occupied for hours; top-tip, take an old dinner knife to split the soft rock and some paper and wax crayons to take rubbings of fossils embedded in big rocks. For more great ideas and free fossil identification sheets visit East Barnby Outdoor Education Centre, two miles from Runswick on the Whitby road. (📞01947 893333 🖥 www.outdoored.co.uk).

On busy days, parking can be a problem at Runswick Bay, so consider parking at East Barnby and walking the four miles to Runswick (all downhill), via Goldsborough Roman signal station and the Cleveland Way cliff-top path. You will be rewarded with magnificent views and the half-hourly number 5 bus takes you back up the hill to East Barnby.

🍴 FOOD & DRINK

Black Bull Ugthorpe YO21 2BQ 📞01947 840286. 'Where do the locals go to eat?' is what I'd ask, and the answer is here. A very friendly, family-run village local with great value food and fine beer. Book early, especially for the Sun carvery.

Fox and Hounds Goldsborough YO21 3RX 📞01947 893372 🖥 www.foxandhoundsgolds borough.co.uk. What was a fabulous pub is now an excellent restaurant (shame it couldn't be both). The daily changing menu features local game and Whitby fish. Open Wed–Sat evenings.

The Royal Hotel Runswick Bay 📞01947 840215 🖥 www.royalhotelrunswick.com. Decent food and drink and possibly the best view from any pub in Yorkshire.

16 STAITHES

In many ways Staithes could qualify as a miniature Whitby – a tidal river slicing its way to the sea through steep cliffs, multi-coloured fishing cobbles bobbing at their moorings behind the harbour's stone piers, and the same mass of orange pan-tiled houses, jostling shoulders for space between the cliffs and the water. The two-towns-in-one principle is also at work again, this time officially, with Staithes proper only on the south side of the beck. Not only do the houses on the other bank belong to the separate village of **Cowbar**, they aren't even in North Yorkshire. The county boundary runs across the middle of the small footbridge over Staithes Beck, and Cowbar is in Cleveland. Just to confuse the issue further, the **Staithes lifeboat** is housed here on the Cowbar side.

"En route *you should see oystercatchers on the mussel beds of Penny Steel, ironstone and jet mines, and alum quarries.*"

Staithes' most famous son is undoubtedly James Cook who, after a childhood just inland, probably had his first smell of the sea when he worked as a teenage shop assistant in the village. An old harbourside cottage bears a 'Cook Trail plaque' but in reality, the shop he worked in was washed away along with 12 other buildings in the great storm of 1745.

A few yards from Captain Cook's cottage is the labelled entrance into **Dog Loup**; quite probably the narrowest named thoroughfare in the country, and a good start to a wander around the back alleys, squares and streets. On your exploration look out for the nautical themes in house names, including imaginative ceramic plaques, and the **Heritage Centre** on the High Street. I also recommend crossing the bridge to climb Cowbar Bank for the best bird's-eye view of Staithes to one side, and the mighty **Boulby Cliff** on the other, returning via the allotments footpath and stepping stones.

One of the best short walks in the North York Moors heads off in the opposite direction, but the tide needs to be in your favour to complete it safely (follow the ebb tide out). The route couldn't be simpler; climb the steps at the far end of the harbour, walk along the rocky shore below the cliffs for a mile to **Port Mulgrave** and then return along the Cleveland Way. *En route* you should see oystercatchers on the mussel beds of Penny Steel (and surfers on one of the most testing reef breaks in the country if there are waves), ironstone and jet mines, and alum quarries. You can also experience the best fossil and rock-pool pickings along the whole coast.

If you would prefer expert local guidance in this very wild environment, it doesn't come any better than from Sean Baxter (☎01947 840278 🖱 www.realstaithes.com), local fisherman, member of the lifeboat crew and passionate champion of the town. 'I'm desperate to counter the doom-and-gloom merchants who claim the natural world is dying,' Sean explained. 'It's just not true; there are more fish, whales, dolphins and peregrines around here than ever and I want to show people this rich natural diversity – and tell them about the amazing maritime heritage of my town.' You can accompany him baiting long-lines and emptying lobster pots, ultimately eating your catch as a picnic at Sean's fisherman's hut in Port Mulgrave.

The landlocked city of Leicester wouldn't be many people's prediction of a major lifeboat sponsor but the good people of that city have bought eleven over the years, the most recent being *The Pride of Leicester*. This is the Staithes and Runswick Inshore Lifeboat, to give it its full title, an 'Atlantic 75' class boat which sits on a trailer attached to its amphibious tractor, in a shed in Cowbar. Being the bustling focal point that it is, with crew members often pottering around, the doors are usually open and you are welcome to go in and nose around there and in the RNLI shop which is just a couple of doors down. One certainly shouldn't wish for a lifeboat call-out, but if the pager call from the coastguard goes out, the launch is exciting to watch. There's no 'maroon' (a loud firework to alert the crew) to hear these days but the sight of grown men racing down the hill from all sides of the village is a bit of a giveaway. You'll have to be quick to witness the launch as the Staithes crew pride themselves on being out of the harbour within five minutes of their pagers going off. More predictable is crew training, 18.00 on Mondays in summer, and 10.00 on Sundays in winter.

🍴 FOOD & DRINK

Captain Cook Inn Staithes Lane ☎01947 840200 🖱 www.captaincookinn.co.uk. A very uninviting-looking hostelry at the top of the bank by the old railway (formerly Station Inn) but don't be fooled: the 'Cook' is an oasis. The best selection of real ales within a ten-mile radius, and cheap and cheerful bar food. Regularly hosts a wide range of festivals: folk music, sea shanties and beer, pies and sausages. Regular jazz.

Cleveland Corner High St ☎01947 841117 🖱 www.clevelandcorner.co.uk. For many years a basic café, this is now a great little restaurant specialising in seafood. Also offers dog-friendly B&B.

Cod and Lobster High St ✆01947 840295. Notable for its position, it must be one of the closest pubs to the sea in the country – storm-damaged on more than one occasion. Nostalgic photos line the walls, and three or four cask ales usually on tap. Food available.

ARTS & CRAFTS

Kessen Bowl High St. A gift shop in a quaint little corner building, named after fishermen's glass floats and selling an eclectic mix of products including artists' materials and pharmaceuticals.

Staithes Gallery High St ✆01947 841840 ⌁ www.staithesgallery.co.uk. A fine display of contemporary artists' work inspired by the old masters from the celebrated Staithes Group. Offers residential weekend courses for artists and co-ordinates an excellent weekend art festival every Sep (⌁ www.staithesfestival.com).

17 BOULBY CLIFF

> The king was borne, hoary hero, to Hronesness (Whale Hill).
> And firm on the earth a funeral-pile.
> *Beowulf*

Viewed from Staithes, the outline of Boulby Cliff is uncannily like the back of a whale, and I would love to share the belief of some, that this was the burial place of that great hero of the Viking age. What is for certain is that his body is no longer there now, after 1,000 years of natural and human erosion. Despite all this cliff reduction, Boulby, at 666 feet above the sea, is still the highest cliff on the east coast of England, albeit in two steps because of the huge alum quarries. Alum is no longer worked here but **Boulby Potash Mine** is a modern mineral extraction operation close by that breaks records in the opposite direction. It is the deepest mine in Europe, and at its bottom, nearly a vertical mile down, tunnels radiate out five miles in every direction, including out beneath the North Sea – a scary thought. The potash, destined to become agricultural fertiliser, is transported to Teesside factories on the only remaining section of the Whitby to Middlesbrough railway.

The four-mile traverse of Boulby Cliff from Staithes makes a magnificent walk, or cycle, and the steep descent at the far end will bring you to a very singular place. The former mining village of **Skinningrove** will never be described as pretty but it has bags of character, and your arrival takes you past some of the structures it has become famous for

– pigeon lofts. Skinningrove is one of the racing-pigeon centres of the North East with scores of sheds lining the hillside.

At the bottom of the hill, the beck won't fail to catch your eye either, being as it is luminous orange, a result of pollution from the ironstone mines further up the valley – rust, in essence. The entrance to the old mine at the top of the village is worth a visit as it has been converted into the excellent **Cleveland Ironstone Mining Museum** (✆01287 642877 ⊕ http://ironstonemuseum.co.uk). Not far from the museum, a half-hourly bus (5 or 5A) can take you back to Staithes if you have walked. Better still, get the bus here and walk back to Staithes as the views are marginally better. Navigation is easy as the whole route follows the Cleveland Way, which is clearly marked on OS Explorer map OL27.

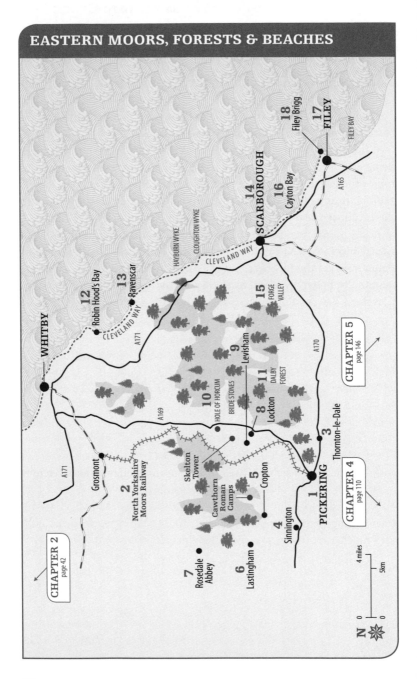

SCARBOROUGH

16 Cayton Bay
14

12 Robin Hood's Bay
13 Ravenscar

WHITBY

HAYBURN WYKE
CLOUGHTON WYKE
CLEVELAND WAY

15 FORGE VALLEY

A171
CLEVELAND WAY

9 Levisham

A170

CHAPTER 5
page 146

10 HOLE OF HORCUM
BRIDE STONES
8 Lockton
11 DALBY FOREST

A169

Skelton Tower

Grosmont

2 North Yorkshire Moors Railway

Cawthorn Roman Camps
5 Cropton

Thornton-le-Dale
3

1 PICKERING

CHAPTER 4
page 110

4 Sinnington

7 Rosedale Abbey
6 Lastingham

CHAPTER 2
page 42

A171

N

0   4 miles
0   5km

3

EASTERN MOORS, FORESTS & BEACHES

This southeastern corner of the North York Moors is dominated by forest, not the natural English oak woodland that was originally here, but hundreds of square miles of coniferous plantation. The almost-linked forests of Cropton, Dalby and Harwood Dale constitute the Forestry Commission's North Riding Forest Park, at 500 square miles the second largest in England. It stretches from Rosedale in the west to the North Sea coast in the east, across an area of plateaux and deep valleys that some inspired geographer gave the perfect label of the Tabular Hills. These uplands don't meet the sea gently, but in a line of precipitous cliffs stretching from **Robin Hood's Bay** in the north to Filey in the south. In the few places where these cliffs relent, there is sand, and where there are beaches there are holiday resorts. **Scarborough**, with two sandy bays, is not only the biggest seaside resort on the Yorkshire coast but claims to be the oldest in the world. Next comes little **Cayton Bay**, literally awash with surfers much of the time, and finally, seven miles south of **Scarborough**, her younger and more modest sister, **Filey**, with the queen of beaches – five miles of glorious Filey sands stretching to the chalk cliffs of **Flamborough Head** and out of North Yorkshire. The only other town in the region is **Pickering**, an old fortified market town sitting just at the point where pancake-flat Ryedale turns hilly: very much a southern gateway to the North York Moors.

SELF-POWERED TRAVEL

CYCLING

I will stick my neck out and suggest that this is possibly the best area in the country for the cyclist, especially **off-road**. It is absolute two-wheel heaven, and **Dalby Forest** is the focus of it all: it is so good that it was selected for staging the World Mountain Bike Championships in 2011. In the last ten years the Forestry Commission has spent over a million pounds developing biking facilities in the forest culminating in a series of six colour-coded and waymarked trails ranging from the two-mile Ellerburn green trail (easy), a perfect gentle intro for young families, to the black trail (severe), which is a challenge for even expert mountain bikers. The most popular route, and it can get very busy, is the 23-mile red route (difficult) which is possibly the best of its kind in the country. Maps of all the trails are available free in the visitor centre at Low Dalby (see page 91).

If you want forest track riding to yourself then just go exploring with the 1:25,000 OS Explorer map OL27. There are literally hundreds of miles of deserted tracks in Cropton, Langdale, Broxa and Harwood Dale forests waiting to be ridden, and the Forestry Commission (bless them) are happy for you to do it as long as you take special care near forestry operations. A rewarding gentle ride, for those allergic to hills, starts at Reasty Hill Top car park near Harwood Dale, and covers a flat four-mile triangular route to Barns Cliff End and back; my children had their first exciting forest bike ride here aged five and seven, and still talk about it. It would be too tame for them now of course, but the route can be extended to Broxa, with the uphill return via the delightful, and delightfully named, Whisper Dales.

"My children had their first exciting forest bike ride here aged five and seven, and still talk about it."

Another more testing favourite of mine is a meandering exploration of the northern end of **Cropton Forest**, taking in Needle Point and Killing Nab Scar. You can reach the starting point either by car from the hamlet of Stape, or from Newtondale Halt on the North Yorkshire Moors Railway (bikes can be taken on the train).

Still off-road, but not under trees, there are lots of bridleways and green-lane routes on the moors. The moors are not as extensive here as further north and west, but two are crossed by bridleways that make for good biking territory. Levisham Moor is one and is accessible from Levisham village or the Hole of Horcum on the A169 Pickering to Whitby road. The other is Brow Moor behind Robin Hood's Bay, where you could make a circular route by using part of the **disused railway line** at Stoupe Brow. This line is a fantastic, recognised cycle route in its own right and rideable all the way from Scarborough to Whitby, 20 miles of easy cinder track with great sea views.

Good **road biking** is less easy to find here, but the best of it is a network of quiet minor roads to the west of Scarborough around the village of **Hackness,** which also link up with the tarmac toll road winding its way through Dalby Forest.

Finally, there is a long-distance cycle trail which incorporates lots of what I have already detailed. The **Moor to Sea cycle route** (⌒ www. moortoseacycle.net) was developed by local bikers for family cycling and provides four days' worth of the best road, forest, lane and rail riding the area has to offer, linking Scarborough, Pickering and Whitby.

CYCLE HIRE ON THE MOOR TO SEA CYCLE ROUTE
Dalby Bike Barn Dalby Forest Courtyard ✆ 01751 460049 ⌒ www.dalbybikebarn.co.uk. Mountain and road bikes for adults and children. Also electric bikes, tandems, child seats, trailers and tagalongs. **Pace Cycle Shop** is next door.
Keldy Forest Cabins Near Cropton YO18 8HW ('via Cropton' for satnavs) ✆ 01751 417510 ⌒ www.forestholidays.co.uk. Bikes, tagalongs, trailer bikes and a tandem for hire.
Trailways The Old Railway Station, Hawsker ✆ 01947 820207 ⌒ www.trailways.info. Bikes, buggies, tandems and trailer bikes for hire. Two hours to multi-day. One-way ride and pick-up by arrangement.

HORSERIDING
The long well-drained tracks here are as good for horses as for bikes, and there are plenty of riding opportunities whether you have your own beast of burden or need to borrow one. The big forests (Dalby and its neighbours) are wonderful venues for riding, and the Forestry Commission welcome you with open arms – free entry into Dalby via the Toll Road for instance. No specific horseriding routes are designated so you are free to use any of the forest roads or bridleways, but colour-coded bike trails are best avoided as they get so busy.

There are trekking/hacking centres at Staintondale, Robin Hood's Bay and Sinnington. If you are bringing your own horse, the North York Moors National Park produces an indispensable guidebook (see page 18).

RIDING CENTRES
Farsyde Stud and Riding Centre Robin Hood's Bay YO22 4UG ✆ 01947 880249 ⌒ www.farsydefarmcottages.co.uk. Hacking for experienced riders on moors, fields and

forests. Trekking is also available on the old railway line for beginners.

Friars Hill Riding Stables Sinnington YO62 6SL ✆ 01751 432758 ⌂ www. friarshillstables.co.uk. Hacking and trekking for those over the age of eight years (but note: not absolute beginners). Also, pony birthday parties and three- or five-day summer camps.

Staintondale Trekking Centre Staintondale YO13 0EL ✆ 01723 871846. Pony trekking for small groups of any ability.

WALKING

Four **long-distance footpaths** or unofficial 'ways' have a terminus here. Whether it is the start or the finish is pretty much up to you, except for the Coast to Coast Walk and Lyke Wake Walk, where the universally accepted direction to travel is west to east, both finishing at Robin Hood's Bay. The other two are the much-frequented, horseshoe-shaped Cleveland Way, which in this area traverses the full length of the coast between Robin Hood's Bay and Filey, and the lesser-known 48-mile Tabular Hills Walk between Helmsley and Scarborough. This route is also sometimes referred to as the Cleveland Way Link as it joins the loose ends of the longer walk to create a circular route of 158 miles.

Shorter day or half-day walks are many and varied, limited only really by your map-reading skills and sense of adventure, because there is a huge network of rights of way and a large area of open access land (see page 10). Avoid busy mountain-bike areas, like some of the bridleways leading into Dalby Forest, and the Moor to Sea cycle route.

Because public transport is so comprehensive here, there are many opportunities for **point-to-point walks** with a bus or train shuttle. I am always more comfortable being driven first and walking back as there is less chance of being marooned and no pressure to make the bus stop or station on time. If you can wangle it so the engine power does more of the uphill than your legs, all the better. A good way to do sections of the Cleveland Way is to use the Scarborough to Whitby bus; Robin Hood's

---

i **TOURIST INFORMATION**

Filey John St ✆ 01723 383636
Pickering The Ropery ✆ 01751 473791
Scarborough Brunswick Shopping Centre ✆ 01723 383636; Harbourside ✆ 01723 383636

Bay to Cloughton perhaps (ten miles), or Cloughton to Scarborough (five miles). The train can do the same job between Scarborough and Filey (seven miles). Away from the coast, a rover ticket on the North Yorkshire Moors Railway allows you to hop off at one station, walk to the next and hop back on – plenty of scope there.

THE SOUTHERN MOORS & FORESTS

Much of this area is virtually uninhabited, wild territory covered by either trees or heather. Around the sole town, **Pickering**, are a clutch of rewarding **villages**: Thornton-le-Dale on the way to Scarborough, Lockton and Levisham towards Whitby and, up the beautiful valley of Rosedale, Cropton, Sinnington, Lastingham and Rosedale Abbey.

1 PICKERING

Pickering first came to my attention as a case study in a geography lesson at school. It is a textbook example of a ribbon development; a town that grows along an important road instead of spreading sideways. What my geography teacher failed to tell me, though, is that the bits of Pickering away from the busy main road are full of unexpected history and quirky character. By far its biggest visitor attraction is the **North Yorkshire Moors Railway**, of which Pickering is the southern terminus, but the shops and arcades of Market Place and Birdgate come a close second. My favourite part of the town is surprisingly little visited, probably because of the steep walk involved. It is the area where narrow old streets lead up Castle Hill to the town's biggest and oldest building **Pickering Castle** itself. My recommended route would be up Castle Road, from where it begins near the railway station, and back down Castlegate to take in the Quaker meeting house. It is worth detouring along Hatcase Lane, not just to celebrate such a wacky name, but because it will lead you to the fascinating **church of St Peter and St Paul**. This would be a humdrum building with little interest but for a chance discovery during renovation in 1852. Lime-wash was removed from an interior wall to reveal 15th-century frescoes underneath which the architectural historian Nikolaus Pevsner described as, 'one of the most complete series of wall paintings in English churches that give one a vivid idea of what ecclesiastical interiors were really like'. The pictures are multi-coloured affairs mainly depicting the important saints of the time, St George of pest control fame, St John the Baptist, St Thomas of Canterbury and a particularly tall St Christopher, who was reputed to stand 12 cubits high.

On emerging from the front of the church you will be back into the bustle of Birdgate. If another dose of peace and quiet is required try **Beck Isle Museum** (Bridge St ✆ 01751 473653 ⌂ www.beckislemuseum. co.uk), at the other end of the marketplace. You don't even need to go in, although it is well worth the small entrance fee, because the beck-side lawn to the front, by the arches of the old bridge, is an ideal place for a tranquil muse or picnic. If you have any interest at all in rural social history, then the 27 rooms of this old agricultural college will keep you well entertained.

Pickering can be a haven of relaxation – it can also be a hive of activity. If you value peace and quiet then don't come here for the Wartime Weekend in October, the Steam Fair weekend in August or whenever the Mountain Bike World Cup is in town. But if you are fine with crowds and noise, then come along and be entertained.

Pickering Castle

Castlegate ✆ 01751 474989; English Heritage.

Pickering's royal connections date back to accounts in a late medieval chronicle of a Briton king called Pereduras living here. A very dubious legend connects him and the origin of the town's name, which involves him losing a valuable ring in the river and it turning up later in the belly of a fish served up on the royal table. The fish was a pike; ring in a pike, pike-ring, Pickering – likely? I don't think so, but there is a pike on the town's coat of arms and a beautifully carved one on a wooden panel in the bar of the White Horse Inn. King Pereduras was around far too long ago to have had anything to do with the present castle but it was a royal residence, having been built at William I's instruction for his personal use when hunting in the Forest of Pickering. Possession of the castle has been passed down the royal line ever since, the present owner being the Duke of Lancaster, better known by her Sunday name – Queen Elizabeth II. English Heritage looks after it for her today.

This is a classic Norman motte-and-bailey castle, with the motte, or mound, crowned by the remains of the keep (the King's Tower).

I particularly enjoy the walk on the path around the outside of the walls to detour into the quarries at the back where the limestone for the building was extracted; the North East Yorkshire Geology Trust have placed information boards explaining how these Jurassic rocks were formed under the sea.

¶¶ FOOD & DRINK

Eleven **cafés** make Pickering a place where it's easy enough to overdose on tea. My top three are **Elizabeth Botham's** Park St (01751 602823), another gem from the Whitby catering family; the very popular **Mulberries**, Bridge St (01751 472337) and **Number 1 Castlegate** Castlegate (01751 474737), off the main street and where the locals go for a quiet lunch.

Cedar Barn Farm Shop and Café Thornton Rd, YO18 7JX 01751 475614 www. cedarbarnfarmshop.co.uk. Angus beef and free-range eggs from their own farm plus veg, pies, cheeses and cakes.

Moorland Trout Farm Newbridge Rd, YO18 8JJ 01751 473101. Rainbow trout, whole, fillets or smoked; just north of Pickering. Feed the fish for 50p.

The Organic Farm Shop Eastgate Sq 01751 473444 www.theorganicfarmshop.com. An Aladdin's cave of good things from home-produced beef to ice cream and groceries.

The White Swan Inn Market Pl 01751 472288 www.white-swan.co.uk. A coaching inn, not a pub, but the place to come if you want comfort and style. The food is locally sourced in the main, and very highly regarded – one customer wrote a poem about it which is framed on the wall.

Willowdene Watercress and Trout Farm West Gate, Carr Rd, YO18 8LX 01751 472769. Traditionally grown watercress and spring water rainbow trout from the door.

Willowgate Bistro Willowgate 01751 476300. For evening eating, this place is hard to beat – not fussy or fancy, just exceptional food and great service. It's very popular so booking is advised.

2 NORTH YORKSHIRE MOORS RAILWAY: PICKERING TO GROSMONT

 01751 472508 www.nymr.co.uk.

Very few people aren't moved to a wistful nostalgia at the sight and sound of an old locomotive in full steam, and this is one of the most popular places in the country to enjoy the experience. Some, me included, would argue that it is best to not actually be on the train but watching from outside, but there is no doubt that either way everybody seems to enjoy steam trains immensely. Waving is *de rigueur* of course.

I once even saw a group of middle-aged travellers all with a handkerchief to flutter at passers-by.

'It's got to be done,' one of them said. 'The nice man in *The Railway Children* did it so we have to keep up the tradition.' Steam travel is somehow very English. Thank goodness for those few passionate and far-sighted enthusiasts back in 1965 who knew that Dr Beeching had made a big mistake in shutting the line. It is them that we have to thank for the continued existence of the railway here because two years later they started a preservation society. In 1972 they took on one full-time paid worker and now they operate a huge business with 135 paid staff and even more eager volunteers helping out.

The scenic route of this railway also adds to its popularity. Most of the journey follows the spectacular valley of Newtondale, a deep and precipitous ravine with the incongruously small Pickering Beck trickling down the middle. This feeble stream is obviously incapable of excavating such a large valley. That job was done 10,000 years ago at the end of the last ice age, when Lake Eskdale overflowed and emptied into Lake Pickering in a raging torrent.

It is 18 miles from Pickering to the official other end of the line at Grosmont, and your journey will call at four stations, each renovated in a different period style. Pickering recreates the 1930s, Levisham has been decorated as it would have been in 1912 and Goathland boasts a 1922-style tea room. Finally, Grosmont has been left how it was in the 1950s just before closure, and also features the fascinating locomotive sheds (see page 53). If you want to complete the story and visit a modern station then stay on the train because some of them now continue the extra six miles into Whitby courtesy of Northern Rail. Carriages are wheelchair-accessible and will carry bikes if there is space (phone to check). Trains run on one of four colour-coded timetables; gold at peak times with nine trains a day on the hour, and red, green or silver, each with six trains a day. Note that some services are diesel-hauled.

"Most of the journey follows the spectacular valley of Newtondale, a deep and precipitous ravine with the incongruously small Pickering Beck trickling down the middle."

If just being a passenger is not enough for you and you don't mind getting your hands dirty, then a Footplate Awareness course would be just the ticket. Over the course of one to five days you get the chance to fulfil many a childhood dream, and drive a steam train.

Fares are reasonable and it's only a few extra pounds to Whitby. Make a full day of it by catching the first train out in the morning and the last one back, taking full advantage of the hop-on hop-off nature of your rover ticket. That way you can explore around each of the station venues for an hour or so and get the next train that comes along.

3 THORNTON-LE-DALE

East of Pickering, Thornton Beck, full of lime from the springs of Dalby Forest, flows between the much-photographed limestone buildings of Thornton-le-Dale. This large village is perennially busy with visitors. On your first visit to Thornton-le-Dale you may well, like me, have a feeling of *déjà vu* with one building in particular seeming very familiar. **Beck Isle cottage** is one of the most photographed buildings in the country so the chances are that you have seen it before on a calendar or jigsaw. It isn't the only photogenic view in the village by any means; the combination of village green with cross and stocks, sparkling beck with 15 bridges and 17th-century almshouses has resulted in Thornton being regularly voted the most beautiful village in Yorkshire. This fame attracts visitors of course so if you need any respite from people then take a stroll on the beck-side footpath upstream past Thornton Mill to the sleepy hamlet of **Ellerburn**. A trout hatchery here takes advantage of the clear, cold, limestone spring water.

A tiny church, part Saxon, has had some unwelcome attention recently due to a wildlife controversy. Rare Natterer's bats live in its roof space, a fact to celebrate you might think, but the bats are not particularly grateful lodgers. Droppings rain down on to the hymn books, sometimes even during the services, and the whiff of bat wee is not really conducive to contemplative worship. The parishioners, understandably, want rid of their guests, but Natural England, also understandably, says no – it's a stalemate at the moment.

If you continue on this route up Thornton beck you will reach **Dalby Forest visitor centre**, a fine walk in itself.

4 SINNINGTON

Travel four miles west of Pickering and you will reach a crossing of the River Seven, a fraction of the size of its West Country namesake and a different spelling. A detour off the main road here to the village of **Sinnington** is worth the effort if only to sit and picnic on the green by the old arched bridge, but there are also many more active things to do if you have the inclination. The walking and biking along the river upstream are both good and pony trekking can be done from here (see page 80). If you keep following the river and you will find yourself in **Rosedale**, a rural idyll now, but a major ironstone mining valley not so long ago.

¶¶ FOOD & DRINK

Fox and Hounds Main St ✆ 01751 431577 ⌂ www.thefoxandhoundsinn.co.uk. An old coaching inn in sleepy Sinnington. Expect homely panelled bars with open fires and modern pub food with a European twist. Cask beers are from North and West Yorkshire: Copper Dragon and Timothy Taylors.

Pearson's Soft Fruits Strawberry Fields YO62 6SL ✆ 01751 433380. Pick your own strawberries, raspberries, gooseberries, redcurrants and blackcurrants or buy homemade jam of all the above. Just west of Sinnington.

5 CROPTON & 6 LASTINGHAM

The main route out of Rosedale passes through the village of **Cropton**, birthplace of the famous Whitby whaling ships' captain, William Scoresby. His local connection is celebrated in the name of a fine beer made in the village, Scoresby Stout. Cropton Brewery is a rarity, a very successful and long-lasting micro-brewery which has been operating from the New Inn since 1984. It still produces the original 'Two Pints' bitter along with numerous other recipes, including my favourite, 'Blackout Porter'.

A gentle two-mile cycle or walk away from Cropton on quiet country lanes is another village of a similar size. **Lastingham** is another one of those 'pub and church but not much else' places, but the Blacksmith's Arms deserves all the plaudits it receives in many good pub guides, and **St Mary's Church** is very special. It does not look unusual from the outside but venture in and you will find that it is in effect one church on top of another. Steps lead from the aisle down to a huge vaulted Norman crypt, extraordinarily unchanged since it was built as part of an unfinished abbey in the late 11th century; you won't come across a more atmospheric place too often. It is the only example in this country of a crypt with a nave and side aisles.

The lane east from Cropton towards Newton-on-Rawcliffe passes **Cawthorn Roman Camps**. Here an assortment of humpy earthworks are the remains of a temporary camp and forts for training Roman soldiers; the Cawthorn Trail is worth following to bring it all to life.

¶¶ FOOD & DRINK

Blacksmith's Arms Anserdale Lane, Lastingham YO62 6TN ✆ 01757 417247 ✆ www. blacksmithslastingham.co.uk. This is almost how you imagine a country pub to be; rambling and dimly lit, very, very old and with legends of a ghost and a secret tunnel to the church crypt opposite. There are always three cask beers on, usually Black Sheep or Theakstons and two other guests, and the food is wholesome and traditional. If there is room then eat in the bar, as it is the most atmospheric part of the building by far.

Cropton Brewery Cropton YO18 8HH ✆ 01751 417330 ✆ www.croptonbrewery.com. Also known as the Great Yorkshire Brewery internationally, this once tiny back-of-a-pub concern is now a big business. Brewery tours are excellent and well worth the entrance fee.

New Inn Cropton YO18 8HH ✆ 01751 417330 ✆ www.newinncropton.co.uk. This is a great beer-drinkers' village inn with its own brewery (see above) and an annual beer festival in November. Food comes in generous portions and is good value and home cooked. Open every day. Accommodation is available in the pub or there's camping in a quiet field behind the brewery.

7 ROSEDALE ABBEY & ROSEDALE

Standing on high ground, and casting an appreciative eye over the fields, folds and pastoral corners of Rosedale, you may find it hardly possible to imagine what has gone on here in the past.

Today, fewer than 500 people live out a sleepy, rural existence in this valley and it was much the same in 1851. Twenty years later that figure was nearer 5,000 as a Klondike-style rush of miners poured in and turned Rosedale into a loud, smoky, and crime-ridden industrial

"Fewer than 500 people live out a sleepy, rural existence and it was much the same in 1851."

centre. It wasn't gold they were after but iron: between 1856 and 1926, millions of tons of high-grade ore were extracted and transported to the blast furnaces of County Durham. How they got it there was both dramatic and ingenious: a railway was constructed which stayed almost level, as railways have to do, by contouring right around the head of the valley at about 1,000 feet up. It then crossed Blakey Ridge and into the neighbouring valley of Farndale where it did the same, hugging a high-

ROSEDALE GLASS – ANCIENT & MODERN

Not long ago, archaeologists unearthed a furnace last used 400 years ago by exiled French glassmakers who plied their trade using local sand and wood fuel. This ancient local craft is celebrated in a thoroughly modern setting at **Gillies Jones glass-blowing studio** in Rosedale Abbey (✆ 01751 417550 ✆ www.gilliesjonesglass.co.uk). Steven Gillies and Kate Jones, partners in life and art, work together to produce exquisite works inspired by the Rosedale countryside. Stephen is the glassmaker and Kate the sand-carver and painter. Drop into the studio to see them at work.

level line round to a point where descent was possible down a steep incline to join the mainline railway system at Battersby. Fortunately for us, the track bed is still there providing a perfect gentle walk or cycle way which is even wheelchair-accessible in places.

The ironstone boom had a major and lasting effect on the only village in the dale: Rosedale Abbey lost its abbey. The ruins of the Cistercian nunnery were dismantled stone by stone to provide building material for mine buildings and houses. Only one small belfry turret survives, but the village boasts two pubs, a café and a glass-blowing studio.

DALBY FOREST & LEVISHAM MOOR

The A169 from Pickering to Whitby has been a route for many centuries, and the name Saltergate, literally 'salt street', refers of course to the journey done in the opposite direction, from Whitby and the coast to Pickering and all points inland, transporting a very important and valuable commodity in times past. Only one part of the A169 still bears that old name, where a hairpin bend takes it past the Saltergate Inn and along the edge of a spectacular crater called the **Hole of Horcum**.

As the road makes its gradual descent from here into Pickering, it bypasses the villages of **Lockton** and **Levisham** to the right, and the wooded ridges and dales of **Dalby Forest** to the left.

8 LOCKTON & 9 LEVISHAM

These two neat and tidy Moors' villages are like a pair of brothers or sisters – close, but separated by a deep valley, always vying with each other over small things, but jumping to each other's defence over matters of importance. In reality the two places are complementary; Lockton has the church and youth hostel, while Levisham provides a railway station and pub. There was a small village shop in Lockton and a post office in Levisham until recently, but both have gone the way of many rural businesses, and sadly closed.

One resource neither village is short of is ground water: wells and springs are all over the place, because of the porous Jurassic limestone hillsides hereabouts. Near one of these named water sources, Rowl Spring, you will find the most mysterious building in the vicinity. **St Mary's Church**, roofless and derelict, is in neither Lockton nor Levisham, but sits between the two in splendid isolation. Local stories claim that there was a village around the church which was wiped out by the plague in the 14th century, but there is no archaeological evidence for this. Whatever the history, St Mary's Church is an evocative ruin in a memorable setting.

"Whatever the history, St Mary's Church is an evocative ruin in a memorable setting."

To the north of Lockton and Levisham is a large area of moor and valley, making up the Levisham Estate, which was in private hands until 1976 when the National Park Authority bought it to safeguard its riches. Such is the wealth of archaeological remains there, tumuli, dykes, enclosures and settlements, that Levisham Moor is the largest scheduled ancient monument in England, though you need to poke around carefully with an OS map in hand to spot its ancient features. It is also designated a Site of Special Scientific Interest, for its rare breeding birds in particular; this is one of the best places in the country to see golden plover and the dashing little falcon, the merlin.

Skelton Tower

There can be few buildings in the North York Moors with as impressive a position and prospect as Skelton Tower. Perched on the lip of Newtondale, a mile north of Levisham Station, it affords magnificent views up and down the gorge, particularly rewarding when a steam locomotive is grunting up the valley hundreds of feet below. In reality the tower was a shooting-lodge-style folly built in 1850 by the Reverend Robert Skelton, vicar of Levisham. The official line is that he retired there for the peace and quiet required to write his sermons, although unofficial local opinion is that it doubled as his secret drinking den.

A walk on Levisham Moor to the Hole of Horcum

OS Explorer map 27. Three possible start points: Hole of Horcum car park (grid reference NZ853936), Levisham village (grid reference NZ833905) or Newtondale Halt on the North Yorkshire Moors Railway (grid reference NZ818910). All are accessible by either bus or train. Refreshment at the pub in Levisham.

Levisham Moor is all open-access land so you can actually walk wherever you like. However, ploughing through deep heather can be tiring so you may want to follow two of the three public rights of way – one out from your start point and another back to it. For the chance of seeing rare flowers, (green-winged orchids in May and dwarf cornel in August) and great views of steam trains follow the Levisham Bottoms

path. For dazzling summer carpets of heather and wide skies go for the moor-top bridleway, and for a close-up view of the enormous natural hollow that is the Hole of Horcum, choose the eastern footpath via Low Horcum and Levisham Brow. The total distance is five to seven miles, depending on which route you choose.

Such is the sinister aura of the ruins now that they were chosen by local author Ian Johnson as home for the murderous goblin Red Cap in his supernatural novel *The Witcher Keys*.

¶¶ FOOD & DRINK

Fox and Rabbit A169, near Lockton YO18 7NQ ℘ 01751 460213 ⌂ www.foxandrabbit. co.uk. Brothers Charles and Toby Wood have got this pub just about right, very welcoming to travellers to and from the coast, three fine Yorkshire beers (Black Sheep, Theakstons and Taylors) and a wide selection of wines. Their food is simple and traditional.

The Horseshoe Inn Levisham ℘ 01751 460240 ⌂ www.horseshoelevisham.co.uk. This is a genuine traditional village pub sitting proudly at the top of the green. Food is similar to the Fox and Rabbit, well it has the same owners, and the beer is from the Dales (Black Sheep) and Moors (Cropton).

SHOPPING

David Stephenson Artist Blacksmith Sunny View, Lockton ✆ 01751 460252 ⌂ www. davidstephenson.org.uk. Hand-forged fireside furniture, frames and weather vanes.

10 THE HOLE OF HORCUM

Levisham Beck starts its life in a series of tributary, spring-fed valleys. In one of these deep dales the springs have eaten back into the hillsides evenly over thousands of years, leaving a dramatic almost circular basin. Our ancestors did not have the benefit of our geographical knowledge and assumed that there must be a diabolical explanation for the phenomenon. The Devil, it is said, in his anger scooped out a vast ball of earth and hurled it over the Moors, the resulting hole being that of Horcum, and the mound where the earth landed, the nearby hill of Blakey Topping.

Plainly visible to the north of the Hole of Horcum is a much more recent monument, the pyramid-shaped radar building of **Fylingdales Missile Early Warning Station**. The 'sandcastle', as it is known locally, is a recent replacement for the original and famous three 'golf balls' constructed during the Cold War. Despite regular peace protests here, and with an ironic twist to what we would normally regard as 'heritage', there was actually a suggestion that the golf balls should be made listed buildings and preserved; certainly they are said to have become the subject of the best-selling postcard in the area.

11 DALBY FOREST

Dalby Forest Visitor Centre YO18 7LT ✆ 01751 460295 ⌂ www.forestry.gov.uk/dalbyforest. This huge area of woodland has become one of the Forestry Commission's beacon leisure forests, so much so that it's easy to forget that it still primarily is a commercial timber production area. The focus of everything here is the purpose-built forestry village of **Low Dalby**, which I am covering in this section with slow transport and economy in mind. You can drive here, but the nearest village by road is Thornton-le-Dale, and that would involve you paying a hefty toll to drive through the forest. By foot, horse or bike, Lockton is the closest access point, and it's free to arrive under your own muscle power. Once you are here you can hire a bike from

Dalby Bike Barn (see page 79) if you have walked in, or treat yourself to a relaxing horse and carriage ride around the forest from **Back in Time**, courtesy of Holly or Maisey (they are the ponies, not the owners).

At Low Dalby the **visitor centre** is designed with all things sustainable and recyclable in mind. It is constructed from wood and glass, has toilet doors made from reconstituted mobile phone cases and is powered by a wind turbine and solar panels. Such a shame then that the architect made it the ugliest box of a building that I've ever laid eyes on. Inside the visitor centre are exhibitions, a shop, an astronomical observatory, the very good **Treetops Café** and information on the bewildering array of things that you can see and do in the forest itself. Outside are barbecue and picnic areas, two adventure playgrounds, a Go Ape ropes course for adrenaline junkies, and free maps for various waymarked trails. One is a permanent orienteering course, and there are also ten walking trails of varying distance, four of which are accessible to wheelchairs. My favourite of these is the Staindale Lake circuit, which I had the privilege of sharing with a group of students from a special school in Scarborough. One of the children, who was using a wheelchair, said, 'This is brilliant. I've seen places like this on telly with explorers

CYCLE TRAILS IN DALBY FOREST

Of everything on offer, off-road biking is Dalby's speciality, and what it is nationally renowned for. The trails available are:

- **Ellerburn cycle trail** (green) – a short relaxing and almost flat route perfect for young families that starts and finishes at the visitor centre (2½ miles).
- **Adderstone cycle trail** (green) – a longer easy circular route starting at the Adderstone field, a five-mile tarmac road ride from the visitor centre (six miles).
- **Dalby blue trail** (blue) – a long intermediate circular route starting at the visitor centre. Still easy

terrain but one or two steep hills (eight miles).

- **Dalby red trail** (red) – very long and difficult. One of the best of its kind in the country and justifiably popular. Don't be tempted on here without decent equipment and skills (21½ miles).
- **Dalby black trail Dixons Hollow Skills Park** and **Dalby Downhill** (black) – if you are good enough, then you will already know about these, if not, then don't even think about it!

going through the trees and mountains. Now it's me, I'm here and I'm the explorer.'

Staindale is also the best start point for another short expedition of less than a mile, this time to just outside the forest, on the adjacent moor. The **Bride Stones** are a series of wonderfully sculpted sandstone blocks and buttresses, that wouldn't look out of place in a Hollywood western movie, such is their desert-style, wind-eroded profile. Each stone has ended up perched delicately above the heather on an undercut pedestal, and they are in the care of the National Trust, who manage this area as a nature reserve.

Near the new Dalby visitor centre is the building that used to house the old one, now called The Courtyard, and home to various Slow or crafty businesses. The Dalby Bike Barn and Pace Cycle Shop are here, as is a paper-making workshop and an annex of Treetops Café.

There is a full calendar of events going on throughout the year, from ranger-led nature trails to car rallies and summer rock concerts.

SHOPPING

Pulpitations ✆ 01751 460134 ⌂ www.pulpitations.co.uk. Niki Hampson describes herself as a paper artist and runs this gallery, shop and workshop where you can have a go at making paper yourself.

ACTIVITIES

Back in Time ✆ 01751 460315 ⌂ www.lowdalbywood.co.uk. Horse and carriage rides of 30 or 75 minutes along a quiet forest road off the tarmac.

Go Ape ✆ 0845 6439215 ⌂ www.goape.co.uk. High-adrenalin, high-wire forest adventure or gentle exploration on a segway 'bike'.

ROBIN HOOD'S BAY TO SCARBOROUGH

In the 20 or so miles between Whitby and Scarborough, **Robin Hood's Bay** is the only place of any size on the coast. Such is the ruggedness of this coastline there is not even any road access to the shore anywhere else, and the few small villages that exist are perched on top of the cliffs, like **Ravenscar**, or set back inland, like Cloughton and Burniston. Then suddenly there's big, sprawling, friendly **Scarborough**, very much a different world.

12 ROBIN HOOD'S BAY

🏠 **Boggle Hole YHA** (see page 201) and **The Pigsty** Fylingthorpe (see page 201)

Let's get one thing straight from the start. Robin Hood, if he ever existed, never had anything to do with this place. Wild theories abound as to the origin of the name, but not one scrap of evidence that he even came here on holiday. Even the locals in a gesture of embarrassed denial have dropped the Sherwood Forester from the name. 'Bay' or 'Baytown' is what they call their home. Confusing names apart it is certain that there have been outlaws here, in fact in the 17th century it appears that most of the population were actively involved in smuggling. There were tunnels linking cellars, secret passages and hidey holes for both people and contraband. It is said that a bale of silk could pass from the dock at the bottom of the village to the top, without seeing the light of day. If you are feeling adventurous it is still possible to scramble up part of this route by following the beck from the beach up into the tunnel a few hundred yards. All you need is a pair of wellies, a torch and a sense of adventure.

Modern-day Bay is very different from those times when it was considered a more important place than Whitby. Fishing has all but gone, the railway is closed, and no alum or jet is mined here any more. Robin Hood's Bay is now entirely dependent on the tourism industry for its livelihood, but it has embraced it with enthusiasm and does it tastefully in the main, celebrating its own history and heritage well. Of course having the wonderful scenic surroundings and prolific wildlife of a national park on the doorstep helps. The village, or town as some claim it to be, is tucked into an almost sheltered corner of the coast, behind the Ness (Viking for headland) also called North Cheek. South Cheek sits proudly, three miles across the wide, sweeping bay with the village of Ravenscar on top. In between, when the tide is out, lie the limestone scars of the shore. I hesitate to say 'beach' because sand is in short supply; there is some, but nothing to compare with Scarborough or Filey. The silver lining is that this is the best **rock pooling** territory in the region. This whole section of shore is protected as part of the Yorkshire and Cleveland Heritage Coast.

As for the town and by that I mean the **old village** on the hillside, not the more modern development at the top, my favourite means of exploration is by semi-formal potter. Wandering up and down the many ginnels and alleys on both sides of the main street, seeing which are interconnected and which are dead ends, is the best way to

READ ALL ABOUT IT!

The residents of Robin Hood's Bay form a close-knit community. There is a real family feel to the place, including 'adoptees', those repeat visitors that come back year after year to the many guesthouses and holiday cottages. Part of the 'glue' that sticks them all together is the monthly town magazine that almost everybody subscribes to. *Bayfair* can tell you virtually everything you need to know about the place, from tide times and local events lists to nature or history articles and details of over 80 places to stay.

'I took it over in 1995 after finishing work at HM Customs and Excise,' said Jim Foster, the editor/designer/printer. 'It was a great move; I was ready to retire but needed something to keep me busy and interested, and *Bayfair* certainly does that. Bay has a real magical quality about it, with its history and all the maritime connections. It draws people in and they stay. I suppose with *Bayfair* we're trying to sprinkle a little bit of that magic about – and inform of course – as this is one of the most aware communities on the coast I think. It's time consuming but I try not to do the real hard work; that's the job of the regular contributors who do a great job.' If you are planning to stay in Robin Hood's Bay then *Bayfair* is an invaluable reference and fantastic value at 33p. You can even order it online (www.bayfair.co.uk) before you come.

make sure you see everything, and make no mistake, there is lots to see. Among the old cottages at Fisherhead, for instance, you will find in the old mortuary the village's tiny **museum**, a whale's jawbone in a garden and ship's portholes as windows. In the maze of alleyways on the other side of King's Beck, look out for a plaque to mark the spot of John Wesley's sermon, and cottage walls sporting insurance company fire marks, which directed the fire brigade to those houses that had paid to have fires put out, and those unfortunates that hadn't. The abruptly ending King Street is near here, and was the town's main street until its northern end fell into the sea in 1780.

All alleyways and streets lead down to **the Dock**, now the only access to the shore since the 1975 sea wall was built, and still a focal point. On either side of the slipway sits the Bay Hotel, the eastern terminus of celebrated walks writer Alfred Wainwright's Coast to Coast Walk (the other end is St Bees Head in Cumbria), and the Old Coastguard Station, now a National Trust visitor centre. For added spice, do your pottering after dark, from pub to pub maybe, and you will stand a good chance of bumping into some of Bay's other night walkers – badgers. Apparently the population of the local sett has taken to raiding bins; they are very bold about it and quite easy to see. If you are staying in town, don't leave your front door open late in the evening as one local resident did, to later find a badger wandering around in his upstairs bathroom.

At the top of the bank you are still in Robin Hood's Bay but a part with a completely different feel to it. It is newer in the main, with many of the Victorian buildings springing up when the railway arrived in 1865. There is not much of interest up here, save one or two good eating houses and the old railway station itself, which is the home of a few Slow businesses and organisations.

The Bay

Any Cleveland Wayer worth his or her salt, when heading south from Robin Hood's Bay, would choose to walk on the seashore rather than the official cliff-top path, if the tide allows. Not only is it the flat alternative,

SEALS

I had heard about the seal colony at Ravenscar, near Robin Hood's Bay, so one clear crisp day in March I went to investigate for myself. It was cold enough to see my breath as I picked my way down the steep cliff path but thankfully there was no wind or I would have needed much more than the thin fleece I was wearing. I heard the seals before I saw them, a slightly forlorn-sounding strangled wail every now and again. At least I knew they were here. I headed towards Peak Steel, the rocky outcrop where the noise seemed to be coming from, and found that I wasn't alone. 'Hello there,' said a man who turned out to be Callum Foster, 'have you come to see the seals as well?'

Callum lives in Robin Hood's Bay where he and his wife run a B&B, but this was his day job and he was accompanied by 12 schoolchildren from York who were staying at nearby East Barnby Outdoor Education Centre. 'We usually take the children on seashore walks nearer the centre but I thought we'd come here today for a change and see the seals,' Callum explained. 'This colony hasn't been here that long. Five years ago, all we'd see were odd individuals out in the bay now and again. But then a few more came from somewhere and started hauling themselves out on the scars here. One winter we noticed some small pups with white furry coats among the rocks and realised that they had started breeding. Numbers have increased dramatically, to the point now ... how many have we counted today kids?' 'Sixty-five!' piped up the ten-year-old voice of Emma, 'but these are different to the two we saw yesterday. These are grey seals 'cos they've got big noses like Romans, and yesterday's when we were canoeing on the river were common seals 'cos they had faces like dogs.'

BIG SKIES

Few places in England can compete in the landscape stakes with this corner of Yorkshire. Clear air, lofty hills and panoramic vistas abound, from the Cleveland Hills in the north to the southern Wolds.

1 One of the great viewpoints of England: Sutton Bank's Whitestonecliffe with Gormire Lake far below. (WTY) 2 May sunshine and a bluebell carpet at Roseberry Topping, the Matterhorn of Yorkshire. (NYMNPA/CC)

WHERE THE LAND MEETS THE SEA

It's no wonder that the whole of the North Yorkshire seaboard merits Heritage Coast status. Glorious cliff and bay scenery, fascinating industrial archaeology and a rich and diverse wildlife to match.

1 The wide sweep of Robin Hood's Bay with 'Baytown' in the distance. (ss) 2 One of Flamborough Head's puffins with a mouthful of sand eels. (s/mm) 3 A young member of the grey seal colony at Ravenscar near Robin Hood's Bay. (tl) 4 You're likely to see gannets at Bempton Cliffs Nature Reserve, home to England's only colony. (s/mk) 5 The sheltered waters of Runswick Bay are ideal for dinghy sailing and lobster fishing. (wty/cm) 6 The high point of Whitby's social calendar is the annual Rowing Regatta with fireworks on the last night. (nymnpa/cc)

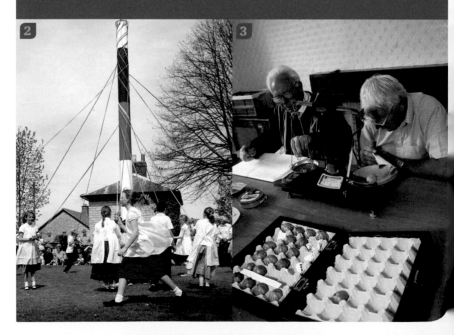

COMMUNITY

The rural communities of the Moors and Wolds are long-lived and tough. Old traditions bind folk together and are valued. Heritage isn't being rediscovered here – it never went away.

1 Monthly farmers' market in Malton, home to the annual Malton Food Festival. (WTY)
2 Slingsby's celebrated 41ft maypole in full swing. (SV) **3** The famous Egton Gooseberry Show, scene of a world record-winning berry in 2009. (MH/A)

it is also a delight – part sand, part rock-ledge, but always with the tang, noise and excitement of the sea right by your side.

The first half mile to Boggle Hole could be busy, as this is a popular stroll, and not just with those staying in the youth hostel. This imposing building was originally a big Victorian watermill, built to take advantage of the latent power in the beck that spills on to the beach here. Fewer people make it to the next beach stream, another half mile on at Stoupe Beck, but there is a route on to the cliff-top back to civilisation and even a nearby road.

You are likely to have the remaining three miles of shoreline to yourself – well, you and the oystercatchers, fulmars and turnstones – as there is no escape up the cliffs until Old Peak. I find it incredible that where the looming cliffs are at their steepest, with waterfalls tumbling over the edge, there was once a harbour. A couple of centuries ago, this was

---

Emma was right; the Ravenscar colony are grey or Atlantic seals, *Halichoerus gryphus*, which literally means hooked-nosed sea pig, and they probably came as colonists from the big population on the Farne Islands in Northumberland. The adult bulls, at 10 feet long and weighing 300lb, are our biggest wild land animal, if you count lounging on beaches now and again as being terrestrial. They eat 10lb of fish per day which doesn't make them popular with local fishermen – just do the sums, 10 x 65 x 365: that is a lot of fish in a year. Callum is happy to see them here though. 'I think there's a big opportunity here for someone with a boat; "trips across the bay to see the seals" would go down a storm with the trippers. I might even do it myself!'

The common or harbour seals that Emma and her friends had seen the day before in the tidal section of the River Esk are much smaller than grey seals. Their nearest breeding colony is 20 miles north on Seal Sands in the Tees estuary, but adventurous individuals often appear along the Yorkshire coast. They are quite happy to venture up rivers, especially when their favourite food of sea trout and salmon are doing the same. Up to five seals take up residence at times, on a grassy bank of the river, halfway between Ruswarp and Whitby. They are visible from the train, so keep your eyes peeled if you are on it, just after Ruswarp Station, or take a riverside walk up from Whitby.

If you want more than a fleeting glimpse from a train, then call in at the Sea Life Centre, Scalby Mills, Scarborough. They operate a seal rescue centre which takes in sick, orphaned or exhausted seals, and pampers them for a bit before releasing them back into the wild.

where ships loaded up with alum, a chemical extracted from the shale rock that was quarried from Stoupe Brow, hundreds of feet higher up. The remains of the quarries and works are still there to be seen, owned and ably interpreted by the National Trust, both on-site and in their Peakside Centre (see page 99).

ⵐ FOOD & DRINK

Dolphin King St ☎ 01947 880337. A rambling old pub on two levels. This fine no-nonsense establishment has a range of real ales and big portions of basic traditional pub food. The Robin Hood's Bay Folk Club meets here every Fri evening.

Grosvenor Hotel Station Rd ☎ 01947 880320 ⵐ www.thegrosvenor.info. A hotel with a popular lounge bar, pool table and regular live music; Sun is quiz night. Bar food includes fish and chips and local lobster.

Laurel Bay Bank ☎ 01947 880400. The smallest pub in town but with bags of olde worlde character. The menu is simple and wholesome and the beers always good. Open every day; quiz night Wed.

The Old Bakery Tea Rooms Chapel St ☎ 01947 880709. The best café in town and in a great position overlooking the beck. Home-baked snacks are particularly good.

Swell Café Bar Chapel St ☎ 01947 880180 ⵐ www.swell.org.uk. A relatively new and innovative venture in an old chapel with superb views across the bay from the café balcony.

SHOPPING

Jet Black New Rd ☎ 01947 881206 ⵐ www.jetblackjewellery.co.uk. A range of jewellery made of the prized local Whitby jet.

The Woodcraft Workshop Station Workshops ☎ 01947 881111 ⵐ www.marklaycock. co.uk. Artisan sculptural furniture made from English hardwoods.

FOSSILS

North East Yorkshire Geology Trust Station Workshops ☎ 01947 881000 ⵐ www. neyorksgeologytrust.com. Provide fossil guides, talks and regular Sunday guided walks for a small fee.

13 RAVENSCAR

🏠 **Oscar** Cloughton (see page 201) and **Worfolk Cottage** Staintondale (see page 201).

There is a major crack in the earth's surface here, well known among geologists as the Peak Fault, and it has a lot to answer for. It has indirectly led to Romans and seals taking up residence here and a Victorian property company going out of business. What the fault did was raise

A coastal walk from wyke to wyke

❄ OS Explorer map OL27; start: either Wyke, grid reference SE018952.

Between Ravenscar and Scarborough, the walk along the wild section of coast from Hayburn Wyke to Cloughton Wyke (❄ grid reference SE018952) and back is a most rewarding one ('wyke' means 'bay' incidentally). It's two miles each way, and you can start at either end; refreshment at the Hayburn Wyke Inn and Station House Tea Rooms may influence your route plans. Tea halfway and beer at the end or vice versa – that is the question. There's good rock pooling at Cloughton Wyke and at Hayburn Wyke, a stream gushes on to a boulder-strewn cove backed by high cliffs.

the land level to the south 600 feet higher than that to the north, where the bay now is, and it brought different, more resistant rocks to the surface (apologies to geologists, I know it's a lot more complicated than that). The Romans consequently had a convenient high vantage point to build one of their chain of coastal signal stations, where the Raven Hall Hotel is now, and the seals got a protective shelf of hard rock to shelter behind (see page 96).

As for the property company, this was a group of Yorkshire businessmen who formed the Peak Estate Company in 1885, with the bright idea of creating a seaside resort at Ravenscar to rival Scarborough and Whitby. They spent a small fortune laying out a road system, putting in water mains and digging sewers and then put 1,500 building plots up for sale. Call it naive, but what they hadn't accounted for was that holidaymakers would not want to walk 600 feet down (and more importantly back up) to a beach that was predominantly bedrock and boulders. They sold eight plots and went bankrupt. Details of their ill-fated scheme, and much more about this cliff-top village, can be found in the National Trust's little visitor centre (☎ 01723 870423) near the hotel entrance gate. Retracing the planned road system makes an interesting potter and can be extended down to the old alum works.

⚑ FOOD & DRINK

Hares Leap Farm Burniston YO13 0DB ☎ 01723 379059 🖱 www.haresleapfarm.co.uk. A farm shop-cum-café in one of the farm's converted barns. Very good value food and a wood-burning stove that's a godsend on cold winter days.

Hayburn Wyke Inn Hayburn Wyke YO13 0AU ☏ 01723 870202 ⌂ www.hayburnwykeinn. co.uk. A welcoming pub, that also allows walkers to park their cars there while they go out for the day. Extensive, traditional menu with a Sun carvery.

The Station House Tea Rooms Station Lane, Cloughton YO13 0AD ☏ 01723 870896 ⌂ www.cloughtonstation.co.uk. Set in the old railway station with half an acre of garden. Open fires, tempting cakes, low prices and good service – what more could you ask for?

14 SCARBOROUGH

🏠 **Troutsdale Lodge** near Hackness (see page 200).

Scarborough has an old provenance: a Roman signal station, a Viking name, a Norman castle and the tourist industry that started in the 17th century. It is also a modern seaside resort, and a 'fast' one at that, with many visitors coming for the nightclubs, amusement arcades, lager and speedboat trips. The words 'go slow' and South Bay seafront fit together as comfortably as, well, a square peg and a round hole. It is all relative though, in the loud-brash-tacky stakes it is not in the same league as Blackpool or Margate and you can still savour its genteel Georgian class in some hidden, serene corners.

A good place to begin is the Spa at the foot of South Cliff, where the original therapeutic spring was discovered in 1626. Behind the elegant **Spa complex**, with its concert hall and café, **South Cliff Gardens** cling to the steep hillside. You could easily spend half a day exploring the three miles of zig-zagging path on foot, or by wheelchair or bike (there are no no-cycling signs) and enjoying stunning views over the sea. In summer you can walk down and take the **Spa Cliff Tramway** back up. Even on busy days the gardens are remarkably quiet, especially at the non-town end. For the more intrepid a walk in this direction does not need to stop at the end of the gardens but could continue along the shore, on to Black Rocks and around White Nab, tide permitting. South of town, the cliff-top is accessible again at **Osgodby Point** and your two-mile return follows the Cleveland Way path. This route crosses debris from the 1993 landslip, when a huge section of cliff suffered a 'rotational slip' taking the Holbeck Hall Hotel with it. You can find out all the details and much more about local geology in the **Rotunda Museum** near the Spa.

> *"In the loud-brash-tacky stakes it is not in the same league as Blackpool or Margate and you can still savour its genteel Georgian class in some hidden, serene corners."*

If you can brave crossing the seafront (on the beach itself is the most pleasant route) the other end of **South Bay** has Scarborough Castle on the headland. From the top of this promontory you can see down on to Scarborough's other beach in **North Bay**, where you can enjoy more sand and less people. Halfway round North Bay, where the road ends, is Peasholm Park, once a huge tourist attraction but now dilapidated and scheduled for redevelopment. Two welcome exceptions here are the **Peasholm Glen Tree Trail** (get a map from the tourist information centre) described in the National Tree Register as 'one of the richest and most diverse tree collections of any English town', and the **North Bay Railway**. Scarborough itself is not in the North York Moors National Park but the boundary comes close to the town in the north near Cloughton, and especially the west, where Raincliffe Woods and Forge Valley are very accessible.

The Rotunda Museum

Vernon Rd ✆ 01723 353665 ✍ www.rotundamuseum.co.uk.

Historically and architecturally, this is one of the most important small museums in the country, but the Rotunda is a real riches-to-rags-to-riches-again story. It was built in 1829 to the specific design of the remarkable geologist William Smith, who almost single-handedly produced a geological map of England and Wales, the first of its kind in the world. Near the end of his career he wished to celebrate his discoveries, and the rich fossil beds of northeast Yorkshire, by displaying his huge collection in the same vertical layers that they occurred in nature, the youngest on the top floor and the oldest in the basement. This graceful 50-foot-high Doric-style building with a viewing spiral staircase was the consequence, and a roaring success in Victorian society.

> "Historically and architecturally, this is one of the most important small museums in the country."

Simon Winchester lamented in his 2001 biography of Smith, *The Map that Changed the World*, that in recent years the building had become a shadow of its former self and had lost its fossils. To their eternal credit, Scarborough Museums Trust have since done a fantastic job of returning the Rotunda to its former glory, and in 2008 it reopened as the William Smith Museum of Geology.

Scarborough Castle

Castle Rd ✆ 01723 37245; closed Tue and Wed in winter; English Heritage.

On the lofty headland between North Bay and South Bay, this is such a textbook defendable site it's no surprise there has been a fort here since Iron Age times. The Romans also had a signal station here and finally the Normans built the present building. Actually, to call it a building is stretching a point a bit, because little is left except the barbican, curtain walls, and the tottering remains of the keep. Parliamentarians did most of the damage in the Civil War, and that was added to last century by the Germans – not as you may suspect, World War II aerial bombing, but an artillery attack from a battleship in 1914. What is left is a big castle site but not an awful lot to see. It is a great place for a family picnic though, with plenty of grassy space for the little ones to run around in, and English Heritage produces free activity sheets for them to do while you sit and have a cup of tea in the café.

Just outside the castle entrance is another building worth a visit, especially for those with a literary bent. **St Mary's Church** is old, but not remarkable, save for a much visited grave outside. It is a memorial to part of the tragic family history of the Brontës, being the resting place of Anne. She moved to Scarborough in May 1849 to take the restorative sea air and try to avoid the fate of her brother Branwell and her sister Emily who had already died from tuberculosis, or consumption as it was known then. It didn't work; she died of the same disease within the month and was buried in St Mary's graveyard. To add insult to injury, there were five errors on her original gravestone which her surviving sister Charlotte replaced with the present one, but even that has a mistake – she was 29 at her death not 28 as the stonemason's engraving claims.

A seafront tour

The best of what Scarborough has to offer is by the sea, between the Spa and Scalby Mills, but these two are almost three miles apart. That's a little too far to walk there and back, and probably the last thing you would want to do is even attempt to drive through town. Here is a suggested multi-transport tour of the seafront, starting at either of Scarborough's park-and-rides, although it could just as easily start at the Scalby Mills car park.

Pack your bags for the day, and take the **park-and-ride bus** into town, getting off at Aquarium Top. Just around the corner is the Spa where you can catch the **Shoreline Suncruiser bus** (every 15 minutes between March and October) and enjoy the open-top views, weather permitting. This will take you around South Bay, the harbour, the kittiwake colony on the castle headland and North Bay to **Peasholm Park**. Just across the road from the park, in Northstead Manor Gardens is the southern terminus of the **North Bay Railway** (⌂ www.nbr.org.uk), a narrow gauge line dating from 1931, where you can take a short ride to Scalby Mills. If you have to wait for your train, then there are always the pedal boats nearby, or a cup of tea in the fantastic **Glass House café**. At Scalby Mills you may be tempted into **Sea Life Scarborough** (reduced entrance fee on production of your train ticket), but it was a little too much like a zoo for me, so I had a pint in the excellent Scalby Mills Hotel instead, and took a stroll along the cliff-top path to watch the seabirds.

¶¶ FOOD & DRINK
Cafés
Scarborough probably has more than a hundred cafés, so to find out which were the best, I approached Sarah Dowey and Victoria Addis-Brown, two locals who review cafés for the local paper in their spare time. Here are the best three in the experts' opinion:

Bonnets Huntriss Row ✆ 01723 361033. In the heart of town, adjacent to its own famous chocolate shop, Bonnets is definitely the cream of Scarborough cafés. It offers a tantalising choice of homemade cakes and light meals and with its chocolatier heritage, deserves a visit for the hot chocolate alone.

The Glass House North Bay ✆ 01723 368791. Tucked away opposite Scarborough's miniature railway, the Glass House is a hidden gem. With its selection of freshly made meals and speciality theme nights this bistro is definitely worth making a stop for.

The Stained Glass Centre Tea Rooms Killerby Lane, Cayton YO11 3TP ✆ 01723 585146 ⌂ www.stainedglasscentre.co.uk. Nestled at the bottom of a rambling country lane, the Stained Glass Centre Tea rooms have a relaxed country atmosphere. The idyllic views offer the perfect retreat to enjoy the unobtrusive service and generous homemade fare.

Pubs
Old Scalby Mills Scalby Mills Rd, YO12 6RP ✆ 01723 500449 ⌂ www.oldscalbymills.co.uk. Popular seafront local frequented by Cleveland Way walkers, Sea-life Centre visitors and the odd sea kayaker. A good range of beers includes a house beer (North Bay ale) from Wold Top brewery. Not renowned for food, though.

Valley Valley Rd ✆ 01723 372593 ⌂ www.valleybar.co.uk. For a Yorkshire pub to be voted the best in the whole country for cider and perry, something special has to be going on. This is first and foremost a drinker's pub, with eight ciders, six draught beers and 100 Belgian bottled on offer. Food is homemade and very good value, especially the locally caught fresh fish. Accommodation available.

BOAT TRIPS

Three boats make sightseeing trips:

Hispaniola West Pier slipway ✆ 01723 355480. Short cruise around South Bay. Easter–end Oct, every day weather permitting.

Queensferry Coastal Cruises West Pier slipway ✆ 01723 379126 / ✆ 07834 410309. A 37ft open launch offering 1hr 45mins trips to seal colonies. Easter–Sep, daily from 11.00.

Scarborough Pleasure Steamers Lighthouse Pier ✆ 01723 363605 / ✆ 07855 381139. A big boat with covered bar, food and entertainment. An hour-long trip up or down the coast, depending on the weather. Seasonal.

15 FORGE VALLEY

The River Derwent follows one of the weirdest routes of any river in the country. It rises on Fylingdales Moor near Robin Hood's Bay, a mere two miles from the sea, but then decides to wander inland and south for another 50 miles, finally joining the River Ouse to empty into the Humber. Before the last ice age it was a normal and much shorter river, finding a fairly direct route to the sea at Scalby Mills. All changed when this exit was blocked by the massive North Sea ice sheet and the river was dammed to form a lake in the Hackness Valley. Water always finds a way out and the lake eventually overflowed south cutting a new channel through the Tabular Hills – the gorge we now know as Forge Valley.

What we are left with is a steep-sided wooded ravine with a flora and fauna rich enough to warrant its designation as a National Nature Reserve, and a crystal-clear trout stream babbling along its centre. Forge Valley really is a delightful place, the only intrusion into its wildness the traffic noise from the road that follows its whole length. Natural England has provided excellent boardwalk paths for walkers and wheelchairs (but not bikes), and riverside picnic areas with feeding stations that attract masses of woodland birds.

Special flowers to look out for are broadleaved helleborine, and birds' nest orchids; exciting birds you may see include woodwarblers, redstarts and woodpeckers. The wooded section of Forge Valley is only a mile long but if you are walking here it is worth extending your route a

CORNELIAN – A YORKSHIRE GEM

Cornelian, or carnelian, is a semi-precious stone with a deep orange colour, often found on the beaches of North Yorkshire. One beach, between Scarborough and Cayton Bay, is a particularly good hunting ground and has earned itself the name Cornelian Bay. Geologists class cornelian as iron-oxide-stained chalcedony – rusty quartz in other words – but that doesn't stop it polishing up into beautiful jewellery. The cornelian pebbles have had a long and eventful journey to these beaches because they do not originate from the local Jurassic cliffs. They have actually been washed out of the cliff-top boulder clay which was left here by the last North Sea ice sheet 10,000 years ago. The ice must have brought the pebbles from the nearest source of cornelian – Scotland!

little to include the remains of Ayton Castle (small but picturesque) and Raincliffe Woods (extensive and quieter than the main valley).

¶¶ FOOD & DRINK

Three pubs in surrounding villages stand out:

The Anvil Inn Sawdon YO13 9DY ✆ 01723 859896 🖰 www.theanvilinnsawdon.co.uk. This welcoming little hostelry is housed in a 200-year-old forge in the back of beyond, with the bar where the blacksmith's workshop was. The food is inventive and locally sourced, and the beer all from Yorkshire too (Daleside and Copper Dragon). A place worth seeking out, off the A170. Open every day, not Mon lunch.

Coachman Inn Snainton YO13 9PL ✆ 01723 859231 🖰 www.coachmaninn.co.uk. The York–Scarborough mail coach stopped here in Georgian times and it's still old fashioned, but in a 1930s Arts and Crafts style now. The food is excellent and decidedly modern, leaning towards local game and fresh fish. Cask beers are from the local Treboom brewery. Closed all day Mon, and Tue lunchtime.

Moorcock Inn Langdale End YO13 0BN ✆ 01723 882268. An absolute rural gem and local institution. Langdale End is a tiny, isolated hamlet, between Forge Valley and Dalby Forest. Food is traditional bar meals with the steak pies especially popular. Yorkshire micro-brewery ales served through hatches to both bars. Can be busy in summer; winter opening hours are sketchy, so ring first.

6 CAYTON BAY

This small beach resort has changed dramatically within the past 20 years. Back in the days when Butlins and Pontins were fashionable, Wallis's Holiday Camp at Cayton Bay was very popular and the beach here almost an east coast Blackpool. There is still a large caravan park but a big new road separates it from the beach which is consequently much quieter. The beach is a classic in the holiday-postcard tradition, a small, almost perfect semi-circle of soft sand, but with a rocky reef in the centre of the bay that makes this one of the best surf spots on the Yorkshire coast.

Not having any of your own gear is no excuse for not having a go in the waves, as **Scarborough Surf School** (🖰 www.scarboroughsurfschool. co.uk) has a base here. The cost of a lesson includes equipment hire, 2½ hours coaching, a shower and a hot drink; it is only a little more than hiring the gear yourself and doing your own thing, so it adds up to fantastic value. Stand-up paddle-boarding and coasteering are also offered.

"The beach is a classic in the holiday-postcard tradition."

If the idea of squeezing yourself into a rubber suit and venturing into the cold North Sea fills you with horror, then head to the quiet north end of the beach. You can bask in the sun or rummage among the pebbles for gemstones.

Just inland from Cayton Bay lies the village of Cayton, nice enough but unremarkable – except that is for a small craft business tucked away down the back lane to Killerby. The Stained Glass Centre (🖰 www.stained glasscentre.co.uk) is run by Valerie Green, keeping her family tradition going, as her grandfather was a master glass stainer in 19th-century Bradford. Valerie and her team produce stained glass and leaded lights for businesses all over the country, but also sell items in the centre shop and run very popular courses so you can learn to do it for yourself. The tea shop is excellent.

SOUTH FROM SCARBOROUGH: FILEY BAY

Filey Bay is huge, stretching ten miles from **Filey Brigg** in the north to **Flamborough Head** in the south and straddling not just two counties but two geological time zones. The brigg marks the end of the Jurassic series of rocks, while Flamborough, in East Yorkshire, is the start of the Cretaceous chalk that makes up the foundations of the Yorkshire Wolds. **Filey** itself is the only settlement on the bay at all, and it is tucked away at the northern end. The wide sweep of the rest of the bay is backed by fast-eroding clay cliffs and is not fit for any permanent buildings, so consequently it is capped by a rash of caravan parks and holiday villages – decidedly non-Slow.

17 FILEY

As part of the Yorkshire Riviera, along with Scarborough and Whitby, Filey has been a holiday venue for many years. It was the planned destination of my mother and her friend Ena on a hare-brained tandem trip in the 1940s. They never got there as it turned out (brake failure before even leaving Lancashire, and recuperation in Blackburn Royal Infirmary) but, had they managed it, their first impressions would have been pretty much the same as today. Filey seems to exist in a time warp of sorts and its very old-fashionedness is what many of its visitors like.

'I hope your book won't go bringing more people here,' commented Bella, the elderly lady with whom I shared a park bench, 'We don't want anything changing. It's just right as it is thank you very much.'

Parts of the resort are crowded, like the short seafront, but not on the scale of Scarborough or Whitby, and there is always some deserted tranquillity just around the corner. Between the buildings of Beach Road and the rest of the town are a line of public gardens which make a pleasant walk between two wooded valleys at either end of the town. Martin's Ravine is at the southern end and The Ravine to the north. The latter was the pre-1974 boundary between the old North and East Ridings with most of the houses on one side and the church and graveyard on the other. This led to the cryptic traditional saying, 'Yon'll straightly be off t' North Riding,' meaning so and-so's not in good health and could soon find themselves in the graveyard. The old fishermen's cottage community of Queens Street is nearby, two of which have been converted into **Filey Museum**, a fine local collection (℡ 01723 515013 🖰 www.fileymuseum.co.uk). Don't be put off by the motto over the door; 'The fear of God be in you' was a reminder to 17th-century fishermen, not a dire warning to us.

Naturalists may well wish to visit **Filey Dams** (🖰 www.ywt.org.uk; open all year round; free entrance), a freshwater marsh nature reserve on the inland edge of town. It is managed by the Yorkshire Wildlife Trust, mainly to protect its rare newts, dragonflies and plants, but it is also a magnet for migrating birds, and a long list of unusual visitors has been seen from the hides.

ⵙ FOOD & DRINK
Pubs
Good pubs are in short supply in Filey, but this one definitely meets the standard:
Bonhommes Bar Royal Crescent Court ☎ 01723 514054. Named after the ship of the American rebel, John Paul Jones, the *Bonhomme Richard*, which sank in Filey Bay. This hidden-away gem is worth searching out. It is a friendly and lively local with music, quizzes and a rotating range of guest cask beers, including brews from Filey's own East Coast Brewery Company. No food.

Cafés
The café picture is very different as there are loads to choose from. These are my best five:
Brontë Vinery Café Belle Vue St ☎ 01723 514805. Good all round and fair value.
The Clock Café Station Av ☎ 07786 634480. A cosy café, particularly recommended for breakfasts but the cakes are nice too.
Country Park Café Northcliff ☎ 01723 514881. Serves free-range and fair trade products. The sandwiches and vegetarian dishes are particularly tasty.
Frothies Coffee Shop Union St ☎ 01723 514114. Wide range of teas and coffees and good-value snacks sold.
The Lighthouse Belle Vue St ☎ 01723 512191. Homemade cakes and scones, and proper fresh ground coffee in a traditional tea room.

18 FILEY BRIGG

Filey owes its existence as a fishing settlement to this narrow promontory of hard Jurassic limestone, as it keeps the worst of the North Sea's waves from reaching the town's boat landing areas and essentially converts Filey Bay into a huge harbour. It forms part of North Cliff Country Park where a caravan park with shop and café sits cheek by jowl with a large car park. There is a big green space here for children to be let loose in, but for me the place to head for (with care) is the cliff edge. Unofficial descent points here are used by anglers and youths in wet suits engaged in the dangerous sport of 'tombstoning' – leaping off the cliff into the sea.

"You can easily spend hours watching people pursuing their contrasting leisure activities, ships and seabirds passing or just waves thundering into the rock wall below."

You can easily spend hours watching people pursuing their contrasting leisure activities, ships and seabirds passing or just waves thundering into the rock wall below. Or you could amble along this end section of the Cleveland Way but, unfortunately, not down to the wave-wasted rocks of the brigg-end itself. Erosion has caused the steep end path to collapse so access has to be across the beach from the other end of the country park, via the yacht club. It is worth the effort though; it's an exhilarating place to be, especially in heavy seas, and the rock pooling here is excellent. There are some huge tame prawns in the upper shore pools who will investigate a wiggling finger or even take food from your hand. Take binoculars: the strong currents off the end of the brigg attract seals and porpoises.

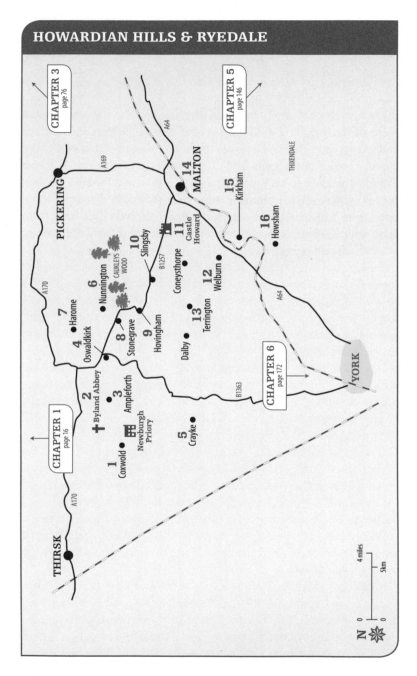

HOWARDIAN HILLS & RYEDALE

CHAPTER 3
page 76

CHAPTER 5
page 146

CHAPTER 1
page 16

CHAPTER 6
page 172

THIXENDALE

A64

MALTON

14

15 Kirkham

16 Howsham

11 Castle Howard

10 Slingsby

B1257

PICKERING

A169

CAUKLEYS WOOD

6 Nunnington

7 Harome

12 Welburn

Coneysthorpe

13 Terrington

4 Oswaldkirk

8 Stonegrave

9 Hovingham

Dalby

A170

A64

B1363

YORK

2 Byland Abbey

3 Ampleforth

Newburgh Priory

1 Coxwold

5 Crayke

THIRSK

A170

N

0
0

4 miles

5km

4
HOWARDIAN HILLS & RYEDALE

If Yorkshire is England in miniature, then this is its Cotswolds. The Howardian Hills are gentle, rolling and agricultural, with more than their fair share of trees; no big forests but some sizeable woods and lots of clumps and copses, dark pillows lying on a rumpled patchwork quilt of a landscape. This arable pastoral embroidery hides a scattering of honey-coloured hamlets and villages, one of which was my home for a while. It is no coincidence that the look and feel of the place is so similar to the Cotswolds as it is the same Jurassic limestone that underlies both, prompts a similar land use, and forms the warm, yellow stone walls of the old buildings.

This is archetypal well-off countryside: sleepy, self-contained and quintessentially English, with each village seeming to have its old manor house, very old church and huge vicarage. I can easily imagine Miss Marple taking tea with the Colonel in Bulmer or cycling past the green in Hovingham. The Edwardian landed gentry feel to this place is no illusion. Feudal old England is alive and well here, with a fair proportion of the Howardian Hills still owned and run by three families as their country estates. The Wombwells rule the roost in the west at Newburgh Priory near Coxwold, the Worsleys' family home is Hovingham Hall but pride of place for pomp, opulence and grandeur must go to the Howards. Not only do they have a castle named after the family, but a range of hills named after their castle; now that is true arrogance – oops, sorry, I mean influence.

Nunnington sits alongside the River Rye just as it leaves the Howardian Hills Area of Outstanding Natural Beauty (AONB) and slides lazily out into the floodplain of its own making, Yorkshire's fenland. Scenically, lower Ryedale is nothing to write home about. Most people would go as far as to say it was boring, unless they had a thing about crop

SLOE MOTION

Hedgerows in the Howardian Hills are often full of dazzling white flowers in April, and tiny wild plums in autumn. These are sloes, the fruit of the blackthorn bush, and although they are far too sour to eat as they are, they make a delicious natural flavouring for other foods and drinks.

Jonathan Curtoys and his colleagues have made a business out of the sloe taste. Their company, SLOEmotion (☎ 0844 800 1911 🖰 www.sloemotion.com), is based at Green Farm, Barton le Willows (south of Howsham), and collects sloes using an army of local pickers, before making them into a range of rich and fruity products. Traditional sloe gin is their biggest seller, but have you ever tried sloe vodka, sloe brandy, sloe whisky, sloe chutney or sloe truffles? No, I hadn't either and I didn't know what I was missing – they are delicious. Buy online or from farmers' markets, shows and good specialist food stores.

rotation, yields per acre or the relative merits of David Brown tractors over Massey Fergusons, because this is prime arable farming country. It does have attractions though; its rivers, the Rye and its tributaries, are wonderful linear reserves of nature and tranquillity.

The River Rye empties into the bigger River Derwent. Three miles below this confluence sits the town of Malton, on the north bank, with its twin Norton facing it from the other side of the river. This has always been an important river crossing even back to Roman times, and Malton is still very much the social hub of this region. When people from **Terrington**, **Hovingham** or **Welburn** say that they are going into town, this is where they mean; likewise, local farmers taking their beasts to market will also head this way. **Malton** is a market town, but a real one that still does what it says on the tin.

Downstream from Malton the River Derwent winds its way south, through Kirkham gorge and away down the western edge of the Wolds, finally joining the sea at the Humber estuary.

SELF-POWERED TRAVEL

CYCLING

It is mixed news on the two-wheeled front. The good news is that **road biking** in places is superb, mainly because the minor roads around here are so quiet. I once cycled from home in Barton le Street, in the middle of the day on a circular route, through Butterwick, Brawby and Salton.

The sun was out, skylarks and yellowhammers were singing throughout the whole nine miles over minor tarmac roads, and I did not see a single motorised vehicle; come to think of it, I did not see another person at all. Ryedale has the added advantage of being flat as a pancake mostly, so is very forgiving for the less athletic biker.

The Howardian Hills half of the region is not quite so gentle; the clue is in the 'hills' bit of the name. There are still some lovely quiet road circuits like Hovingham to Stonegrave to Gilling East to Coulton and back to Hovingham, or west from Terrington along Bonnie Gates Lane and back via Steersby and Skewsby, but some of the hills on the way are killers. Dalby Bank, up from the beck to the hamlet, is my nemesis, but what the heck, there is no shame in getting off and pushing every now and again.

Off-road biking is less promising. The areas of the OS map devoid of bridleways suspiciously correspond to the biggest estate lands. Gilling Castle and Newburgh Priory estates seem to have been particularly good at keeping peasants off their land in the past, which is reflected in the lack of rights of way today. A decent network exists elsewhere, with Castle Howard lands being surprisingly rich. One of my particular favourites is a circuit linking Hovingham and Coneysthorpe, with much of the northern leg following the Centenary Way, and the parallel southern return on the Ebor Way. This is a lovely nine-mile ridge route predominantly under trees and with lots of alternative options to shorten or lengthen the ride. Wildlife encounters are likely, with hares lolloping away from you across every field you pass and buzzards soaring on the up-draught at any point on the ridges. If you are early or late in the day you have an excellent chance of seeing badgers bumbling along the track side, roe deer melting into the trees or barn owls drifting along hedgerows. Other recommended off-road hill routes are Caulkleys ridge from Nunnington and a circumnavigation of Welburn.

Down on the flats of Ryedale, off-road biking is not recommended unless you can see from the OS map that the bridleway follows a farm track. The chances are that those marked in bold green across the fields, or along riverbanks, do not in reality exist on the ground, or are complete quagmires. I have had some nightmare walks-with-a-bike in swampy fields between Butterwick and South Holme and, worse still, had my bike gears completely destroyed by wheat stalks that had been planted over a bridleway, jamming in the mechanism.

CYCLE HIRE

Golden Square Campsite Oswaldkirk YO62 5YQ ✆ 01439 788269 ⌂ www.goldensquare caravanpark.com. Off-road bikes.

R Yates and Sons Railway St, Malton ✆ 01653 693215 ⌂ www.yatescycles.co.uk. Off-road and town bikes available.

HORSERIDING

Sadly, and surprisingly for such a horsey area, there is a dearth of facilities for riders here. **White Rose Riding School** at Park House Farm near Coxwold (✆ 01347 869001 or 07764 575249 ⌂ www. whiteroseridingschool.co.uk) is the only one offering horses, hacking and lessons, although there are four not so far away in bordering regions. These are at Sinnington (see page 80) and Hawnby and Helmsley (page 18). It is good riding country though, so if you can bring your own horse you will have a field day. Grazing, feed and a secure tack room are available at Manor Farm, Old Byland (✆ 01439 798247) and other horse accommodation can be found in neighbouring areas at Boltby, Gillamoor, Hawnby, Helmsley, Pockley and Sproxton (see *Chapter 1*) and Appleton le Moors, Cropton, Ebberston and Sinnington (*Chapter 3*).

WALKING

Although the options for walks are more limited here than in the neighbouring North York Moors, the quality is high. Because the Howardian Hills are so compact and small-scale, one walk can visit a variety of landscapes in a short distance. The brief section of the Centenary Way north of Welburn is a good case in point. Within two miles it crosses arable farmland, follows a small beck through ancient deciduous woodland containing a fen nature reserve, visits classically managed parkland, cattle and sheep pasture and finally dark conifer plantations. The drawback is that this is the whole list of what the area has to offer; you won't find proper hill-tops or fast flowing rivers, and the only open access land is a small area of woodland near Yearsley voluntarily opened by the Forestry Commission.

Three **long-distance footpaths** visit the area in passing, the Ebor Way *en route* from Helmsley to Ilkley, the Centenary Way from York to Filey and the Foss Walk briefly, through Crayke.

As for shorter and more practically achievable ventures, the Howardian Hills AONB authority has produced four excellent leaflets with suggested

---

i **TOURIST INFORMATION**

Malton Tourist Information Centre Malton Library, St Michael St ✆ 01653 600048
Howardian Hills AONB Office Wath YO62 4NN ✆ 0845 0349495 🖰 www.howardianhills.
org.uk. The website is a great source of information and useful downloads like walks leaflets.

---

representative **circular walks**. The start points are Hovingham, Welburn, Nunnington and Terrington with the walks ranging from three to nine miles. The leaflets are available online (🖰 www.howardianhills.org.uk).

Point-to-point walks using public transport are possible, but require a bit of forward planning, because buses are so few and far between. The simplest strategy is to catch a bus from Malton to Welburn, Castle Howard, Terrington or Hovingham and walk back. It is best done this way round with unreliable buses, to avoid being marooned in the sticks. For shorter walks, the 'Street' bus can be caught for a few stops, and the return made along the Centenary Way ridge, Hovingham to Barton (five miles) for instance, or Slingsby to Appleton (four miles).

The **Rye**, with its tributaries, is a lovely river, so it is worth trying to search out the few footpaths that follow them. Pickering Beck south towards Kirbymisperton is a delightful stroll, as is the mile along the River Seven from Marton to Normanby, or vice versa, but the longest and best stretch is the Rye itself from Helmsley to Nunnington via Harome. This convoluted five miles can be extended by one more to West Ness, or two more to Salton.

The **River Derwent** suffers the same problem of pathlessness, especially upstream of Malton, but there are places where you can stroll along the banks. My favourite of these is the three mile stretch from Kirkham Priory to Howsham Bridge, an added benefit being the choice of return routes – either the quiet country lane through Crambe village or via the sylvan delights of Howsham Woods.

AN ABBEY ROAD
– FROM COXWOLD TO OSWALDKIRK

Where the northern edge of the Howardian Hills butts against the southern slopes of the Hambleton Hills the village of Gilling East sits astride a narrow gap often called the Gilling Gap. Its centuries-old use as a transport route is not surprising: as well as having a road and disused railway line, it is a known Roman route. What is not quite so clear is why it was such an ecclesiastical magnet, as within six short miles, from **Oswaldkirk** to **Coxwold**, are two abbeys (**Ampleforth** and **Byland**), two very old churches (Oswaldkirk and Coxwold), and a priory at **Newburgh**. This little corner's pulling power does seem to have waned though, as it never seems anywhere near as busy as nearby Helmsley, Sutton Bank or Nunnington. For us lovers of undisturbed walks or traffic-free cycling this is no bad thing of course.

To the south of Coxwold lies the quietest corner of the Howardian Hills, with the hill-top village of **Crayke** perched at its edge.

1 COXWOLD

'I am as happy as a prince in Coxwold, and I wish you could see in how princely a manner I live. Tis a land of plenty.' So wrote Laurence Sterne, vicar of Coxwold in the 1760s, and this small village is still a very desirable place to live, and was rated in the top ten best villages nationally on TV's Channel Five *Property List*.

I would also rate it highly in a list of desirable places to visit, but the two are very different things. At first sight it seems like just another Cotswoldy village typical of this corner of the Howardian Hills but beneath the surface lies a rich vein of quirky eccentricity. **Shandy Hall** at the top of the village is the best example; a singular building that was lived in by a very singular man, Laurence Sterne himself. As vicar of the village he spent a good deal of time, though not as much as he should have spent apparently, in **St Michael's Church**, the next large building down the main street. He almost certainly spent too much time in a building opposite the church, the Fauconberg Arms, although it was not called that then. The pub name has followed the family name of the residents of nearby **Newburgh Priory**, being the Bellasis Arms in Sterne's time although it has not so far changed to the Wombwell Arms in honour of the present family name. Two lines of honey-coloured stone buildings lead down the broad main street with an ancient crossroads at the bottom. Wakendale Beck crosses

"At first sight it seems like just another Cotswoldy village typical of this corner of the Howardian Hills but beneath the surface lies a rich vein of quirky eccentricity."

the road by the old schoolhouse, changes its name to Green Beck and passes the old mill it used to power. The Old Schoolhouse is now the Schoolhouse Tearooms.

Shandy Hall

✆ 01347 868465 🖥 www.laurencesternetrust.org.uk; open May–Sep, Wed and Sun afternoons only.

Shandy Hall is the oldest building in Coxwold, and looks it. A wonderfully rickety maze of a place, it would merit preservation in its own right, but the reason it is a museum is not for what it is but for who lived here. In 1670 this was the Parsonage, and the new parson, Laurence Sterne, was part-way through writing what would become his most famous novel, *Tristram Shandy*. He finished it in this house along with *Sentimental Journey*, both books written in a surreal comedic style way ahead of their time and a touch ribald for a country vicar. Sterne enjoyed eight years of fame, and a little controversy, before succumbing to ill health and dying in 1678. After Sterne's death the renamed Shandy Hall became a place of literary pilgrimage and in the 1960s was bought by the newly formed Laurence Sterne Trust, which has looked after the house and gardens ever since. The present curator Patrick Wildgust lives in the house with his wife Chris. 'My job is to celebrate the life of this great writer and introduce other people to his work, but there are things here to appeal to all sorts. Sterne was never a dedicated gardener, as he said himself he would sometimes "weed, hack up old roots or wheel away rubbish", but the gardens he has left us are lovely. Much like the man really, a complex contradiction; two acres of old-fashioned roses, formal walled garden, and semi-wild old quarry.

"Shandy Hall is the oldest building in Coxwold, a wonderfully rickety maze of a place, it would merit preservation in its own right."

St Michael's Church

The Pope wrote to the King of Northumbria in AD757 instructing him to repair Coxwold Minster so we know this is a very old church site – in fact there was probably a pagan temple here before then. The present building is not that old (1430) but some really unusual features inside and out justify an exploration. As you would expect, there are lots of connections with the Bellasis/Fauconberg/Wombwell family – monuments, memorials, tombs and the like – but Laurence Sterne has also left his mark. He installed a three-decker pulpit (now reduced to two) and box pews, and his gravestone sits just by the porch outside. In a bizarre chain of events typical of Sterne, he was buried three times: firstly in Westminster Abbey, then again after his body was stolen for medical research but reclaimed, and finally in 1960 when the London graveyard he lay in was built on. The Laurence Sterne Trust obtained permission to bring his head up to Coxwold and its final resting place near his beloved Shandy Hall.

Newburgh Priory

☎ 01347 868372 ◌ www.newburghpriory.co.uk; open Apr–Jun Wed and Sun afternoons.
Just south of Coxwold, this house is one of those places whose brilliance lies in its differentness. For a start, it is not a priory but a stately home, and a refreshingly un-heritage one at that. The building is a hotchpotch of styles with some of it derelict and roofless, and the grounds are very randomly set out with no apparent plan, but the whole place has a serene, informal air about it.

It is a special place for me because I so much savoured a sense of discovery, chancing upon it with no pre-knowledge of its existence, and just turning in off the road on spec. I was lucky as opening times are very singular; and it was late afternoon on a Sunday when I was greeted at the entrance shed by a dapper, elderly gentleman dressed in slacks, shirt and straw trilby. He listed the attractions, each with a vague directional point. 'There's the lake of course, but you can see that. The walled garden is splendid at the moment (it was). The basin pond and water garden are over there (vague point), and should you feel like you can tackle the hill behind the house, you will find a view over to the Hambleton Hills (cursory wave) absolutely marvellous.'

'Is there a map or guidebook at all?' I asked.

'Oh no – it's very much a go and find it for yourself experience here,' was the reply. So I went and searched, and in the walled garden I found leeks growing in tubes, new potatoes part-harvested, a pink climbing rose with an overpowering perfume, a lily pond with dancing blue damselflies and newt tadpoles just below the surface. At the side of the house, a series of 'Royal Trees' were planted by visiting monarchs, and a small fenced-off area near the water garden contains the graves of family dogs.

Inside the house is just as quirky and interesting. The compulsory tea-shop visit at the end was, as expected, very non-National Trust. The handwritten sign 'Tea Shop' directed us through the old servants' quarters and into the dining room with its faint smell of lavender and mothballs. Old paintings lined the walls; each small table had a single rose in a small vase and the clock on the wall tick-tocked slowly. Such was the peaceful atmosphere in the room, the two people already there were actually whispering.

The rest of the house has the usual lines of family portraits, wood panels and Chippendale-esque furniture, but then suddenly you come face-to-face with the death mask of Oliver Cromwell on an attic vault door, with his headless corpse inside by some accounts.

¶¶ FOOD & DRINK

Coxwold Tea Rooms The School House ☎ 01347 868077 ⏛ www.coxwoldtearooms. co.uk. Basic, cosy café handily placed at the bottom of the village near the craft workshops. Also does B&B accommodation.

Fauconberg Arms ☎ 01347 868214 ⏛ www.fauconbergarms.com. On Coxwold's main street, this ancient inn was rescued from closure in 2006, and had new life breathed into it by the present owners, the extended Rheinberg family. They have done a great job. I was informed independently by three family members that 'This is a pub first and foremost, but we do very good food,' and they are right on both counts. Top-quality Yorkshire cuisine and (bravely, I feel) Thwaites Lancashire beer. Dog-friendly accommodation and a mini-theatre with regular varied events.

2 BYLAND ABBEY

Byland YO61 4BD ☎ 01347 868614; English Heritage.

Two things catch your attention on first sighting the ruins of Byland Abbey. The first, from a distance, is the amazing rose window (the first of its kind to appear in England), or rather half rose window, and the question of what is keeping it up, as it looks so precarious. The second, with a closer view, is likely to be the size of the place; the site is huge with the abbey church alone as big as some cathedrals. Other features to look for are the 13th-century ceramic mosaic floor tiles, still in their original position and made on site, and said to be of World Heritage significance as far as ceramics go; and a medieval doodle of the rose window scratched into the wall beneath the window itself, on the left as you come in (not at all easy to spot without some expert guidance).

NOT ALL MONKS ARE NICE

Byland Abbey has boasted many colourful characters over the years, too many to mention, but one story in particular deserves to be told. The 'most audacious acts and merited misfortunes' of Wimund the Blind Monk were recorded by William of Newburgh.

Although of humble origins, Wimund learnt to write and became a monk at Furness Abbey. His 'ardent temper, retentive memory and competent eloquence' resulted in quick promotion (sounds like a few politicians I can think of). After a meteoric rise he became bishop of the Isle of Man but still yearned for greater acclaim and more power (definitely a politician, then). He announced that he was the rightful heir to the earldom of Mowbray and that the King of Scotland was depriving him of his inheritance. Gathering an army of followers he invaded Scotland, 'wasting all before him with rapine and slaughter'. Sensing military defeat, the king of the Scots decided on a more subtle strategy that would use Wimund's own arrogance against him. He granted large areas of land, including Furness, to the rebel knowing that Wimund would not be accepted by those who once knew him as a low-born monk. Sure enough, as he was parading his army around the area, a trap was set and he was captured. His punishment was to be blinded, castrated and sent to Byland Abbey as a lowly monk once more (politicians take note). He remained there, humiliated but unrepentant until his death, moaning to all who would listen of his woes: 'Had I the eye of the sparrow, my enemies should have little occasion to rejoice at what they have done to me.'

The fact that the abbey was built here at all is down to a strange series of 12th-century events and a long journey by 13 Savignac monks. Amazingly, we know all their names; they were: Gerold the Abbott, Robert, Tocka, John, Theodore, Hormi, Roger, Alan, Wido, William, Peter, Ulfus and Bertram (an interesting study in which names survive nearly 1,000 years and which don't – I certainly don't know any Widos or Hormis). The 13 were sent out from Furness Abbey in Lancashire to found a new abbey, and tried four sites before ending up here. Their penultimate choice was five miles due north of the present abbey at a place still called Old Byland. The apocryphal reason for them leaving there after only four years was that they were too close to Rievaulx Abbey and their church bells clashed with those of the established Cistercian community. The monks finally settled near the village of Wass, converted to Cistercianism and, in 1170, started to build their magnificent monument. During the next 370 years Byland prospered and became a very rich and powerful organisation/landowner until the catastrophic Dissolution in 1538.

3 AMPLEFORTH

Ampleforth is an unusual and not overly attractive place, or should I say, two places. There is a village, but mention the name of 'Ampleforth' and most people will think of the abbey and associated private college. These two are tenuously attached to the village but very definitely culturally separate. The whole lot is strung out along two miles of busy and often congested road. Surprisingly, the village is much older than the abbey and college, it being mentioned in the Domesday Book whilst the latter was only founded in the 19th century.

Ampleforth Abbey is one of the few living and active Benedictine monasteries in the country, and certainly the largest. Until recently, the monastic community kept its slow and peaceful lifestyle pretty much to itself and the students of the college. But, times have changed, and an outreach venture that has really taken off in the last year or two has been the sale of abbey produce. At the heart of this has been Father Rainer and his cider-making, which made the columns of the national press back in 2008.

¶¶ FOOD & DRINK

Ampleforth Abbey Tea Room YO62 4EN ☎ 01439 766868 ⌂ www.hpo.ampleforth.org. uk. A pleasant modern room decked out with Mousey Thompson wooden tables and serving home-produced scones and cakes. Fruit from the abbey orchard features prominently. Closed Sun mornings.

4 OSWALDKIRK

This tiny village clings precariously on to the hillside known, not too flatteringly, as Oswaldkirk Hag. Most of the village buildings sit on the slightly less steep south side of the road and fall within the jurisdiction of the Howardian Hills AONB, whereas those on the other side lie within the North York Moors National Park.

Oswaldkirk has two buildings of note and these are, as is so often the case, the church and the pub. I suppose for decency's sake I ought to deal with the **church** first, especially as the village was named after it. It is a lovely, peaceful little building, especially the side away from the road where the sloping graveyard allows panoramic views across the vale. There was probably a wooden Saxon church here originally but the present building is a humble mixture of Norman and more modern stonework.

There are no prizes for working out that the church is dedicated to St Oswald but the story of the man himself is much more obscure. He was a Saxon king of Northumbria in the 7th century, and one of the

AMPLEFORTH CIDER

Ampleforth Abbey has a historic five-acre organic orchard with more than 40 varieties of apple trees, which until recently was largely unloved and untended; most of the apples went to feed autumn wasps and blackbirds. Father Rainer Verborg had other ideas, first producing apple juice to sell at local farmers' markets, and then moving on to cider-making. The production plant, in old abbey farm buildings, now makes over 3,000 litres a year, but could sell twice that amount, such is the popularity of the distinctive pale, dry brew.

During the production months of July–November, the orchard is open to visitors on Monday and Friday afternoons and the cider mill likewise on Tuesday and Wednesday afternoons, but ring to check if you are planning to visit (✆01439 76000). Father Rainer's cider is available in the abbey shop and various delis locally such as Castle Howard farm shop and Hunters of Helmsley. Look out also for the excellent Ampleforth cider brandy and Belgian Trappist-style beer.

original 'Christian soldiers'. It was he who invited St Aidan to establish the original monastery at Lindisfarne. In the year AD642 King Oswald was killed in battle against the heathen King Penda and he was sainted soon afterwards. A cult surrounding him developed, resulting in many St Oswald's churches in the Saxon areas of eastern England. His head, as a prized relic, was taken to Lindisfarne and, when the Viking raids threatened, was put into St Cuthbert's coffin for safekeeping. It is still in the coffin now, buried in the foundations of Durham Cathedral.

I like old churches, but I love good pubs and the **Malt Shovel** is one of my favourites, with a real two-buildings-in-one feel to it. The side by the road has two dark, low-ceilinged rooms, one a cosy bar and the other a flag-floored pool room and, during many visits to the Sunday quiz, this is all I saw. It was only when my neighbour, on a sunny day, suggested a pint from the back bar to be drunk in the beer garden, that I saw the original front of the building – and it is magnificent. From here its origins as a manor house are obvious, a storey higher than the back because it is lower down the hill, and with stunning views over the terraced gardens and patchwork of fields and woods in the vale.

The Malt Shovel looks as if it should be haunted, and apparently is. The official ghost is of a five-year-old boy, Thomas Bamber, who died in the house in the 1890s and whose mother, unable to accept the death, kept his body for weeks. He is still said to be there, in his bedroom – now the ladies' toilets. 'I've never seen Tom,' said the landlady as we chatted in the lounge bar. 'But I have seen a bloke in here. No idea who he was but he drifted across the room and through the wall there. It doesn't bother me – they can't hurt you can they? That only happens in films.'

🍴 FOOD & DRINK

Malt Shovel YO62 5XT ☎ 01439 788461. A gem of a place (see opposite) and the cheapest beer in Yorkshire courtesy of Sam Smith's Brewery. Not renowned for its food, but that's not why you would come here.

5 CRAYKE

The charming village of Crayke sits on top of a little eminence with staggering views across the Vale of York. This isolated Howardian Hill, cast adrift from the rest, is thought to be the one that the Grand Old Duke of York famously marched his 10,000 men up and down.

Crayke has very strong ties with County Durham; in fact until 1844 it was still officially a remote enclave of the county. St Cuthbert founded a monastery here, giving his name to the church, and the Prince Bishops built the original castle which is now a private house. It is said that the saint's body was hidden from marauding Vikings here before its final burial in Durham Cathedral.

🍴 FOOD & DRINK

Durham Ox Westway ☎ 01347 821506 🖱 www.thedurhamox.com. This is an unashamedly high-quality food and wine establishment and it does it brilliantly. Seafood and local game are their specialities.

LOWER RYEDALE

Part of what is now called the Vale of Pickering, Lower Ryedale a few thousand years ago was Lake Pickering which stretched some 20 miles from Ampleforth in the west to Scarborough in the east, making it probably the biggest lake in Britain at the time. Lake sediments make fabulously rich farming soils and agriculture here is productive and very lucrative. Stand atop one of Lake Pickering's old islands, now small hillocks, like Great Edstone or Normanby Hill, and turn through 360°; all you will see is a flat carpet with a repeating pattern of wheat, barley, spuds, hay, wheat, beans and barley – thank heaven for a break in this monotony. The saving grace is the River Rye itself, and its tributaries the Dove, Seven and Costa Beck. They are ribbons of oasis in the desert, willow-fringed and hidden away behind flood banks. Wherever footpaths and bridleways meet them it is a joy, especially so to float down in a kayak or canoe in the few places not policed by landowners or fishermen. In summer they're bejewelled by iridescent blue and green damselflies, and in winter, when they burst their banks to temporarily re-form Lake Pickering, they're alive with cackling and honking flocks of ducks and geese.

6 NUNNINGTON

All most visitors see of Nunnington is its stately home. Granted, Nunnington Hall is well worth a visit, but there is more to explore here. The hillside village is bigger than it seems: you could spend a pleasant hour pottering up and down its two lanes. The **church of All Saints and St James** at the top of the village is unremarkable except for two stories recorded in the porch; one of a local St George-style dragon slaying and the other a framed piece of writing that I found particularly moving. It was a 'thank you' note to the villagers, and his guardians in particular, from a war-time evacuee (or 'vaccy', as they were known), with an accompanying drawing of the church that he did himself as a child in the 1940s.

Not far down from the church is the Royal Oak. Some pubs just belong exactly where they are, and this one, slotted into a row of other hunched, yellow, limestone buildings, does just that.

The River Rye winds its way lazily around the bottom of Nunnington. I have seen it cold, brown and uninviting after winter rain, but in summer it is delightful. Leaning over one of the village's three bridges and gazing into the gin-clear water, with its long slowly waving tresses of water crowfoot and hanging trout shadows, can be an hypnotic experience.

Nunnington Hall

Nunnington YO62 5UY ✆ 01439 748283; open daily except Mon in summer, weekends only in Nov and Dec, and closed all Jan and Feb. Entry to the tea shop and tea gardens is free and if you're not visiting the hall there's a reduced fee for the garden. National Trust.

By the standard of its near neighbours, this is not an exceptional stately home. Hovingham Hall is bigger, Castle Howard is more spectacular and Newburgh Priory is older. What Nunnington Hall has though, is

NUNNINGTON'S WATER BATS

The hall is closed, the car park is empty and the crowds have gone: this is the best time to enjoy the River Rye, a balmy summer evening with the last yellowing of the sky reflected in the water under the old bridge arches. Wait a few minutes longer, if you can bear the attention of the dusk midges and mosquitoes, because these insects will soon tempt out some of Nunnington's special residents. In crevices and crannies in the stonework of the bridge lives a healthy population of bats, and not any old flitter-mice either; these are Daubenton's bats, a species that loves to live near, and hunt over, water. When they appear they are unmistakable, whizzing around in circles and figures of eight, inches above the river, sometimes setting off ripples as they grab a hapless insect from the water's surface. You will get about half an hour's watching in before the light goes; the bats will carry on hunting of course, but you can retreat to the pub to enjoy a glass of wine or beer and scratch your new midge bites.

a just-rightness and great charm, with everything that a stately home should have – stone-flagged floors, oak panelling, old paintings and tapestries, a giant, creaky staircase and a haunted bedroom. The restored walled garden, with a local-variety apple orchard and flower beds, is a balanced mix of practical and ornamental and the hall's location, tucked into a bend of the River Rye, is serene.

"What Nunnington Hall has though, is a just-rightness and great charm, with everything that a stately home should have."

So it is not surprising that the National Trust accepted the hall and gardens from the Fife family in 1952, or that it is one of their most popular properties with visitors. Many come here specifically for what is in the attic, the old servants' quarters, which houses a permanent exhibition of miniature rooms and buildings (the Carlisle Collection), that has nothing to do with Nunnington; it is just a convenient place for the National Trust to store it. Other attic rooms house constantly changing exhibitions from rock musicians' photographs to Victorian cartoons.

It can get very busy here, especially early afternoon with folk calling in *en route* from Castle Howard to Helmsley, or vice versa. Being such a small place, crowds can spoil the experience here so my advice would be to go midweek if you can, or if not, be first at the door when it opens in the morning.

THE STAR INN

For a little backwater village, Harome is becoming very well known, even beyond the bounds of Yorkshire. This fame is almost solely down to one man, Andrew Pern and his wife Jacquie. Put simply, Jacquie is the landlady of the village pub, the Star Inn, and Andrew is the chef. In reality the two of them are at the helm of a burgeoning business that is fast becoming an empire.

It all started in 1996 when the pub came up the sale and the newly wedded Perns, working for another nearby pub, had their offer accepted. It was a brave move, as Andrew remembers. 'It was knee-high in weeds and ridden with mice. We left the Milburn Arms on 10 June, 1996, and were faced with opening our new venture just ten days later. There was just me in the kitchen, Jacquie out front and her mum behind the bar. We were serving off plates that were our wedding presents, and washing them at once to serve the next customer. On the first day we ran out of food, beer and change as an avalanche of people fell into the place. The encouraging thing was that the avalanche never stopped. We worked 18-hour days for 20 months virtually without a break, until our first child, Daisy, was born.'

Their hard work paid off in 2001 when the Star Inn was awarded a coveted Michelin star with more to come in 2006 when it was rated the best gastropub in the country by Egon Ronay. The success of Andrew and Jacquie's business has allowed them to expand to the point where it seems like they are taking over the village. They now have catered accommodation at Cross House Lodge, Black Eagle Cottage and The Farmhouse, and have opened The Corner Shop opposite the pub selling specialty foods and local produce. Their most recent acquisition is the village hotel, The Pheasant.

Andrew is very aware of the importance of his local roots, and values not just the quality but the 'localness' of his supplies. 'Taste and smell are potent in their ability to evoke faces and places, times and events. Looking back to my childhood on a farm, I can instantly recall the waft of bacon frying, the aroma of roasting beef, the gamey scent of partridge in the oven, and the tang of blackberries as I plucked them, purple-fingered, from the hedgerows. The North York Moors was an idyllic place to live and learn about nature's larder: seafood from the North Sea, lamb, beef and pork reared by people with pride in their produce, game from the rough shoots alongside the Esk Valley and especially grouse from the purple-cloaked moors of Egton, Rosedale and Danbydale. The food you were eating was teaching you about the seasons.

¶¶ FOOD & DRINK

Nunnington Hall tea room This was originally a dining room and it has been restored with the original dark décor which makes it a bit dingy, and service is quite formal. In good weather, the tea garden by the river is much the better choice. Usual National Trust good quality and value, locally sourced produce.

Royal Oak Church St, YO62 5US ✆01439 748271 ⌂www.nunningtonroyaloak.co.uk. Warmed by log fires and with an assortment of jugs, flagons and old keys hanging from the beams, this is a little too much restaurant and not enough pub for me but has very good food and well-kept local beers.

7 HAROME

This must be one of the most mispronounced place names in the country. I have heard 'Ha-rowm', 'Ha-rom' and 'Har-rowm', to name but three, but the correct one apparently is 'Hair-um'.

One of the village's claims to fame is its seven thatched cottages, the most of any place in Yorkshire, giving it more of a West- rather than North-country feel. What brings most people to Harome though is not its chocolate-box look but the gastronomic delights available in the Star Inn, Pheasant Hotel and shop, all run by the Pern family.

¶¶ FOOD & DRINK

Pheasant Hotel Mill St ✆ 01439 771241 ⌂ www.thepheasanthotel.com. A country hotel in buildings that were once barns and a blacksmith's workshop. This is part of the Pern family stable and head chef Peter Neville came from the Star Inn, so high-quality service and food are both guaranteed; they're also open for morning coffee and afternoon tea.
Star Inn Main St ✆ 01439 770397 ⌂ www.thestaratharome.co.uk. Possibly the best food anywhere in Yorkshire, in a low, rambling building with a nicely old-fashioned bar as well as a sleek dining room and plenty of space to sit outside; decent beer too. Gastronomic Michelin-starred heaven, but meal prices reflect the quality so save it for a special occasion, like a birthday, anniversary or holiday. See box, page 126.

THE 'STREET' VILLAGES

The Romans were famously good road builders. Contrary to popular belief though, their roads did not always follow the straightest route, but they did invariably choose the easiest course. Consequently, when they decided to link the garrison town of Malton (Derventium) with Aldborough (Isurium) near Boroughbridge, they avoided the direct line across the steep ups and downs of the Howardian Hills. Instead they followed the flat land to the north, through Lower Ryedale and the Gilling Gap, but just uphill enough to avoid the swamps. This is the course of the present B1257, known locally as the 'Street' in recognition of its antiquity. A string of old **villages** punctuates this road, from Broughton in the east to Hovingham in the west, with two of them, Appleton and Barton, even having 'le Street' tacked on to their name to distinguish them from nearby Appleton le Moors and Barton le Willows.

8 STONEGRAVE

I have a rule: any place that I pass through on a busy road thinking 'Ooh, this looks nice', by definition isn't, and what spoils it is the very busy-ness of that road. Stonegrave suffers from this phenomenon unfortunately as the whole hamlet is strung out along the well-used Malton–Helmsley road, the B1257. There are three consolations though: a lovely short circular walk nearby, a truly ancient church, and the rarest native tree in England.

The walk is a tour of **Caukleys Wood** east of the hamlet; go clockwise if you prefer your uphill bit first, along the top of the wood, with panoramic views of the moors to the north, then down Caukleys Bank to return under the trees at the bottom of the wood. Do it in reverse if you need a warm-up before any ascent.

Any church with Minster as part of its name is usually very old or has been very important at one time; **Stonegrave Minster** is both. Sadly, the building has suffered many 'modernisations' over the years so only part of the tower is original Saxon, but you can see fragments of intricately carved 9th-century crosses on display just inside the porch.

9 HOVINGHAM

⌂ Cold Harbour Shed (see page 201)

This is arguably the prettiest village in the Howardian Hills, and certainly one of the most popular with visitors. Hovingham is a sunny-Sunday sort of place, somewhere to lounge and stroll, because to be honest there is not an awful lot else here to do. It has more than enough to be a living, working village – a hotel, a pub, two shops, two cafés and a bakery – but for me its biggest attractions are the buildings themselves. It does 'grand', notably **Hovingham Hall** itself which dominates the village green, and **All Saints' Church** with its impressive Saxon tower, but it is the little buildings that make Hovingham special for me, especially some of the tiny cottages hidden away behind the church and the strangely Gothic primary school. Historically, the hall and church were the epicentres of the community, but now on most days, and especially weekends, the focus is the **Spa Tea Room** and adjacent beck. Everybody seems to gravitate there, grown-ups to sit with a cup of tea outside if it's warm, inside if it's not, and children to paddle and fish for bullheads in the limey waters of the brook.

Hovingham Hall

YO62 4LX ☎ 01653 628771 ✐ www.hovingham.co.uk; open 1–28 Jun only.

Most stately homes are extravagant status symbols, built to be viewed as much as to view from. To this end almost all of them sit in splendid isolation, with a definite front on display to the world.

Hovingham Hall is an exception. It is right in the middle of the village, presenting a not very imposing façade to the main road, but neither is the other side particularly impressive. The odd reason for this is that Hovingham Hall was never built as a house at all, but comprises a huge, ornate riding school and stables with the living quarters tacked on as an afterthought. The man responsible, back in the 1750s, was Thomas Worsley, known as Thomas the Builder to differentiate him from the other five Thomases. The Worsley family, incidentally, are an amateur genealogist's nightmare, specialising as they do in duplicate names. Since 1563 there have been six Thomases, six Williams, six Roberts and we are now on a run of Marcuses in the present day.

Thomas the Builder is regarded as an eccentric today, but when he was alive he was considered completely disreputable by his fellow aristocrats, for two reasons. Firstly, he married a servant, his half-sister's governess,

THE BLACK POPLAR

I will be honest; I was not overawed when I first saw the Howardian Hills' only surviving black poplar tree. It is a handful of feeble re-growing shoots sprouting from an old dead stump of the original tree that blew over in 1996. But, such is its value as a sole survivor that cuttings were taken and pampered lovingly in local nurseries, and are now being replanted in hedgerows around the region. Black poplars need this helping hand because they have lost the ability to germinate from seed and are very fussy about the soil they grow in – it has to be silt over gravel. So if you are walking in the Yearsley, Brandsby or Hovingham areas and see a ditch-side sapling with a protective mesh guard, then the chances are it's one of the VIP baby poplars.

The parent tree is in a hedgerow just south of Stonegrave village on the Cawton road, with an AONB information board telling you all about it.

but more seriously, his riding school did not teach proper riding for hunting, but strange prancing about that Thomas had seen on his travels in Europe – dressage to you and me.

Two generations after Thomas, in the 1800s, one of the Williams changed the layout of the building to make it more habitable for humans, but its equine origins are still very obvious.

The next obsession to shape the house and grounds was cricket. Sir William number five was a cricketer of note, captaining the Yorkshire county team in 1928 and 1929. He had the field behind the house made into a cricket pitch and converted one of the rear stables into a pavilion. An indication of Sir William's priorities can be seen in his proclamation that, if a batsman broke a window in the house with a strike for six, then five pounds was payable, not by the player to cover the damage, but *to* him as a reward for such a good shot. This area in the hall's history is commemorated by one of the village pubs. In the Worsley Arms, facing the hall on the main street, the Cricketers' Bar has old photos of famous visiting teams, signed bats and other memorabilia.

"Hovingham Hall has a pleasant family-home feel to it, basically because it still is."

Like Newburgh Priory, Hovingham Hall has a pleasant family-home feel to it, basically because it still is. On my last visit, the guided tour had reached one of the staircases just on the hour, and we were listening to an antique grandfather clock playing an intricate baroque tune which echoed around the domed stairwell. As we stood there we were joined by the baronet Sir Marcus himself, just passing through. He offered a prize for anyone who could recognise the tune, and breezed off again.

All Saints' Church

'There is a church and a priest here' said the Domesday Book of Hovingham in 1080, and there still is, although the priest is now a vicar shared with the other three 'Street' parishes. Most of All Saints' Church is a Victorian rebuild, but a very sensitive one that has incorporated many of the original medieval features and, thankfully, left the fantastic Saxon tower completely untouched. With a bit of searching inside and out you should find other even older relics which show that the Saxon church was itself a replacement of a still more ancient church. Here is your tick list: an Anglican cross above the west doorway, a Danish wheel cross over the South Belfry opening, and a Viking carved cross on the altar.

The Worsley family obviously had a strong influence on All Saints' from the 1500s onwards, paying for the Victorian rebuild for instance, so it is no surprise to see memorials aplenty, of various baronets and ladies, and the family mausoleum in the churchyard.

¶¶ FOOD & DRINK

Malt Shovel High St ✆ 01653 628264 ⌂ www.themaltshovelhovingham.com. You are always guaranteed a friendly welcome and decent pint of Black Sheep here. Also very popular for food.

Spa Tea Room High St ✆ 01653 628898. A very welcoming and popular café with bakery attached. Everything is well done but the bread and pastries are particularly good, as you would expect.

Worsley Arms Hotel High St ✆ 01653 628234 ⌂ www.worsleyarms.co.uk. There is a restaurant but I much prefer the atmosphere in the Cricketers' Bar for eating and drinking. Food is very good, beer is well-kept local Hambleton Ales and the owners are justifiably proud of their well-stocked wine cellar.

10 SLINGSBY

This is the largest village in the Howardian Hills but also one of the least well known. Even temporary residents on its two caravan sites tend to use the place as a base from which to go and visit more entertaining places, but its castle and its maypole make it worth a look.

Slingsby has a tradition of impressive **maypoles** which probably goes back over a thousand years, but the first one to be documented was in 1799.

The tallest, at 91 feet high, was erected in 1895 but the villagers are just as proud of the current 41-footer, which stands on the village green right in front of the primary school entrance. If you want to see the pole in action, then go on May Day Bank Holiday Monday. You will see Slingsby completely out of character, in a frenzy of fertility-rite excitement, with the maypole the central attraction of a bustling village fete. With a summer fair in early July being the only other exception, Slingsby soon settles down after May Day to its normal, quiet existence with life just ticking along.

I find **Slingsby Castle** fascinating because it is a ruin; not just in the sense of having no roof and not being lived in, but in its state of utter dilapidation. There are no mown lawns or interpretive signs here, but a series of completely overgrown and dangerously teetering walls and tall towers. Underlying these is a series of interconnecting, vaulted, basement chambers and the whole lot is surrounded by an intact but dry moat. At twilight, with owls hooting and bats emerging from the cellars, it is like a scene from a Gothic novel – a hugely memorable place.

The castle is owned by the Castle Howard Estate, and unfortunately has no public access, but public footpaths pass close enough for you to get a distant glimpse.

CASTLE HOWARD & AROUND

11 CASTLE HOWARD

YO60 7DA ☎ 01653 648333 🖱 www.castlehoward.co.uk.

Castle Howard still does what it was always designed to do – dominate and impress. What is in effect one building is the focal point of the whole area, having for instance more attached shops than the nearby villages of Terrington, Welburn, Bulmer, Crambe, Whitwell and Coneysthorpe, put together. As for its origin, well I like to imagine the scene. It is 1699 and Charles Howard, the third Earl of Carlisle, is in London and sitting in the Trumpet Tavern with other members of the Kit Kat Club. Drinking brandy with him is a chancer, ex-soldier and playwright John Vanbrugh, and they are discussing the Earl's intention to build a house on his Yorkshire estate.

> Vanbrugh: So Charles, who is going to design this big house of yours?
> Charles: I don't know. None of the chaps I have so far have come up with anything I like.
> Vanbrugh: Really ... now that is interesting. Charles, I'll do it for you.
> Charles: Would you? Splendid! How many similar projects have you done before, John?
> Vanbrugh: Erm ... not many, but what say, how difficult can it be?
> Charles: John, exactly how many buildings have you ever designed?
> Vanbrugh: Well, none – but I am a quick learner ...

It reads like a *Blackadder* script, with Rowan Atkinson as Vanbrugh, Hugh Laurie as the Earl, and Mrs Miggins hovering nearby with pies, but astonishingly it is more or less true. Quite how Vanbrugh managed to convince Charles Howard he was the right man for the job is anyone's guess but he did, and over the next ten years their joint dream became a magnificent reality, probably with more than a little help from a lowly clerk of works who happened to be Nicholas Hawksmoor, one of Christopher Wren's apprentices.

Oddly, the iconic great dome, such a signature feature of Castle Howard today, was not part of the original design, but added almost as an afterthought well after the building work had begun, and was reconstructed after World War II. Vanbrugh died in 1726 and the third Earl followed in 1738, but their work was continued by two subsequent earls and various architects and landscape gardeners, during the rest of the 18th century. Castle Howard in its entirety, that is the mansion, park, lakes, temples, mausoleum, road and monuments, was complete by the start of the 19th century.

All that has happened since then has been tinkering really, and a massive repair project after a fire in the main building in 1940. World War II nearly saw the end of Castle Howard. First the disastrous fire reduced the mansion house itself to a burnt-out shell and the dome was destroyed, then the heirs to the title began to drop like flies in the war in Europe. Mark, the eldest son, died on the Normandy beaches and the next in line, Christopher, was killed flying with the Dambusters.

Things were looking so bad for the estate that the trustees began to sell off the mansion's contents, assuming that it would never be lived in again. Enter a hero; George, the third son, returned wounded from the war and turned everything around. He moved into the house and set about the mammoth task

"The house and gardens were opened to the public in 1952 and the estate has not looked back since."

of repairing the damage and restoring the building to its former glory, dome and all. The house and gardens were opened to the public in 1952 and the estate has not looked back since. The palatial grandeur of the house, inside and out, is instantly familiar to anyone who has seen the filmed version of Evelyn Waugh's novel *Brideshead Revisited*, either the wonderful 1981 TV 11-hour adaptation or the 2008 movie.

Today, Castle Howard is a multi-million-pound business run by a private company, of which two of George Howard's sons, Nicholas and Simon, are the directors – and business it very definitely is. At the stable courtyard, your first port of call if arriving by car or bus, you'll find a café and five castle shops selling books, gifts, local farm produce, plants and chocolate. Tours and talks, constantly changing exhibitions, events and outdoor concerts are on offer throughout the year; in fact no end of expensive things to do with lots of other people.

The **grounds** are big enough to escape the crowds and get lost in. Public rights of way thread through the wider estate, allowing you to get some choice glimpses for free of the house, the majestic 20-column mausoleum, and Palladian splendour of Temple of the Four Winds from a distance. The hamlet of **Coneysthorpe**, built for estate workers around an oblong green, makes a handy starting point for walks, with scope for getting close up to the house and lake to the south and a fine section of the Ebor Way to the north, which offers choice views of the Vale of Pickering.

"Public rights of way thread through the wider estate, allowing you to get some choice glimpses for free of the house."

There is **wildlife** here, especially around the lakes where there are breeding flocks of greylag and Canada geese all the year. The Great Lake is even more of a magnet for birdwatchers in winter when large numbers of migrant waterfowl arrive; pochards, wigeon, goosander and goldeneye brightening up the chilly season. For those interested in furry, as well as feathery, flyers, some of Castle Howard's ancient hollow oak trees are important roost sites for noctule bats.

Castle Howard has a high season (March–October and December) when the house is open, while in other months just the gardens are available. There is no getting around it, entrance fees are very high so consequently many people don't get past the free café and shop area, making do with distant views of the house. Fortunately those wanting more affordable parkland walking can find it in the nearby arboretum at half the price.

The Yorkshire Arboretum

Castle Howard YO60 7BY ℘ 01653 648598 ⊕ www.yorkshirearboretum.org; open Mar–Nov.
This delightful rural escape is always a lot less crowded than the big house next door, but it is rapidly being discovered by more and more people. Although it is sited on the Castle Howard estate and was set up by the Royal Botanic Gardens at Kew, the arboretum trust is independent of

both. It exists to manage the huge collection of trees planted here in 1975, and to entertain and educate visitors in all things woody. There is lots to do here, especially for families, with the most obvious being a walk to see the trees, either on the one mile short trail or on the long trail of 2½ miles into the wild corners for the more energetic. For keeping children entertained, the treasure hunt, leaf bingo and orienteering course work really well. I overheard one lad, running past me with a map, say to his mate in a broad Leeds accent, 'This is mint, innit? Much better than that castle place wi t'fountains over t'road.'

The trust have worked hard to make everyone welcome – those with an artistic bent can enjoy a community sculpture trail, visitors with limited mobility can hire a motorised buggy, and dogs and their walkers are actively encouraged.

¶¶ FOOD & DRINK

Arboretum Café Castle Howard ℅ 01653 648767. Very welcoming and cheaper than the nearby Castle Howard Stables Courtyard Café. More importantly it is much quieter, with seating inside and out and wide, green views over the arboretum park. Open daily Mar–Nov.

12 WELBURN

What a difference a pub and a shop make. Bulmer has neither and Welburn has both, and consequently the latter is very much the livelier and busier of these two neighbouring villages. There was a time though when the balance of power was reversed, when the church was the focus of village life and Bulmer's old St Martin's served both villages as a joint parish. Welburn got its own church in 1865 thanks to monies from the then Earl of Carlisle: its recent resurgence is almost solely due to its proximity to Castle Howard. Two routes to the 'big house' passed through Welburn, the present public road being originally for aristocracy only, as it took them from the private Castle Howard railway station at Crambeck. This now sadly defunct station was built for one visit of Queen Victoria to the castle in 1850. The proletariat's route by road from the main York road, now the A64, to Welburn was from near Whitwell village (❀ grid reference SE725665) along what is now a green lane and a very pleasant cycle or walkway. As it broaches the ridge-top above Welburn you get your first view of Castle Howard. Such was the impact of this first sight that a gateway was built for extra emphasis and the posts of the 'Exclamation Gate' are still there for you to lean on and frame your photos of the castle.

Welburn is the base for another series of excellent AONB 'History and Habitats' walks (see page 115), although their selection of three by no means exhausts the wide choice of others nearby. A particularly nice two-miler circles the village keeping your walk's-end refreshment venue in sight most of the way round, whether at Pattacakes café or in the Crown and Cushion pub.

¶¶ FOOD & DRINK

Crown and Cushion Main St ☎ 01653 618777 ⌂ www.thecrownandcushionwelburn. com. Recently reopened as the latest addition to the fine North Yorkshire Provenance Inn stable and back to its excellent best for food and drink. Dog-friendly.

Pattacakes Main St ☎ 01653 618352 ⌂ www.pattacakes.biz. Good value tea shop, bakery and deli. Also runs popular full-day bread making courses.

13 TERRINGTON & AROUND

On the face of it Terrington seems much like other nearby villages of a similar size, with neat limestone houses set back on the wide main street, a relatively modern looking church on an old site, a big Victorian rectory building and one central pub.

What is different here is the modern bustle about a place that has had a very slow and uneventful past. As one local historian put it, 'History has its place in Terrington, but nothing big ever happened here.' It has never had a castle or an abbey and the Victorian railways were always too far away to have any influence. Other villages have had, and lost, these exciting things and feel as if they are having a well-earned rest; Terrington gives the impression of waking up after a big sleep. Much of this new life is centred on the shop, **Terrington Village General Stores**, the only proper shop for five miles in any direction and consequently one of those admirable sell-a-bit–of–everything sort of places. It also has a café attached and a little art gallery around the back with the no-nonsense name Back o' the Shop Art Gallery.

The road west out of Terrington runs along one of the Howardian Hills ridges, giving spectacular views to Sheriff Hutton and the Vale of York beyond. The best place to enjoy this vista is just on the edge of the village at the **Yorkshire Lavender Farm**, or you can carry on for a

THE CITY OF TROY

Eight ancient turf mazes survive in England, and this one, the smallest in the whole of Europe, sits by the roadside near the hamlet of Dalby. It is a seven-ringed puzzle based on the classical labyrinth of Crete, and named after the walls of the Trojan city. Why it is here, when it was made and by whom, is a mystery.

couple of miles to the hamlet of **Dalby** and the church of St Peter. This has to be one of the most serene little buildings anywhere; plain, unassuming and so quiet you will feel obliged to whisper. The view from the porch, through the trees and down the hillside, could grace any calendar.

If you travel east on Terrington's only road you will first pass the enormous rectory that later became Terrington Hall, and since 1920 has been a private preparatory school. A mile down the road is the hamlet of Ganthorpe, birthplace of Richard Spruce, an apt name for an eminent Victorian botanist, who is buried in All Saints' churchyard.

My preferred choice for exploring around Terrington, though, is on foot rather than by car, and North Yorkshire County Council have obliged by producing two **walks** leaflets (see page 115).

Yorkshire Lavender Farm

Terrington YO60 7PB ℡ 01653 648008 🖰 www.yorkshirelavender.com; open daily; free entrance.

What started off as a plant nursery specialising in herbs has evolved over the years into an award-winning celebration of all things lavender. Everything in the café and shop is either coloured or flavoured lavender, including the walls, the chairs, the cake, the tea and even the custard! I found it all a bit death-by-mauve but loved the outside, wandering around the gardens, watching the children feed the deer and admiring the 'Spirit of Yorkshire' cricket game sculptures – all with the heady scent of fresh lavender in the warm summer air.

🍴 FOOD & DRINK

EJ's Tea Room Yorkshire Lavender Farm, YO60 6PB ℡ 01653 648008 🖰 www. yorkshirelavender.com. You could just have a coffee and a biscuit, but where else is it possible to have lavender cake, lavender and blueberry cheesecake, and a lavender scone washed down with lavender tea? It wouldn't be quite right not to try at least one.

MALTON & THE DERWENT VALLEY

When asked where I live, my reply of, 'Near Malton', usually prompts the response, 'Isn't that the place that flooded? Where exactly is it?' Malton is not a well-known place outside of northeast Yorkshire, even though tens of thousands of holiday visitors pass close by every weekend on the A64 or railway on their way to Whitby, Scarborough and Filey. This is not a place geared to mass tourism and that, I think, is where its attraction lies. **Malton** is very much a small work-a-day, rural market town serving the people of Ryedale and the Wolds.

14 MALTON

Getting to know Malton takes time because of its very strange and confusing layout; it took me months to get my bearings when I first moved here.

What most people describe as Malton town is actually three separate places welded together, Old Malton, Malton and Norton. Even Malton proper is confusing as it has no one obvious centre but a scattering of focal points that reflect areas of shifting importance through history. The Derwent bridge and adjacent fort was the Roman town centre, but emphasis shifted in medieval times to Castlegate where the Lodge Hotel now stands on the old motte and the roads from York, Beverley and Helmsley all meet at the old crossroads. The marketplace was the hub in days past, and still is on Saturdays, but the cattle market is now a shadow of its glory days. Like most towns of its size Malton has its fair share of necessary but not very welcome 'new', like 1950s housing estates, high-street chain shops and the Ryedale Borough Council offices, but it is slow and sleepy enough to have retained some genuinely old-fashioned traditional shops and businesses.

Town trails

Four town trails are detailed in an excellent leaflet produced by the tourist information centre, three on the Malton side of the river and a fourth around Norton. To be honest, I got the impression that the Norton Trail was a token one included so as not to offend the good people south of the river, as most of the interest is on the north bank. The shortest trail, barely half a mile long, stays within the town centre and can be done easily in an hour. It visits both of Malton's old parish **churches** and five historic **pubs**, including one with a medieval hospice crypt (the Cross Keys) and one with an excellent micro-brewery (the Crown hotel or 'Suddabys'). It will also lead you up two alleyways; Chancery Lane, downhill from the marketplace, has Charles Dickens connections. Also here is the fabulous small, traditional, **Palace Cinema**, a very informal, family-run establishment where you can relax with a glass of wine or cup of tea while watching your film – very civilised.

Uphill from the market is **The Shambles**, like its more famous namesake in York, an historic site of butchers' shops. There are none there today, but just around the corner is the acclaimed Derek Fox's, a traditional butchers, and supplier of the extraordinary Yorkshire Pot. This is a local delicacy produced at Christmas and by order only, comprising four boned birds, one inside the other in order of size, and ready for roasting. One Christmas I shelled out £60 for a partridge in a pheasant in a duck in a turkey; it was delicious and lasted for weeks.

The intermediate town trail extends the short one by a further hour and will take you along a short section of the **River Derwent** and over both the town's bridges. It also allows you to explore the sites of Malton's old **fortifications**, first the Roman legionary camp of Derventio followed by Malton Castle. Don't get too excited – there are no buildings left to see at either place, just mounds, banks and ditches. Having said that, Orchard Fields, where the Roman fort was, and Castle Gardens are very pleasant and peaceful green areas and the nearest

"Chancery Lane, downhill from the marketplace, has Charles Dickens connections."

Malton has to a park. Information boards are on hand explaining the strategic importance and huge size (22 acres) of the Roman fort, and the turbulent history of the castle.

The long town trail is a further loop tacked on to the previous two taking you through the lovely riverside trees of **Lady Spring Wood** to Old Malton. Boardwalks keep your feet dry as you visit the limestone springs and marshes, and a mosaic trail marks the route. Take care in wet weather; the water meadows here become lakes when the river gets very full and even the boardwalks won't stop your feet getting wet.

Old Malton

A confusing name this, because it is in fact younger than 'new' Malton's Roman settlement, but presumably this was the bigger of the two places

TWO ARTISTS IN WOOD

One small outlet on The Shambles in Malton is, quite literally, the shop window for the art of **Mark Bennett**, working under the name of Woodlark (✆ 01653 691124 www.thewoodlark.com). Mark is a genius at producing, he would say 'finding', the beauty in wood. In his nearby workshop he works in many different timbers, sometimes in-laying metals and gemstones, and combining several different types of wood. No matter what the finished product, whether it be a functional ash and yew jewellery box with gold inlay, a bog-oak toilet seat or just a hand-carved ornamental spiral, they are all beautiful.

In complete contrast, **Nick Nixon** (✆ 01653 695525 www.nixoncricket.co.uk), in his workshop 50 yards away from Mark's shop, works with two sorts of wood only, willow and cane, and makes just one finished product – cricket bats. These aren't just any bats though, they are handcrafted, bespoke items, shaped by an ex-player who loves the game and knows his stuff. Nick makes over 600 bats a year, and though they are only used for whacking a lump of leather around, each one is a work of art. As Nick says, 'There are only two ways of making a bat worthy of the great game, the wrong way and the right way'.

in Saxon times when the new non-Latin names were given. It was certainly a very important place in the 1150s when the large **priory of St Mary** was built here on the site of an earlier church. What was unusual was the monks that occupied it; they were Gilbertines, an exclusively English order that had 26 priories or churches across the country. All are now complete ruins except St Mary's; it is considerably reduced in size from its original but it is the only Gilbertine church in the world still in use, and incidentally the only church that I know of with a medieval barn-owl nest box built into the tower wall (see box, page 161). Such was its importance in its heyday that it spawned two chapels of ease in 'new' Malton, that later became the joint parish churches of St Michael's and St Leonard's. In 1971 the Church of England had a rush of ecumenicalism and donated, or should that be returned, St Leonard's to the Roman Catholic Church.

The remainder of Old Malton village consists of the main road into Malton (from the A64) with two pubs positioned almost next door to each other, and some rather attractive, old stone buildings, two of which are thatched.

Just outside the village though, and on the other side of the A64 dual carriageway, squats a very singular museum. I say 'squats' because the buildings of **Eden Camp** (✆ 01653 697777 ◌̂ www.edencamp.co.uk) are all low, single-storey Nissen huts, which would be very inconspicuous were it not for the banking spitfire suspended above the entrance. This excellent World War II museum is housed in an old prisoner-of-war camp from that very conflict. It is open daily.

▯▮ FOOD & DRINK

Malton has a regular **Saturday market**, and a big **farmers' market** (✆ 01653 692151) on the last Saturday of every month except August and December. The Malton Food Festival takes place in May.

Grapes Inn Great Habton YO17 6TU ✆ 01653 669166 ◌̂ www.thegrapes-inn.co.uk. Northwest of Malton, this is not the most inviting of buildings or villages, but there's always a warm welcome and excellent food. Very good value as well, lots of thoughtful extras for the price. Closed all day Mon and weekday lunchtimes.

Leoni the Coffee House Wheelgate ✆ 01653 691321. A fabulous place. Voted best coffee shop in Britain back in 2006 and still run by award-winning barista Simon Robertson. 'I want good coffee to be seen in the same light as good food,' said Simon. 'Just like food, the difference between good coffee and bad coffee is passion. Like a chef I am passionate about creating something beautiful.' Leoni also does food with an Italian slant, snacks and lunches made from listed local sources.

Malton Relish Market Pl ✆ 0845 116 1378 ◌̂ www.maltonrelish.co.uk. This delicatessen sells specialist foods from Yorkshire and beyond. Sit at one of the small tables in the corner with whatever takes your fancy from the shop and wash it down with a brew from behind the counter.

The New Malton Market Pl ✆ 01653 693998 ◌̂ www.thenewmalton.co.uk. Possibly the most popular eating place in town. Sophisticated, but not fussy, food at very reasonable prices. Dog- and beer drinker-friendly.

Thai House at the Cross Keys Wheelgate ✆ 01653 696117 ◌̂ www.crosskeysthai. co.uk. Stuart, the landlord, moved his successful Thai food operation from the Bay Horse in Terrington over to here in 2008, and has been turning away customers ever since on the frequent occasions when it fills to capacity. The all-you-can-eat buffet on a Mon evening is particularly good value, but book early. This is still also a proper pub with a traditional food menu and real ale. Closed Tue.

Pubs

Malton's pub story is a sad but familiar one. Ten or 15 years ago the town was regarded as a haven for the traditional inn lover, with a string of town pubs to rival York. Most of these have now gone night-clubby downhill or out of business, save for a few oases in the desert, notably:

Royal Oak Town St, Old Malton ✆ 01653 699334 🖰 www.royaloakmalton.co.uk. This is a very welcoming village pub with a comfortable ambience, especially in the front snug or back beer garden. A well-kept range of Yorkshire beers are served and food is also sourced locally. Meals are served Wed–Sun. Closed Mon–Tue.

Spotted Cow Cattle Market ✆ 01653 692100. As befits a pub in the middle of the cattle market, this has a country farmers' inn feel to it. Excellent beer, and bustling on market days. Limited food.

Suddaby's Crown Hotel Wheelgate, Malton ✆ 01653 692038 🖰 www.suddabys.co.uk. A Grade 2 listed coaching inn which has been run by the Suddaby family for 138 years. The brewery was, until recently, in the old stables behind the pub but has now outgrown the building. One of the house beers, Double Chance, takes its name from a Grand National winner once stabled here. Don't come for décor and comfort; Suddaby's is a basic boozer, but the beer quality is second to none, whether it is brewed on the premises or not. It hosts three beer festivals a year (Easter, summer and winter), and an attached shop stocks over 200 bottled beers and some wine. No food.

THE DERWENT VALLEY: 15 KIRKHAM & 16 HOWSHAM

🏠 **Yew Tree Cottage** (see page 202).

🏕 **Jollydays Luxury Camping** Scrayingham (see page 202).

Not long after leaving Malton, the River Derwent enters Kirkham Gorge and reverts to its wild state after the last 20 or so miles of agricultural straightening and urban encroachment. This is the start of the river as a linear nature reserve of national importance, because the wildlife here is so rich. The Derwent was one of the few rivers where otters never died out in the 1970s and they are now thriving, sustained by more than 20 species of fish that swim in these clean waters – including salmon, which are making a comeback (see box, page 188). Although this is an historical navigation route all the way up to Malton from the sea, no boats use the river now as it has been designated a Site of Special Scientific Interest and the right of navigation removed.

"The Derwent was one of the few rivers where otters never died out in the 1970s and they are now thriving."

The only way to see the delights of this waterway is on foot or by train; the Malton–York line accompanies the river through the gorge. **Walking**, it's almost possible to hug the riverbank all the way from Malton to Howsham by following the Centenary Way for five miles to Kirkham on the left bank, then swapping to the right bank for the remaining three miles. No buses run to either of these places and sadly, the train no longer stops anywhere between Malton and York, so a point-to-point walk is awkward.

Kirkham is best known for its Augustinian Priory (✆ 01653 618768; English Heritage), its riverside situation as glorious the building itself. It is open in summer except Tuesday and Wednesday, but open every day in August.

The OS map does not indicate much of interest in **Howsham** but that is misleading. The small village is quiet and pretty and the Old Hall was a private school until recently, but the real interest is down by the river. Canoeists and kayakers have long known about the weir here as a play spot, but since 2004 it has been the mill it serves next door that has hit the headlines (see below). Once the river water has done its job at Howsham Mill it slides downstream towards the fantastic floodplains of the Lower Derwent, but out of our area.

Howsham Mill

✆ 01653 619712 ⌂ www.howshammill.org.uk; open most weekends in summer.

Howsham Mill was built in 1755 in the Gothic revival style and was operational until 1947 when it was abandoned. In 2004 it was taken over by the Renewable Heritage Trust. 'This is a wonderful Grade 2 listed building that desperately needed rescuing back then,' explained Dave Lister, one of the volunteer restorers. 'Our plan was not just to restore it but to put it back to work harnessing energy from the river. This time it would generate "green" electricity via the waterwheel, plus two modern Archimedean screw turbines, enough for the whole thing to be completely self-sustaining. The building could then be given over to use by the community – a residential environmental centre. We got enough support for the idea to actually win the Northern England round of the BBC's *Restoration Village* programme in 2006 – that was a massive boost. Since then it's just been a lot of hard graft by a few dedicated volunteers. We've had ups and downs (mostly vandalism) but we're getting there. The Archimedes screw is in and working, funding everything now – the electricity it generates we sell to the National Grid, £15,000 a year would you believe? Things are looking good.'

To visit the mill, cross to the east side of the Derwent bridge at Howsham, follow the path under the bridge and then upstream along the boardwalk. After a few hundred yards of pleasant riverside walking, you will cross a small footbridge to the mill on its own little island.

Ryedale Vineyards

Farfield Farm, Westow YO60 7LS ☎ 01653 658507 ⑦ www.ryedalevineyards.co.uk.

England is now firmly on the map when it comes to producing wines of internationally recognised quality but most of the commercially viable vineyards tend to hug the southernmost regions of the country. Ryedale Vineyards have crossed that north–south divide by becoming the most northerly commercial vineyards in Britain.

Close to the village of Westow, the vineyards are owned and run by Stuart and Elizabeth Smith, an established name in the commercial world of grape growing, as the Smiths have been running a vine-supply business for over 20 years.

The vineyards began in 2006 when seven acres of a gently sloping hillside were planted to vines. Said Elizabeth, 'Before we bought the land, we made regular trips over the course of 12 months to see the plot in all different weathers – to see if it sat in a frost pocket in early morning for example, which could be extremely damaging to the vines. But the vineyard is on a south-facing slope, the ideal orientation.' With such a lovely rural spot, the Smiths are keen to enhance the wildlife and are working with the RSPB to ensure that bird species such as tree sparrows and barn owls are protected by their activities.

"Ryedale Vineyards have crossed that north–south divide by becoming the most northerly commercial vineyards in Britain."

A selection of modern, disease-resistant red and white grape varieties are grown at the vineyard in addition to some small test plantings of the more familiar French Pinot Noir and Chardonnay grapes, in the hope of producing some delicious sparkling wine in the future. 'Because we are so far north, our vines have been selected specially to ripen early, before the harsh frosts arrive, although we try to put off harvesting for as long as possible to raise the sugar levels in the grapes, which makes a better-quality wine. The Pinot Noir and Chardonnay grapes tend to ripen later in the season so they are being trialled to see what happens.'

Their first commercial vintage was produced in 2008, most of which sold out instantly. 'We were really thrilled to win several awards with our first vintage,' said Elizabeth. 'Our rosé, "Yorkshire Sunset" won a

UPDATES WEBSITE

You can post your comments and recommendations, and read the latest feedback and updates from other readers online at ⌐ www.bradtupdates.com/northyorkmoors.

national award and our aromatic white, "Wolds View", won a trophy as the best dry white wine in a regional competition.'

The public are invited to help out with the harvest – a very sociable occasion with a privileged opportunity to witness a lesser-known aspect of North Yorkshire. For those who prefer to sit back and hold a glass of wine, there are vineyard tours. Wine tastings are also available to guests staying in the adjacent farmhouse B&B that Elizabeth runs. Wine can be bought from the vineyard by prior arrangement.

There is also the opportunity to rent a vine, which includes a name plaque on a row of vines, a bottle of wine from the following harvest and an invitation to a special preview tasting when the wines are released.

THE YORKSHIRE WOLDS

CHAPTER 3
page 76

SCARBOROUGH

Filey

A170

CHAPTER 4
page 110

MALTON

A64

11
GREAT WOLD VALLEY

12
FLAMBOROUGH
HEAD

A165

9
Wharram Percy

10
Sledmere

BRIDLINGTON

A64

8
THIXENDALE

A166

A614

A165

7
GARROWBY HILL

5
Pocklington

6
Millington

Kilnwick Percy

A164

POCKLINGTON
WATER

A1079

4
Goodmanham

A1035

3
Market
Weighton

A1079

2
Beverley

A165

A614

A1033

KINGSTON
UPON HULL

M62

A63

RIVER HUMBER

Barton-
upon-Humber

1
Humber
Bridge

A15

0   4 miles
0   5km   N

5
THE YORKSHIRE WOLDS

'Wold' is an Anglo-Saxon word meaning wooded hill, which is odd because this is an area noticeably lacking in woods, especially on higher ground. The Yorkshire Downs would be a better name perhaps, as these rolling uplands bear a distinct similarity to the hills of Sussex, Hampshire and Berkshire.

Bedrock is the key. The Yorkshire Wolds are rooted on an extension of the same chalk that is found under the North and South Downs, the most northerly chalk in Britain, in fact. An arc of these chalk hills extends from the Humber estuary in the south to a precipitous terminus in the northeast where **Flamborough Head** meets the North Sea. To the east lies the plain of Holderness and to the west the Vale of York, with the River Derwent a handy boundary on that side.

These are not the hills that a hardened Dales fell walker would recognise. The summits, in fact, are where the least interest lies. The rich, limey soil here has been ploughed and planted for millennia, resulting in the tame, rolling landscape familiar from David Hockney's paintings. There is a wildness here, but it hides away in the deep flood-cut valleys – land too steep to cultivate and left to harbour native woodland or rough grazing for sheep.

SELF-POWERED TRAVEL
CYCLING

Big skies and quiet roads. These two attributes of a good Hockney painting are also what makes the Wolds such a desirable venue for **road biking**. Perhaps it's no coincidence that the young painter himself spent two childhood summers cycling up and down the deserted lanes around the village of Huggate. The serious cycling fraternity has long known of the potential here, and recently their secrets have been shared with the rest of us. Big Skies Cycling (⌖ www.cycleyorkshirewolds.com) is a great website promoting two-wheeled travel, with the 146-mile circular Yorkshire Wolds Cycle Route their jewel in the crown. The southern section of this route, from Pocklington to Bridlington, also corresponds with the final leg of an increasingly popular coast-to-coast route, the Way of the Roses ride.

For us lesser mortals who prefer to be in the saddle for a few hours or a day at the most, the Wolds bike people have also produced ten short (20 miles or so) circular routes starting from Bridlington, Hunmanby, Malton, Sledmere, Pocklington, Market Weighton, Beverley, Driffield, Stamford Bridge and Hessle. Excellent little route maps are downloadable from ⌖ www.visithullandeastyorkshire.com.

Off-road biking here is a lot less rewarding, but not impossible. Arable farming country is often poor in bridleways, so you will have to search hard for a completely off-road circular route – there's usually some tarmac to put up with to get back to your start point. Having said that, areas with the greatest scope for mountain bikers are between the top end of Millington Dale and Huggate, and the network of green lanes encircling Wetwang and Garton on the Wolds.

HORSERIDING

With such an equestrian tradition hereabouts, you would expect there to be lots of hacking and trekking opportunities in the Wolds – not so unfortunately. You may well see thoroughbreds on the gallops near Malton and Norton or even witness the famous race at Kiplingcotes (see page 154), but centres or stables where you can ride yourself are few and far between and all on the periphery of our area.

_i_ TOURIST INFORMATION

Beverley 34 Butcher Row ✆ 01482 391672
Bridlington 25 Prince St ✆ 01482 391634
Humber Bridge Country Park, Hessle ✆ 01482 640852
Malton The Library, St Michael's St ✆ 01653 600048

RIDING CENTRES

Fairfield Stables Bishop Wilton YO42 1SF ✆ 07557 503626 ⌂ www.fairfieldstables.co.uk. Not just pony trekking and hacking but all sorts of other horsey fun, like horse and carriage rides to the pub and kids' pony parties.

Woldgate Trekking Centre Bridlington YO16 4XE ✆ 01262 673086 ⌂ www. woldgatetrekking.co.uk. Pony trekking for beginners through to experienced riders on a variety of rural routes.

WALKING

Wolds walking is very different to hiking in the Dales or in the Lake District. It's usually gentle, tending towards the potter or the ramble, rather than a scramble or clamber. What the area may lack in excitement it more than makes up for in its peace and quiet quotient. It's very easy to have a day's walk in the Wolds and not see another soul, especially if you wander off the paths in open access areas – 'wild' patches of land, not on the hill-tops as you might expect, but in the deep, dry valleys in between. What isn't so easy is finding enough public rights of way to link into convenient circular walks. For much of the area, the best option is to follow sections of the 79-mile **Wolds Way**, a National Trail from the Humber Bridge at Hessle to Filey Brigg. Another well-used unofficial long-distance trail links the two ministers of Beverley and York and is called, not surprisingly, the **Minster Way**.

In places, open access land can link footpaths and bridleways to create a rewarding **loop-walk**. Three good examples (all on OS Explorer map 294) are:

- From Huggate (✿ grid reference SE882554). A three-mile walk using Horse Dale to the north.
- From Fridaythorpe (✿ grid reference SE874592). A two-mile walk using West Dale to the west.
- From Warter (✿ grid reference SE868504). A two-mile circuit of Great Dug Dale.

THE SOUTHERN FOOTHILLS

On its completion in 1981, the Humber Bridge became the longest single-span suspension bridge in the world, linking Lincolnshire's Barton-upon-Humber to Hessle in Yorkshire. I have it on the good authority of an engineer friend of mine that this is the only place that the bridge could possibly have been built as the north tower needed the solid rock here as foundation; anywhere else it would have sunk into mud and clay. This rock happens to be our first chunk of Yorkshire Wolds chalk.

As the Humber Bridge road heads north towards **Beverley**, the Yorkshire Wolds Way footpath veers to the west following the chalk. On its journey inland it gains altitude and interest, especially near the **villages** of Brantingham, South Cave and the Newbald twins (North and South). By the time it reaches **Market Weighton** we are in the Wolds proper, and the deep valleys are turning wilder – at their most beautiful near Millington, east of Pocklington town.

1 HUMBER BRIDGE

From Hessle you get a terrific view of this vast structure, with its main span of 7,283 feet (nearly 1.4 miles) and holding the title of the world's longest single-span suspension bridge until 1998. Its opening in 1981 was the culmination of more than a century's campaigning by Hull businesses after a road tunnel in 1872 came to nothing. It replaced a 20-minute ferry crossing and was the very first suspension bridge to have concrete towers, standing to a height of 510 feet. It went massively over budget, partly because of interest rates and spiraling inflation, and the construction loans are not expected to be paid off till around 2032.

National Cycle Route 1 crosses the bridge on its journey from Hull to Fakenham (Norfolk), giving cyclists and walkers the chance to appreciate the views as they cross via the cycle path, happily separated from traffic.

2 BEVERLEY

The chapter has barely started, and already I've wandered out of the Wolds. It's forgivable I think, because Beverley is such a delightful place, bursting with history, tradition and culture, and as 'Slow' a town as you'll find anywhere in Yorkshire.

Beverley's coat of arms gives a clue that this is a lowland town – a beaver over three wavy blue lines representing water. The nearby River Hull once formed a vast area of lake and marsh, thriving with beavers, hence the town's name since medieval times.

What turned Beverley from being a bustling market town into a nationally important settlement (the town was the tenth largest in England, at one stage) was the foundation of the monastery of Inderawuda, later to become **Beverley Minster**, one of the largest parish churches in the country. The less visited **St Mary's Church**, on the north side of the town centre, has a feast of medieval carving on its bosses and misericords, and a gregarious painted panelled ceiling with depictions of English kings.

With its medieval fortified bar, snickelways, and ancient pubs, the town is very much like a mini-York. It even has a quaint racecourse, about half the size of the one by the River Ouse at Knavesmire.

Much of the appeal of Beverley is derived from wandering around at will and enjoying its numerous, mostly Georgian, terraces. **The North Bar**, the sole survivor of five gateways in the long-vanished town wall, is a handsome specimen of medieval brickwork, beyond which 18th-century shop frontages line Saturday Market, as the marketplace is known, with its elaborate market cross. In Register Square, the imposing classical Grade 1 listed **Guildhall** (free entrance) is worth a look for its magnificent courtroom with intricate stucco work by Giuseppe Cortese.

Beverley Westwood certainly contributed to the town being voted the 'Best place to live in England' a few years ago. Sounding more like a Hollywood film star, this is actually a lovely area of parkland complete with meadows and a windmill, and easily walkable from the town centre.

Beverley also has a lively cultural scene, with annual festivals for food, real ale, early and folk music, and literature. The poet Philip Larkin features prominently in the last of these. His home city of Hull is only eight miles down the road, and he regularly called in on Beverley.

Beverley Minster

Minster Yard North ✒ www.beverleyminster.org.uk; entry to the minster, Quiet Garden and churchyard is free; small fee for church and/or roof tours and photography permit.

Although officially only the parish church of St John and St Martin, Beverley Minster is larger than many cathedrals and a masterpiece of Gothic architecture, renowned above all for the quality of its medieval stonework. The present building is uncannily like a smaller scale version of York Minster.

The building owes its existence to an East Yorkshire cleric named John, who is still here incidentally, buried under the nave. He was a contemporary of Abbess Hilda of Whitby, and rose through church ranks to become Bishop of York in AD706. When he died in 721 his remains were buried in the monastery that he had founded in Beverley, then known as Inderawuda. Supposed miracles associated with his remains caused a cult to develop and Bishop John was canonised in 1037. The present church was built over his tomb, starting in 1220 but with the construction work spanning 200 years. Much of Beverley's subsequent prosperity has been a consequence of St John's fame and popular pilgrimages to venerate his bones.

"Beverley Minster is a masterpiece of Gothic architecture, renowned above all for the quality of its medieval stonework."

Besides the magnificent aura of the space inside the Minster, other things to see are the 68 ornate misericord seats dating from the 16th century, the extraordinarily delicately carved Percy tomb canopy and the Saxon Sanctuary Chair or frith stool (one of only three in England), which entitled anyone who sat on it to sanctuary from the law for 30 days.

¶¶ FOOD & DRINK

The Pipe and Glass Inn West End, South Dalton HU17 7PN ☎ 01430 810246 ⌂ www. pipeandglass.co.uk. Not actually in Beverley but a village six miles to the northwest. What tempts most travellers out to this isolated 15th-century inn is its Michelin star (enough said). Also offers accommodation.

The White Horse Inn Hengate ☎ 01482 861973 ⌂ www.nellies.co.uk. Known to its many fans as 'Nellies', after a long-serving previous landlady, this pub serves very cheap and drinkable Sam Smiths beers and basic pub food. What makes it an exceptional place is the quite astonishing building itself. Sitting in one of the pokey gas-lit rooms or navigating the warren of rickety wooden corridors and staircases is like stepping back in time. This is no mock-up though, the interior of the White Horse has remained virtually unchanged for nearly a century.

3 MARKET WEIGHTON

In 1251, Henry III granted Wicstun a Royal Charter, allowing it to have a market. The locals were presumably so proud of the accolade that they added 'Market' to their town's name and one has operated here ever since. Friday is the current market day, with a local producers' market on the third Saturday of each month.

Most of the town centre is made up of humble brick buildings dating from Georgian times with the Norman All Saints Church a notable exception. All-in-all, nice but nothing special. If that was it I suspect that few folk would have heard of the town, but one man put paid to that. He was born in 1787 and became known as the Market Weighton Giant. By the age of 20 **William Bradley** stood at 7 feet 8 inches tall and weighed 27 stone. A bit of a celebrity in his own lifetime, William made a living touring the country as part of a travelling show. Before he died, aged 30 from tuberculosis exacerbated by his medical condition, he met George III, who presented him with a gold chain. A **Giant Bradley Heritage Trail** around the town starts at William's specially adapted house on York Street (big doorways!) and includes his grave in the church. This was originally in the graveyard, but was moved into the church after worries that his skeleton may be stolen. One of his boots is in the York Castle Museum.

During the rail heyday, Market Weighton sat at the junction of two routes, the York–Beverley line and the Selby–Driffield line. Sadly, both are now gone and Market Weighton is rail-less, but one of the old track beds (eastwards towards Beverley) doubles as a public footpath and permissive bridleway. The full ten-mile trip to Beverley completes the Hudson Way, named after the Victorian railway entrepreneur who built the original line. This fine day's excursion takes you past the historic village of Goodmanham and two excellent little nature reserves owned by the Yorkshire Wildlife Trust. Rifle Butts Quarry is famed for its geological features and Kiplingcotes Chalk Pit boasts many rare meadow flowers and ants. Whichever direction you choose to do the walk, the hourly X46 bus can take you back to your starting point. Cycling the Hudson Way doesn't give you the bus-back option but there is an excellent quiet minor road return route.

¶¶ FOOD & DRINK

Sadly, Market Weighton is not a gourmet's paradise so it is probably worth travelling out of town to eat and drink, to Sancton or Goodmanham.

The Star Sancton YO43 4QP ℰ 01430 827269 ⌂ www.thestaratsancton.co.uk. A fine village pub, two miles from Market Weighton on the main road to Hull. Yorkshire beer from Great Newsome or Copper Dragon breweries and food even more local – much of the fruit and veg is grown in the pub's own garden and village allotments. The meals aren't cheap but are top quality.

ENGLAND'S OLDEST HORSE RACE

The 21 March 2013, as befits the first official day of spring, was sunny, with an icy chill in the air. More importantly, that year it happened to be the third Thursday in March, which in this neck of the woods can only mean one thing – the Kiplingcotes Derby.

This race has been run over the same course on the same day for 494 consecutive years, making it the oldest flat race in the country. The starting post is an old stone marker near Kiplingcotes railway station, with the wooden finishing post at Londesborough Wold Farm. The intervening course is a relatively straight four miles of minor road verge and farm track.

So far so odd, and there are further quirks. The prize money for the winner is £50, but the second placed horse wins the sum total of all the £4.25 race entrance fees, which can in theory be more than the winner's prize money. This all depends on how many entrants there are and no-one knows for sure what this figure will be until the start of the race, as any horse and rider turning up before 11.00 can enter.

For the record, in 2013 the race was won by Woteva, ridden by Carolyn Bales, with the wonderfully named Eeyore in second place. As there were 13 riders that year, Eeyore's mount, Geoff Bridges, did indeed take home more prize money that the winner!

4 GOODMANHAM

Market Weighton is an old town, but the nearby village of Goodmanham is not just very old, it's ancient. It was probably the natural springs emanating from the chalk here that drew the first Stone Age or Bronze Age settlers, who left behind their burial mounds on Howes Hill. To the Celts that followed this became a religious site, with two holy springs, now known as Lady's Well and St Helen's Well, and a temple on the hill where **All Hallows Church** now stands. The name of the village originates from *godo* (temple) and *mynnydd* (hill).

The historian Bede recounts that this pagan shrine, later dedicated by the Anglo-Saxons to their god Woden, became a church in AD627 during the reign of King Edwin of Northumbria, the high priest Coifi starting the demolition personally using an axe. A wooden bench near St Helen's well carries an inscribed verse inspired by this conversion, starting with the evocative line: 'From dark to dark through fire-lit hall flies the axe that strikes the shrine.'

That first Saxon church was wooden but the Normans, as was often their want, rebuilt it in stone, and most of their work survives as the present Grade 1 listed building.

¶¶ FOOD & DRINK

Goodmanham Arms Main St ✆ 01430 873849 ⊕ www.goodmanhamarms.co.uk. From the outside of what looks like a small, boring brick house, you would never guess how good this place is. Going inside is a trip back in time – tile floors, wood fire, home-cooked food and very reasonably priced beer from their own brewery. The landlord's passion for vintage motorbikes is obvious and there are plans for a museum behind the pub. Not surprisingly this is a regular winner of the CAMRA Best Village Pub of East Yorkshire.

5 POCKLINGTON & AROUND

🚉 **Skipwith Station** North Duffield and **The Wolds Retreat** Kilnwick Percy (see page 203). Pocklington may be one of the largest of the Wold-foot towns but in terms of regional importance it is a shadow of its former self. When the Romans arrived here 2,000 years ago they found the capital of the kingdom of the Parsii tribe, and by Norman times it was still the second largest town in Yorkshire after York. Now it's just a pleasant market town that benefits from not being particularly on the way from anywhere to anywhere else. Pocklington Beck flows right through the middle of town, but you wouldn't know it as for most of its route as it's hidden in culverts beneath the buildings. It reappears to the south and becomes a feeder for the **Pocklington Canal**, once an industrial boon to the town – now a great place to walk and cycle, and a linear nature reserve.

Burnby Hall Gardens

Pocklington YO42 2QF ✆ 01759 307125 ⊕ www.burnbyhallgardens.com; open daily.
What Pocklington does possess that is definitely out of the ordinary is Burnby Hall Gardens, a floral gem on the edge of the town centre. Major Percy Stewart was an extraordinary man, although he didn't think so himself. 'We are terribly dull people', he said to his wife. 'Let us travel around the world so we shall have something to talk about.' They did, and he became one of those Victorian polymaths – traveller, adventurer, collector, scholar and philanthropist but most important of all a gardener par excellence.

The major and his wife Katherine bought the Burnby Hall Estate in 1904 and, in between their world tours, set about creating the luscious gardens seen today. They include an aviary, formal Victorian garden, and exotic woodland, but without doubt the centrepiece is the pair of lakes with a national collection of water lilies from around the world. Midsummer is the best time to see them in their full glory.

The Stewarts never had children and left the estate to the people of Pocklington in their will. The hall was never anything special and has become council offices, but the gardens have given pleasure to thousands of people over the years.

Give yourself at least half a day if you come here – time to visit the interesting little **museum** (featuring artefacts collected by the major on his adventures) and have a brew and a snack in the café.

Pocklington Canal

⌂ www.pocklingtoncanalsociety.org.

Although it wanders out of the Wolds and into the Vale of York, the Pocklington Canal has such special qualities that I feel I must mention it. Like most English canals it was dug in the early 1800s to link Pocklington with the rest of the national waterway system via the River Derwent, 9½ miles away. Competition with the railways led to its gradual decline and complete abandonment in 1932.

> *"Dragonflies and damselflies dashed and hovered everywhere, and swans drifted serenely by."*

My first experience of the Pocklington Canal was on a glorious sunny day's canoe exploration, upstream from the River Derwent, and what a revelation it was. Where the river water was brown and silty the chalk stream fed canal was crystal clear and teeming with fish – that is where we could see the water. Most of the canal's surface was draped with a blanket of water-lilies whose yellow and white flowers were in full bloom at the time. Dragonflies and damselflies dashed and hovered everywhere, and swans drifted serenely by.

Back in the 1960s, all this could have been lost if a proposal to dump industrial waste into the canal had been approved. Hurrah for the Pocklington Canal Amenity Society (PCAS), as it was they that blocked the idea and have looked after this delightful waterway ever since. The main aim of the PCAS is to restore the canal back to fully-navigable along its complete length. At present they have managed about half, from Melbourne to the Derwent and offer 30-minute trips on their narrowboat *New Horizons* (payment by donation). You can explore the rest of the canal on foot along the well-maintained towpath, and bikes are allowed along the first 2 miles at the Pocklington end.

Madhyamaka Kadampa Meditation Centre

One of Pocklington's more dubious claims to fame is that it was the site of the last burning at the stake of witch in Britain. Thankfully the locals are much more tolerant of other religions these days, and the village of Kilnwick Percy just up the road is home to one of the largest Buddhist meditation centres in the country.

Tiny Kilnwick Percy itself comprises merely a church, a stately home and the estate farm that served it in the past. The oldest part of **Kilnwick Percy Hall** dates from Elizabethan times but most of this graceful brick building is Georgian. An uneventful history was livened up during World War II, when the hall was requisitioned as a military mail sorting-office, but it was 30 years ago that its most unexpected reinvention occurred. In 1986, Kilnwick Percy was bought by a branch of the Kadampa Buddhist movement and has operated as the Madhyamaka Kadampa Meditation Centre ever since.

This is very definitely not a closed community and the centre actively welcomes visitors to the hall and landscaped grounds. They run the World Peace Café, day and residential classes in meditation and regular community events. Various forms of accommodation are also on offer (see *Accommodation*, page 203).

¶¶ FOOD & DRINK

Of the dozen or so places to eat and drink in Pocklington, here are my favourites in each type of establishment.

Coffee Bean Market St ☏ 01759 301863. Welcoming, traditional café with a good atmosphere.

The Fresh Food Deli Market Pl ☏ 01759 307370 🖱 www.freshfooddeli.com. Houses a café upstairs, but what makes this place special is the food shop downstairs which stocks a wide range of specialty, luxury and obscure comestibles.

Judson's Market Pl ☏ 01759 302548 🖱 www.judsons.co.uk. Officially just a wine bar but its more than that – a classy (if pricey) restaurant and almost a pub.

6 MILLINGTON

This is a delightful little village, boasting the best pub for miles, a classic tea shop and characterful little church. I have to admit though, as much as I love my pint of Everards Tiger Beer in the Gait Inn or tea and toasted bloomer from the Ramblers Rest Tearoom, what brings me to this place time and time again is not the village but the valley that it sits in. Millington Dale is actually a series of dry chalk vales – with names like Pasture Dale, Nettle Dale and Sylvan Dale they could hardly be anything less than idyllic. Most of the dales are open access, meaning that you are free to wander among the grazing highland cattle and meadow flora. One of these little side valleys (Lily Dale) contains an ancient ashwood, such a rarity in these parts it has been designated as a local nature reserve. The **walk** round the wood of just over a mile is highly recommended.

¶¶ FOOD & DRINK

The Gait Inn Millington ✆ 01759 302045 ⌂ www.gait-inn-millington.co.uk. This ancient hostelry has been run for some years by the Stephensons, a local farming couple who have maintained it as a real community pub. Pool, darts and dominoes teams, quizzes and villagers' lunches keep the locals happy but it's also great for the visitor – fine food (especially the locally sourced meat), rotating guest real ales and regular live music.
Rambler's Rest Tea Room Millington ✆ 01759 305220 ⌂ www.ramblersrestmillington. co.uk. A watering hole beloved of cyclists for years, in an old village-centre farm cottage. A new addition is an evening restaurant with attached B&B accommodation.

THE HIGH WOLDS

The old Roman road from York to Bridlington roughly follows the route of the modern A166 up Garrowby Hill to the highest point on the Wolds. Many valleys snake northwards from this summit plateau, some joining up at the village of **Thixendale**. North from here the hills rise again around **Wharram Percy**, an ancient village nestling between the two country estates of Birdsall and Sledmere.

7 GARROWBY HILL

There is very little up here except a stupendous view westwards over the Vale of York and a couple of memorials. The vista has always been well-known but in recent years it has been gazed on by many more pairs of eyes, albeit in an unusual colour scheme. David Hockney's 1998 landscape *Garrowby Hill*, featuring his trademark lurid purples, reds and greens, was painted from here. The Hockney Trail can be followed around the Wolds (⌂ www.visithullandeastyorkshire.com).

The memorials are both marked on the OS map, the most visible being a large wooden crucifix on the edge of the Garrowby Hall woodland. It

A walk from Thixendale to Wharram Percy

✻ OS Explorer map 300; start: the Cross Keys pub in Thixendale, grid reference SE845610.

There are a few circular walks described on the village website (🖱 www.thixendale.org.uk) and in walking guidebooks but my particular favourite is this nine-miler linking Thixendale and Wharram Percy (see page 160). The walking is typical Wolds fare, brilliant in places – where the path follows the bottom of narrow, steep-sided valleys, and tedious when you end up on the flat, arable tops.

With the Cross Keys pub on your left, walk along to the main village street and turn right along it through the village, turning right after the last building on to the Wolds Way footpath. After 1½ miles, where the path meets a farm track and the Centenary Way footpath, turn left. Follow the Centenary Way down a steep hill until you join a tarmac road near the village of Birdsall. Turn right here and follow this minor road for 2½ miles until you reach a row of cottages near a hairpin bend. The Wolds Way joins the road here, but before you turn right to follow its route along a disused railway line, check out the nature reserve in the quarry nearby. The Wolds Way will take you through the deserted medieval village of Wharram Percy and up the valley of Deepdale. Continue up the side of the valley until you reach another junction with the Centenary Way. Turn left and follow the Centenary Way for a last downhill mile back to Thixendale.

was erected in 1956 by Lord Halifax who lived in the hall, in memory of his friend George VI. The other memorial is further up the hill by the summit and is a much more poignant affair. It commemorates the deaths of eight men when a Halifax bomber crashed here in fog during World War II. Seven of them were flying in the plane but the eighth was incredibly unlucky as he was actually on the road when the Halifax landed on the milk truck he was driving at the time. His ghost is said to haunt the hill-top, but not accompanied by gold-tops a-rattlin' in their crates, as his name wasn't Ernie but Arthur.

8 THIXENDALE

🏠 **Manor Farm** (see page 202)

Most people share the view that this is a very special place, but no-one can seem to agree on where the name came from. Some say that six dales feed into the main valley; others count the smaller dale-lets and reckon on 16, whereas Viking history scholars are sure that this was the home of a Norseman called Sigstein. It's still an open debate.

What's not in doubt is that for hundreds of years this has been one of the country's most isolated and least explored corners. Recently though Thixendale has begun to be discovered, mainly by walkers, art lovers and seekers of solitude.

Thixendale's most obvious connection with the art world is an arresting landscape sculpture by Chris Drury. *Time and Flow* can be found just south of the village (※ grid reference SE841598) and is one of a series of sculptures commissioned by the Arts Council to accompany the Yorkshire Wolds Way along its whole route. The other nine are detailed on ⬦ www.visithullandeastyorkshire.com/walks-and-trails. More traditional paint-on-paper art can be found a mile up the Fotherdale Road, at Fotherdale Farm. This is the home, studio and gallery of wildlife artist Robert Fuller (see opposite). Thixendale also features as a subject in paintings by the most famous local artist of all. David Hockney's *Three Trees in the Proximity of Thixendale* was exhibited at the Royal Academy.

🍴 FOOD & DRINK

Cross Keys Thixendale 📞 01377 288272 ⬦ www.thixendale.org.uk. A one-roomed gem of a pub in the heart of the village and regular CAMRA award winner. The real ales are always kept well and food is wholesome, filling and specifically aimed at keeping walkers fuelled up. B&B rooms are in an adjacent annex with excellent breakfasts served in the bar.

Village Hall Teas, scones and cakes served every Sun 11.00–16.00.

9 WHARRAM & WHARRAM PERCY

Almost all the present residents of Wharram live in the village of Wharram le Street, up on the hill-top where the old Roman road ran through – hence the 'Street' tag. This wasn't the case back in the 13th

YORK

York is a history lesson in stone, and quite simply the most complete medieval city in the country. But it's not just the past that attracts, as this is still a vibrant metropolis and the cultural and artistic centre of the county.

1 York Minster, the largest Gothic cathedral in northern Europe, dominates the city skyline. (S/AW)
2 Quality teas at Bettys, a Yorkshire institution. (SS) **3** Stonegate, one of the oldest streets in York, boasts the ancient Olde Starre Inne and its unusual street-spanning sign. (WTY)

NORTH YORK MOORS TOWNS & VILLAGES

It's all Yorkshire, but what variety – from the solid sandstone villages of the Moors to the quaint charm of Ryedale and the windswept spaces of the Wolds.

1 Regular winner of local 'best-kept village' titles, Thornton le Dale has a certain Cotswoldy charm. (ss) **2** It's serious stuff, this game of quoits, and has been for the past few hundred years. (MKP/A) **3** The Black Mill (an old windmill) in Beverley Westwood Park, with the Minster in the background. (VHEY) **4** A peaceful corner of Helmsley, behind the bustling market square. (S/KE) **5** Stepping stones cross the River Esk at the village of Lealholm. (ss) **6** All great villages have a good pub as their social centre. Coxwold's Fauconberg Arms goes one better – it is a theatre as well! (ss)

COASTAL TOWNS

Such is the isolation of this coastline that before the coming of the railways the only access to many towns was by sea. The locals are still maritime folk, proud of their Viking heritage.

1 The ruins of the Norman castle loom over the harbour in Scarborough, North Yorkshire's largest seaside town. (ss) **2** Moored cobles sheltering up Staithes Beck, a view beloved of artists for centuries. (DB)

BARN OWLS

A white owl bounces over
the hedge top
As if on puppeteer's strings
So bright and alive it
illuminates the dusk
So buoyant, it seems its
wings are stretched
To keep the Earth from
losing it
What heart this bird must
have
To fill so slight a body with
such energy...
Mike Bagshaw

Barn owls have inspired poets and artists since ink and paint existed. They provoke conflicting feelings of love and fear, being the nation's official favourite farmland bird but also a traditional omen of death. In living memory they were skinned and nailed to doors to ward off lightning storms. These eclectic birds are in trouble though. Nationally, their numbers have dropped by 75% since the 1930s, yet I have seen more in the last two years in Ryedale than in the rest of my 40-odd years of birdwatching elsewhere in the country. What is it about this part of Yorkshire that suits *Tyto alba?* The obvious person to ask was Robert Fuller. Robert is one of Britain's leading wildlife artists, but also a passionate conservationist with a special interest in barn owls. He directs operations from his home at Thixendale on the Wolds side of the Derwent Valley.

'I set up the Wolds Barn Owls Group with friends a couple of years ago. It's a real hands-on project where we make and put up barn owl boxes on farms on the Yorkshire Wolds. We're an enthusiastic team and have great support from the local community.

Barn owls have had problems from all angles. A lot of their habitats have changed because there are bigger fields these days and different farming methods. And the old traditional brick farm buildings they liked to nest in are no longer used ... a lot of them have been converted, knocked down or have fallen down, so it is important to provide them with an alternative nesting site. Dutch elm disease has been a big problem as well. The elm trees were often important as they had good hollows for owls to nest in, but now all those trees have fallen down and rotted away.

I've designed my own nest box for the project. Normally the male barn owl has to find a new home once the chicks are born and people tend to put out two boxes. My boxes have two compartments with a little penthouse area for the male to live after the chicks arrive. We've put up nearly 200 boxes across our area and about half are occupied – that's a healthy population of owls. It is good to know that, despite the pressures of habitat loss and harsh weather limiting hunting, at least the barn owls won't be short of a place to nest. I've always had a particular affinity for barn owls and they often feature in my paintings – it's nice now to give something back.'

and 14th centuries when the local population farmed a couple of miles away in a village at the bottom of Deep Dale, called **Wharram Percy**. This medieval settlement was abandoned around the year 1500 and is now perhaps the country's most famous deserted medieval village, rediscovered in 1948 by historian Professor Maurice Beresford. The church was always fairly obvious being as it was a fairly intact, if roofless, building but what the professor and his team of archaeologists managed to do was find the rest of the village. Over a period of 40 years they excavated and mapped the foundations of scores of buildings, the grassy outlines of which you can still make out on the ground.

English Heritage, which manages Wharram Percy, has placed useful information boards around the site to explain all the humps and bumps and answer questions like my 'Why was it abandoned?' The answer was a surprising one – nothing to do with the Black Death but an early example of economic land clearance. In the 16th century, sheep became more profitable than crops so the landlord (not the original Baron de Percy but a certain Mr Hilton) turfed out his tenants, replaced them with sheep and demolished the village.

If you enjoy poking around old churches you should find the ruins of St Martin's interesting but don't neglect the current, intact church in **Wharram le Street** because it is even older. Most of St Mary's is Norman with medieval additions but the tower dates back to Anglo-Saxon times. The churches are a mere two miles apart and the very pleasant stroll between them takes you briefly on the bed of an old railway which was built to take out stone from the big chalk quarry midway between the two villages. Like many disused quarries this place is a haven for wildlife; if you are here in early summer it's well worth the short detour to marvel at the hundreds of butterflies feeding on carpets of thyme, rest harrow and orchids (details from the Yorkshire Wildlife Trust ᐰ www. ywt.org.uk).

10 SLEDMERE

YO25 3XG ᐰ 01377 236637 ᐰ www.sledmerehouse.com; house open some days each week Apr–Oct.

There is no genuine village of Sledmere, just a country house and estate belonging to the Sykes family – the old village and medieval hall were demolished in the 18th century by successive 'Lordies' to make way for the big, new house and gardens designed by Capability Brown.

Like many country estates it is run as a business to make ends meet, with house and gardens open to the public and grounds available for weddings and events.

Sledmere does seem to reflect some of the modest and unassuming nature of the Wolds, though, and that's where it differs from big, brash places like Castle Howard. Not that the house is unimpressive; with 30 rooms this is a big building displaying quite a range of architectural styles, partly because of a troubled history. The original early Georgian interior was extended and redecorated 50 years later but then almost completely destroyed by fire in 1911. Fortunately, much of the house contents and the original plans were saved (allegedly by the villagers and staff as Sir Tatton Sykes finished his pudding in the dining room). The inside of Sledmere was reconstructed to the Georgian plans but with an Edwardian twist.

Fourteen rooms are open to the public, including the celebrated Long Library, the drawing and Music Rooms with Joseph Rose plasterwork and the Chinese Bedroom with a Chippendale bed. The quirkiest room is probably the one inspired by the Sultan's apartments in the Yeni Mosque of Istanbul and called (not surprisingly) the Turkish Room.

The entrance charge for the house is not exorbitant and includes access to the gardens. These are arguably more impressive than the house itself, especially the formal patterns of the Parterre and the Georgian walled rose garden. There are parts of the Estate accessible free of charge; these are the shop, café, entrance exhibition and **Waggoners Museum**. This last building commemorates the work of Sir Mark, the sixth Baronet, during World War I – ironically he survived the trenches but died during the 1918 flu pandemic. His body was exhumed from its lead-lined coffin in 2008 to extract DNA for research into flu treatment.

⅋ FOOD & DRINK

The Triton Inn Sledmere ☎ 01377 236078 ⬀ www.thetritoninn.co.uk. Local Wold Top beers and traditional pub food – nothing fancy but good quality. The bar also stocks an unusually large collection of gins from around the world. B&B accommodation available.

EAST TO THE COAST

At their northern edge, the Wolds loom out over Ryedale and the Vale of Pickering as a long escarpment, heading east to finally reach the sea at

Flamborough Head. Behind this high land lies a long dale sometimes known as the **Great Wold Valley**, down which flows the famous Gypsey Race, through the **villages** of Weaverthorpe, Wold Newton, Burton Fleming and Rudston.

11 THE GREAT WOLD VALLEY

⌂ **Wold Cottage**, Wold Newton (see page 202).

My first visit here was a puzzling one. I was armed with my OS map, which had on it a distinct wiggly, blue line – a stream at Kirby Grindalythe that I intended to follow. When I navigated myself to the right place though, there was nothing there, just a dry ditch in a field. The name **Gypsey Race** should have given me a clue really; gypsy – itinerant, wandering, often arriving in spring and then disappearing. This is one of those intermittent streams, often associated with chalk country.

Chalk is no more than a pure form of limestone, and a crucial property of this rock is its permeability, that is it allows water to pass through it. Chalk hills like the Wolds behave as giant sponges, soaking up millions of tons of water a year, which is why we see very little surface water in streams, ponds or lakes. It is only when this water reaches an impermeable layer of rock below, or the underground reservoirs are full to overflowing, that it bubbles out on to the surface from springs. This often happens after heavy rain, but also sometimes mysteriously during dry weather when it is least expected.

Whatever the geological cause, the significance of the Gypsey Race on past human societies here has been enormous historically, and especially pre-historically. Another glance at the OS map reveals a concentration of ancient monuments, clustered along the length of my wiggly, blue line, starting up near the stream's source at Wharram le Street. **Duggleby Howe** (✳ grid reference SE881669), one of the largest Neolithic burial mounds in Britain, is the first. Travelling downstream, you pass **Wold Newton Barrow** (✳ grid reference TA048726), **Willy Howe** (✳ grid reference TA062723), **Little Argham Henge** (✳ grid reference TA096706) and finally the remarkable **Rudston monolith** (see page 166). Current thinking considers the Stone and Bronze Age veneration of springs (see page 165); historians

"The name Gypsey Race should have given me a clue really, gypsy – itinerant, wandering, often arriving in spring and then disappearing."

THE FALLING STONE OF WOLD NEWTON

A man (me) walks into a pub and orders a pint of the local bitter. 'Why the strange name?' he asks the landlord, pointing to the *Falling Stone Bitter* pump-clip. 'Oh, that's to do with what happened in a field near the brewery donkeys years ago,' was the barman's reply. 'Tell me more,' the man said, and joking apart, this is the story he heard.

In the middle of a December afternoon in 1795, farmhands working in the fields behind Wold Cottage Farm, watched aghast as a dark object flashed diagonally across the sky and struck the ground near where they were. The explosion of the impact was heard for miles around, and John Shipley, the nearest worker, was showered with soil. The 56lb rock, still hot and smoking from its supersonic flight, lay buried seven inches into the chalk bedrock.

What these men, and others from the village, had witnessed was the final seconds of the journey of the second largest meteorite ever to land on English soil. Or 'an extraordinary stone that fell from the atmosphere,' as it was reported at the time –

and boy was it reported. By pure chance, the Falling Stone of Wold Newton had happened to land in fields belonging to Major Edward Topham, a farmer, writer and magistrate who also owned a newspaper. The stone became a celebrity, so much so that Major Topham put it on display in Piccadilly, charging a shilling a time to view. Eventually, what was left of the stone after souvenirs had been chipped off was donated to the Natural History Museum in London, where it resides today.

The Falling Stone of Wold Newton remains the only meteorite landing that has ever been observed by reliable witnesses, thus giving the astronomers of the time vital evidence for the cosmic origin of meteorites. Cue top scientific fact of the day – a meteoroid is the rock in flight, a meteor is its visible burning tail and a meteorite is what it becomes when it lands. The landing site is marked by a brick memorial monument erected by Major Topham. It sits on private land with no public access, but paying guests at Wold Cottage (see *Accommodation*, page 202) are able to visit.

reckon that our ancestors probably regarded unpredictable groundwater appearance on this scale, a river appearing overnight, as magical – in other words, Gypsey Race was a major religious site.

'Race' folklore continued into historical times, with floods in particular said to be the harbingers of doom or disaster. A roaring race, or 'woe-waters' as they were known, preceded the Black Death, the beheading of King Charles I, the attack by William of Orange and the Wold Newton meteorite (see above). The last big flood was in December 2012, just before a meteorite shower injured hundreds of people in Russia ... a coincidence of course – or was it?

Most of the time the Great Wold Valley is a sleepy backwater with not much going on besides farming and locals getting on with their lives. Few visitors come here which means that those that do will have a lot of peace and quiet to themselves. Footpaths and bridleways are virtually deserted and road cycling on the very quiet country lanes is a joy.

There are no tourist attractions to see in the string of villages along the valley bottom. Most have small and interesting **churches**, many rebuilt or restored by the Victorian Sir Tatton Sykes of Sledmere House. Particularly worth visiting are St Andrew's in **Kirby Grindalythe**, St Andrew's in **Weaverthorpe**, St Peter's in **Helperthorpe** and the lovely little St James's at **Fordon** (the smallest active church in Yorkshire).

The Rudston Monolith

Frankly, I can't understand why this place isn't a major tourist attraction, for it is the tallest prehistoric standing stone anywhere in Britain. At 25 feet, the Rudston Monolith stands higher than any of the acclaimed Stonehenge stones or menhirs on Orkney, and here it is, hiding down the side of an unremarkable church in a small Wolds village.

Closer examination of the details makes the stone's presence here even more astonishing. For a 25-foot block to stand without falling over it must have a further 15 feet underground, and therefore weigh at least 30 tons. What's more, the stone is not local; it is composed of sandstone, the nearest outcrop of which is ten miles away in Cayton Bay near Scarborough. I find it difficult to imagine the effort it must have taken our ancestors 3,000 years ago to move such a block of stone here, armed only with boats, logs, ropes and ingenuity. I don't think that the religious importance of Rudston can be overestimated.

When Christianity arrived on our shores churches were built on existing holy sites so there is every likelihood that a church has existed here for 1,500 years even though the oldest part of the present building is Norman. Incidentally, the village name is Saxon: not the usual 'ton' for town, but 'ston' for stone, with the prefix rood, meaning cross. It probably commemorates a time when this pagan symbol was converted to Christianity by the addition of a cross on top.

¶¶ FOOD & DRINK

Some of the valley villages have never had a pub in living memory and some have lost them recently; those currently with a place to eat and drink are Weaverthorpe (two), Wold Newton,

Walks round Flamborough Head

✳ OS Explorer 301; start: South Landing, grid reference SE231692.

The obvious walk to do here is one that takes you right around the end of the promontory, and just for a change public transport is on your side if you choose to use it. My choice would be to start on the gentler south coast and finish at the spectacular cliffs further north. The walk begins at **South Landing**, which you can drive to, but its only just over half a mile's stroll from Flamborough village where the Bridlington bus (510) stops every 30 minutes. Facing the sea at South Landing, turn left and follow the coastal path for two miles to **Flamborough Head** itself. After admiring an historic pair of lighthouses overlooking Selwicks Bay, continue along the steadily rising cliffs of the northern shore for two further miles to **North Landing**. While you could catch the bus back from here, the cliff scenery will probably tempt you on for a further mile to where a public footpath leads across the fields and back to Flamborough village. If you did use the bus from Bridlington to get here, then this seven-mile circuit can be extended by another two miles by continuing along the coast to the RSPB visitor centre perched atop the stunning cliffs of **Bempton** (free entry if you arrive on foot). From here, an amble downhill for a further 1½ miles will take you to Bempton railway station, where you can catch one of the nine trains a day back to Bridlington.

Thwing and Burton Fleming. All are good but I would particularly recommend:
Anvil Arms Bridlington Rd, Wold Newton YO25 3YL ✆ 01262 470279. A justifiably very popular pub for both eating and drinking. Food is traditional English and comes in large portions (steak and ale pie world famous). Theakstons and Black Sheep bitters are always available and usually another guest beer.
Bluebell Country Inn Main St, Weaverthorpe YO17 8EX ✆ 01944 738204 🖰 www.blue bellweaverthorpe.com. The Bluebell has always been an excellent beer drinkers venue (Tetleys and Timothy Taylors) but recently the emphasis has shifted to concentrating on high quality food. B&B accommodation also available.

12 FLAMBOROUGH HEAD

Flamborough Head Nature Reserve ⌖ www.ywt.org.uk; open all year; free entrance.
Bempton Cliffs Nature Reserve ✆ 01262 851179; open all year; entry fee per car but
free if you walk or bike there; RSPB.

Pedantically speaking, only the relatively low cliff at the very end of the
headland qualifies for the name but when most people talk of Flamborough
Head they are referring to the whole area of land between Bridlington and
the sands of Filey Bay. This enormous chunk of chalk, an extension of the
Wolds, sticks out a good six miles into the North Sea, with its highest cliffs
an awesome, vertical 400 feet at Bempton on its northern side.

Flamborough has always been a very separate place. Indeed the
Bronze Age people here cut themselves off from the rest of the country

SEABIRD CITIES

This is almost a sensory overload experience I am going through. There is deafening cackling all around and the constant pattering of feet on water, so many individuals are coming and going carrying fish that I cannot keep up, and an overpowering fishy smell pervades everything. Where am I? A busy Scarborough chip shop on a Friday night perhaps? No, I am bobbing on the swell in a small boat at the foot of Flamborough Head cliffs, taking in one of the most spectacular wildlife experiences that Britain, never mind Yorkshire, has to offer. Most of the pattering fish-carriers are members of the auk family; puffins mainly, but also guillemots and razorbills that have surfaced with a beak full of sand eels to feed their young. They manage to get themselves airborne with a whirring of their small wings and a frantic leg-sprint over the sea surface before banking over to their cliff-top nest. As they leave, the next shift arrives and plops beneath the surface. I lean over the side and watch enthralled as one puffin flaps its

way under our boat (they swim by flying underwater), its progress through the clear water visible because of a silver layer of air clinging to its waterproof feathers.

What sound like two sharp gun-shots pull my attention to the other side of the boat, just in time to see the cause of the noise as a gannet folds its wings back at the end of its 30-foot dive and 'thunks' into the water at breakneck speed. Two others surface, both with a wriggling mackerel that they wolf down headfirst – what gannets! There is so much going on it is tiring; a seal's head in the water to port, was that a porpoise fin on the starboard side? Yes, there it is again – two of them! After a while though, childish excitement slackens enough to observe and see order in the apparent chaos. Seven or eight species of bird breed on the chalk cliffs of Flamborough and Bempton, 200,000 in total, most feeding on small fish, sand eels and sprats. Kittiwakes and guillemots are the most numerous and nest on ledges completely by constructing a massive earth wall and ditch now mistakenly known as 'Danes' Dyke'. There is a strong Scandinavian connection here though, with many colloquial terms, stories and traditions dating from Viking times. The annual sword dance that is still performed, even if only by local village schoolchildren now, is probably the most famous of these old traditions.

Flamborough Head's exposed position has always been a hazard to shipping; over 50 shipwrecks are recorded close by, so it's no surprise to find a lighthouse here. What is unusual is that there are two, the present working one built in 1806 and its predecessor, a wonderful octagonal chalk edifice whose beacon was a basket of burning coal. Dating from 1674, this is the oldest standing lighthouse in the country.

high on the most vertical sections of cliff with gannets and razorbills preferring the lower sloping sections. The puffins here are unusual – elsewhere in the country, such as the Farne Islands in Northumberland, they raise their young in soil burrows at the cliff-top. At Flamborough, natural cavities in the rock face do the job and puffins have the unusual experience of tenement living with fulmars as neighbours.

In the past, the vast numbers of birds here were seen as a harvestable resource by locals. Gangs of 'climmers' would make a hair-raising descent by rope from the top of the cliffs to collect both eggs and young birds for food. This sustainable harvesting worked fine until Victorian times when things got out of hand. Shooting birds from boats as holiday sport caught on and many more eggs were collected to supply private collections, but the activity that caused a change in the law was kittiwake collecting. Thousands were massacred to provide feathers for fashion

hat accessories and to stuff mattresses. So to prevent their complete wipe-out, the first Bird Protection Act of 1869 was introduced to the statute book and today the birds are very well protected.

As my boat chugs back to North Landing at Flamborough I marvel at what a special place of superlatives this is. It is the most northerly outcrop of chalk in the country, England's biggest seabird colony, and the only mainland gannet colony in Britain. Most of all, it provides one of the most exhilarating wildlife experiences to be found anywhere.

If you fancy a boat trip to see, hear and smell the birds of Flamborough Head, there are a few options (see page 170) but being afloat is not the only way to experience the birds of course. You can see them with a good pair of binoculars from the beaches at North Landing and South Landing or from the cliff-top path looking down. The RSPB have some excellent viewing points at the top of Bempton cliff.

Other attractions apart, what draws most people to Flamborough Head are its birds. Two nature reserves are dedicated to the protection of the huge seabird colonies here, Bempton Cliffs Nature Reserve (RSPB) and Flamborough Head Nature Reserve (Yorkshire Wildlife Trust).

¶¶ FOOD & DRINK

Ship Inn Post Office St, Flamborough ✆ 01262 850454. The name is apt, as you will feel as if you have walked into the captain's cabin when you enter the varnished, wood-panelled bar. This is a traditional local, with darts, pool, dominoes and cards available to play, and John Smith's and other guest cask ales to drink. The grub cooked here is wholesome and very good value, especially the seafood.

BOAT TRIPS

Emmerson's North Landing slipway ✆ 01262 850575 or 01262 850704. Boat trips to see the birds and caves of Flamborough Head. Summer only.
RSPB Bempton Cliffs From Bridlington Harbour ✆ 01262 850959 🖰 www.rspb.org.uk/datewithnature. Gannet and puffin cruises on the *Yorkshire Belle*. May–Jul weekends.

UPDATES WEBSITE

You can post your comments and recommendations, and read the latest feedback and updates from other readers online at 🖰 www.bradtupdates.com/northyorkmoors.

6
YORK

Caroline Mills

🏠 **Middlethorpe Hall Hotel** and **The Nottingham Trader**, Bishopsthorpe (see page 203)

'The history of York is the history of England,' according to George V, and he was probably right. While the passage of time in other British towns and cities is recorded in books, York's is still there to be seen in bricks and mortar. And yet, with the help of vibrant industries aside from tourism, it has managed to avoid becoming a stereotypical tourist city with little else to offer the wider community.

My first historical encounter with York, long before I lived there, involved eating ice cream – a fine history lesson for a youngster. The delightful block of frozen loveliness, wedged between two rather soggy wafers, was made by the Ebor Ice-Cream Co Ltd (sadly no longer in existence). I was told that Ebor was short for Eboracum, the Roman name for York.

The city and Legionnaire's fortress, built some 2,000 before the ice cream eating incident (though I swear the wafers may have been artefacts from the era), was one of the most important places on the map of Roman Britannia. The remnants are still evident: a column from the Roman headquarters, the remains of the fortress in the basement of the Minster, the **Multangular Tower** – a part of the old Roman bastion – in the Museum Gardens, stone coffins by the city walls and the ghostly figures of a marching army tramping through the basement of the Treasurer's House, heading who knows where along an old Roman road.

However, York is perhaps more famous for its Viking history, with archaeological digging uncovering all manner of important finds. While I lived in York, I really took all this Viking talk for granted. It was not until I visited Trondheim in Norway that everything fell into place. There were distinct similarities – the streets were named gates, the town gateways were *bars* and St Olave, a name that crops up repeatedly around York, stood on a column in Trondheim's centre, the patron saint of Norway. Indeed, the penny dropped – the Vikings made their mark in York. They too are ever-present at the **Jorvik Viking Centre**, one of the city's major tourist attractions following archaeological excavations more than a quarter of a century ago.

Yet these invasions are only the start of York's story, with medieval merchants profiteering from get-rich-quick schemes, infighting royals, men loyal to the royals, guys not so loyal to the royals, highwaymen, railway men, chocolate makers and Quakers all making an impact on the way the city looks today. You don't need an in-depth history of York to enjoy the city's pleasures – partaking of a hot-buttered teacake in a tearoom, aiding the profits of the independent retailers that line the streets or relaxing on a grassy knoll in the Museum Gardens – but a brief understanding does help to explain a few things. Whenever I return to the city, I usually head straight for a walk 'around the block': down **Stonegate** (arguably York's most atmospheric pedestrianised street); along **Low Petergate** for a look back at one of the most classic views of the Minster; to **King's Square**, often frequented by buskers; down the minuscule 'Shambles' towards **Parliament Street** where street markets prevail; and along **Davygate** returning to **St Helen's Square** to visit the civilised world of **Bettys Café Tea Rooms**, where tea drinkers look out through the great glass window on to the world of York. From there a trip to the **Minster** is a must for me, to marvel at the size and scale of the creamy exterior walls and the hundreds of years of craftsmanship that have gone into creating and preserving them. Finally a wander around the **Museum Gardens** would top off a visit, especially on a day filled with sunshine.

Dividing the centre of York into segments is somewhat arbitrary for there are really just two main parts to York – inside or outside the city walls. For the sake of honouring York's chocolate heritage, I've broken

THE YORK PASS

If you plan to visit lots of fee-paying attractions, and you're in town for more than a day, it's worthwhile purchasing a York Pass. The pass is a smart card allowing discounted entry into more than 30 places of interest, including several outside York mentioned elsewhere in this book. Passes can be purchased for one, two or three consecutive days from ⌖ www.yorkpass.com.

the city centre into three bite-size chunks that are more easily digestible by a visitor on foot – Around the Minster, Traders' and Debtors' York, and South of the River Ouse.

FOOD & DRINK

As York's a cosmopolitan city, you can grab a sandwich or a pasty for pavement food, dine in any number of international restaurants or sink a pint of regional brew in one of the many town centre pubs and bars. But this is Yorkshire, and the city has not forgotten its roots, with a plethora of cafés and tea rooms serving a traditional afternoon tea. With such a compact centre you could eat all day moving from breakfast to brunch, lunch to tea and evening drinks to dinner without leaving a street.

The area around Newgate and Parliament Street is the place to pick up goodies in the open air. Newgate hosts a daily **market** while Parliament Street is the scene for **York Farmers' Market** (last Friday of every month) and several **continental markets** held throughout the year, including a large one around Christmas.

¶¶ CAFÉS & RESTAURANTS

The Bar Convent 17 Blossom St ✆ 01904 643238 ⊕ www.bar-convent.org.uk. Quiet café, serving delicious homemade food throughout the day in relaxed surroundings.

Bettys Café Tea Rooms 6–8 St Helen's Sq ✆ 01904 659142; and **Little Bettys** 46 Stonegate ✆ 01904 622865 ⊕ www.bettys.co.uk. The epitome of Yorkshire (see page 174), Bettys overlooks St Helen's Square with a huge curved plate glass window from which to survey the world while listening to some classic coffee shop tunes from the in-house pianist. Little Bettys is much more intimate and cosy, looking like an old shop from a Dickens novel. Both serve excellent food and drinks, and their fantastic bakery products, teas and coffees can be bought to take away from the premises too.

The Blue Bicycle 34 Fossgate ✆ 01904 673990 ⊕ www.thebluebicycle.com. Well-talked-about restaurant specialising in seafood. By no means the cheapest in town but good quality, fresh ingredients used and plenty of ambience.

Café Concerto 21 High Petergate ✆ 01904 610478 ⊕ www.cafeconcerto.biz. A bistro that has gained quite a reputation for good food and ambience; in a prime location overlooking York Minster.

Grays Court Chapter House St ✆ 01904 612613 ⊕ http://grayscourtyork.com. Next door to the Treasurer's House, this is an extra special place to eat for either a relaxing mid-morning coffee, lunch or afternoon tea. The entrance to this magnificent historic building is through a peaceful cobbled courtyard. You can relax on sofas or private window seats in the oak-panelled Jacobean long gallery, or find a table overlooking the garden, itself overlooked by the city walls. My pick of daytime eateries throughout the whole of York.

Treasurer's House Chapter House St ☎ 01904 624247. A National Trust tea room, open to all (not just those visiting the house).

York Minster Tea Rooms College St ☎ 01904 634830 🖱 www.yorkminster.org. Good for people-watching over a coffee, this sits in the zebra-like timber-framed building of St William's College. With a few tables on the pavement outside, it overlooks the east front of the Minster. There's also a nice courtyard away from the crowds.

¶¶ PUBS

If there is a better collection of pubs in any town or city centre in the country, I've yet to see it. Here is the cream of the crop:

Blue Bell Fossgate ☎ 01904 654904. Small, pokey and brilliant. With an interior unchanged since 1903 this is one of CAMRA's elite heritage pubs.

Guy Fawkes Inn High Petergate ☎ 01904 671001. One of the reputed birthplaces of Guy Fawkes in the shadow of the Minster. The tiny bar serves the pub's own beer brewed by Great Heck Brewery.

Kings Arms Ouse Bridge ☎ 01904 659435. Famous as a flood victim. Not the best beer in town but certainly the cheapest (Sam Smiths) and worth visiting if only to see past flood levels marked on the wall.

Minster Inn Marygate ☎ 01904 624499. Not where you might expect it with a name like that, but tucked down the side of the Museum Gardens. An unspoiled, friendly, multi-roomed local and a genuine haven of peace and quiet.

Snickleway Inn Goodramgate ☎ 01904 656138. Another of the pubs claiming to be the most haunted in York.

Ye Olde Starre Inn Off Stonegate ☎ 01904 623063. Prepare for some ghostly sights while mulling over a pint. The pub sign spans the street – one of the few in Britain to do so.

Yorkshire Terrier Stonegate ☎ 01904 676722 🖱 www.york-brewery.co.uk. Pub owned by York Brewery serving their own ales and a few guest beers. In a beautiful old building, the pub sits behind and above the brewery's shop.

GETTING AROUND

Much of the beating heart of York is pedestrianised so the very best way – indeed the only way – to see the main proportion of the city within the walls is on foot, or at least by pedal cycle. Public transport only helps when crossing the city or getting from the outskirts to the centre.

i TOURIST INFORMATION

Visit York Information Centre Museum St ✆ 01904 550099 🖰 www.visityork.org
York Railway Visitor Information Centre Station Rd; contact details as above.
Wheelchair accessible.

BY BUS

Buses from the suburbs to the city centre are run by **First Bus** (✆ 0845 604 5460 🖰 www.firstgroup.com/ukbus/yorkhumber/york). These are colour-coded routes for ease of use, with the main terminus at Station Road outside the railway station and Rougier Street, a five-minute walk from the railway station. These buses won't particularly help you to see the sights of York but they will help visitors staying in accommodation away from the city centre.

However, one way to reach some of the attractions of York is by taking the **York City Sightseeing Tour** (✆ 01904 655585 🖰 www.city-sightseeing.com). It's a hop-on hop-off ride stopping at 18 points of interest. With tickets valid for 24 hours, the tour skirts the city walls and is useful for gathering your bearings, or for those with mobility problems (the buses are wheelchair and pushchair 'friendly'), but it can't replace foot-stomping through the streets.

BY TAXI

Taxis are readily available directly outside the railway station but there are also licensed taxi ranks in various locations around the city centre, including St Saviourgate and St Leonard's Place (useful for evening performances at the Theatre Royal).

BY CAR

Frankly, this is not a good idea. By far the easiest and most cost-effective thing to do with your car if visiting for the day is to use the convenient park-and-ride scheme (city centre car parks are expensive). With free parking in five locations, all well-signposted around the city ring road, the bus, with a reasonable fare, transports you right into the centre, stopping at several points around the city.

CYCLING

To get to York, the National Cycle Network Route 65 (The White Rose Cycle Route) has much **off-road cycling** from Selby to York, connecting with Hull and Middlesbrough, plus several new routes in the offing, including a trans-Pennine route from Manchester to York.

York is officially the safest place in the UK in which to cycle, based upon recent research by the Cyclist Touring Club, and has been granted 'Cycling City' status from Cycling England. There are many traffic-free **cycleways** to keep you off the busy streets, with bike parking facilities in the city centre. **Bike hire** is available from **Europcar** (✆ 01904 656181) at the railway station and from **Giant York** (✆ 01904 622868 🖰 www.giant-york.co.uk) in Lord Mayor's Walk.

As for **maps**, pick up a free copy of York's *Cycle Route Map* from visitor information centres and local libraries or download it from 🖰 www.york.gov.uk/cycling. This details all cycle routes throughout the city as well as off-road tracks for safer cycling.

WALKING

The very heart of York, enclosed by the **city walls**, is compact and easily manageable on foot. With your head down, you could cross the centre from wall to wall in approximately 20 minutes, though in reality you'll take far longer because there is so much to see. It is by far the best way to see York, and many of the main streets are pedestrianised. Rather than cross the heart of the city, you can circle it with a walk along the city walls providing one of the best vantage points from which to view the centre, particularly as an introduction before tackling the core. Originally built by the Romans and beefed-up with stone in the 13th century to keep out the Scots, the castellated walls include an inner parapet-like walkway that is approximately three miles long. They are a significant feature of the York landscape and can make a good short cut in places. My favourite section is to start at **Micklegate Bar**, considered to be the royal entrance to York as it's the gate through which all members of the royal family have passed on state visits to the city, and walk towards **St Leonard's Place**. Besides the superb golden glow of trumpeting daffodils hugging the banks in

"Originally built by the Romans and beefed-up with stone in the 13th century to keep out the Scots, the castellated walls include an inner parapet-like walkway."

springtime, there are fabulous views, when walking this part of the walls, of the curving Victorian arches at the railway station, the beautiful Dutch-looking former headquarters of the North Eastern Railway Company and one of the most magnificent views of the Minster. It's the West Front of the Minster that you see from this particular section of the walls and on sunny afternoons, the stone from the façade glows with such vigour as to bring it to life.

York has built a tourist industry around walking and for visitors who prefer to be guided by a knowledgeable local, there are any number of themed walks provided by various organisations. One of the most notable is **Yorkwalk** (✆ 01904 622303 ⌂ www.yorkwalk.co.uk) which begins its tours from the main gates of the Museum Gardens on Museum Street. Regular walks include useful themes for first-time visitors such as Essential York and Secret York. Other tours are more specific – the Bloody Execution Tour, Roman York, Women in York History and the infamous Historic Toilet Tour, a unique approach to uncovering aspects of social history within the city.

For **self-guided trips**, following the route suggested by Mark Jones in his book *A Walk around the Snickelways of York* is hard to beat. The most recent addition to the trail list is an official one started by (and starting at) York Lucky Cats shop on the Shambles. It links the many cat statues on the old buildings of the city and is proving very popular.

AROUND THE MINSTER
YORK MINSTER
The character and ambience of York is owed to a multitude of fascinating and beautiful buildings with a mix of architectural styles from a wealth of historical periods. But if there is one building that truly sums up York, one that most people think of as 'being' York, it is the Minster. A colossus in stature and fame – one of the largest cathedrals in the world and arguably the most beautiful example of Gothic architecture – it dwarfs anything that stands around it. The Minster can be seen from several miles away in certain directions, a beacon that rises up through the notorious autumn mists drifting across the Knavesmire, the vast open expanse to the south of the city.

This is one of the few positions from which to survey the whole of the Minster. As you move closer to the structure, fragments disappear behind other buildings; even when you are standing right by it, when its sheer size is overwhelming, you cannot possibly see all of it. As you gaze skywards, you'll feel a pain in the neck creep in, unaware just how long it has been that you have studied the delicately carved decorations, mighty flying buttresses and magnificent **stained glass windows**. From inside, these windows glint and gleam with every passing sunlit flicker, as if taking on a life of their own. The rose window in the south transept is one of the most famous in the world, not least for the painstaking restoration that was required following the lightning-bolt fire in 1984 that destroyed this work of art. The window joins the red and white roses of Lancaster and York, a symbol marking the end of the Wars of the Roses, a horrific and bloody period of history during which the Plantagenet families of Lancaster and York spent many a year bickering. When Henry VII married Elizabeth of York, daughter of Henry IV, in January 1486 in York Minster, the two 'roses' were conjoined to create the Tudor Rose.

"From inside, these windows glint and gleam with every passing sunlit flicker, as if taking on a life of their own."

Other windows are equally beautiful, their colours dancing across the gigantic walls and pillars within the Minster, such as the Great West Window, known as 'The Heart of Yorkshire' owing to the shape of the stone carved into it, and the unique Five Sisters Window in the north transept, with five elegant columns of glass. You can take a tour of the Glass Conservation Studio, to view the medieval stained glass at close quarters and see the restoration methods used. Tours of the studio, which is housed in the Bedern Chapel close by, take place on Wednesday and Friday afternoons, leaving from the Group Desk in the Minster.

The **Central Tower** is open for visitors who can manage the 275 steps, giving an astonishingly grand gargoyle's-eye view of the city from 230 feet up.

By far the greatest architectural gem of the Minster is the oldest part, the **Chapterhouse roof**. Above the highly ornate ceiling of the octagonal Chapterhouse (which can be seen simply by walking around the Minster), its roof, an up-turned conical labyrinth of latticed timberwork, stands as high again as the chapterhouse does from floor to ceiling. Its weight is phenomenal, the structural strength of all the wood and lead suspended above the Chapterhouse ceiling mind-boggling. Howard

Mosley, head of the Visitors' Department at the Minster, describes the Chapterhouse roof as 'a giant IKEA kit', the marks still visible where the carpenters laid out and built the timber frame at ground level before piecing it together in situ. Howard explained that should the Minster ever catch fire again, firefighters are requested to save the Chapterhouse roof before any other part of the Minster. It's a shuddering thought to even contemplate, allowing the rest of the Minster to burn purely to save this one roof but when you see it for yourself, and the three enormous oak trees that stand suspended in the middle, one on top of the other (having been placed there goodness knows how in 1260 without the aid of modern lifting equipment!), you begin to understand the sentiment and the reasoning.

The Minster grounds

To best appreciate the acoustic qualities of York Minster, listen to one of the concerts held there occasionally or listen to the attractive peal of the bells on a Sunday morning, slowly dragging persistent slumbering souls into the awoken world. To concentrate on this musical campanology, head for the **Dean's Park**; it's a quiet (but for the bells) and restful green space overshadowed by the north face of the Minster.

Restoring York Minster

The walls of York Minster might have been built almost a thousand years ago, but this most celebrated of buildings could be likened to Trigger's broom, the prop that made an important appearance in the sitcom *Only Fools and Horses*. The unlikeliest of analogies, I know, but in a famous scene Trigger describes how his original road-sweeping broom has lasted for 20 years, adding that the broom has had 17 new heads and 14 new handles. York Minster is a little bit like that. So soft is the limestone used to build and decorate the Minster that every stone only lasts for approximately 150 years. Hence it's difficult to find much genuinely original stonework.

The stone restoration is a mammoth task so the Minster has its own stoneyard, housed on Deangate. Peer through the gates and you're likely to hear the sounds of giant circular blades slicing through stone like soft butter and when the whirring stops (remembering that the original masons didn't have such a useful tool to summon into action), there's the gentle tapping of the stone-carver's chisel and mallet.

The stoneyard is open to the public occasionally. If you're not in town when a tour is planned, accept that you'll get neck ache and take the time to admire the stonework on the Minster. Generations of stone-carvers have plied their trade and thousands of man-hours have gone into making the Minster look the way it does.

I chatted to Geoff Butler, Head Stone-Carver at the Minster Stoneyard, as he carved one tiny section that will sit on the East Front, the area of the Minster currently being restored. The piece of stone Geoff was working on was approximately 16 inches high and 8 inches wide, indicating just how laborious the restoration task is. Geoff was about to carve a crocket, a leaf-shaped decoration that's particular to Gothic architecture, on to a small, decorative pinnacle that had been marked out. He described the process: 'We receive large, sawn-cut blocks from the quarry. The masons put a template on the block and saw away some of the stone and then it comes in to me to carve. From the ground the crockets appear like knobs on pinnacles but when you get close to them (an opportunity afforded to those visitors who climb the steps to the Minster roof), they're quite intricate. We have to put the design back as it was because we're trying to maintain the original medieval pattern.'

It's when designing the decorative grotesques that the carvers can let their imagination run. Each one is entirely unique and doesn't always follow the designs of their stone-carving forefathers. Geoff explained: 'On the latest restoration area, the old grotesques are either missing or too eroded to tell what the designs were. I decided that we would make them into figures from the time of the medieval carvers that originally worked on the cathedral and then base them upon illnesses of the time. So we have figures that are suffering from the plague, toothache or backache.'

He pointed to a magnificent decorative figure hanging over the workbench being sick, the figure's smoothly carved, hunched back appearing to be desperate for some tender hand to relieve his suffering. Geoff continued, 'That one is the Black Prince, a character from the period when this section currently being restored was built. He represents dysentery as that is what he factually died from and we like to make the detail historically accurate on whatever we are carving.' Accurate indeed, the Black Prince's coat of arms was intricately carved on to his shield, the poor wretch clutching at his stomach with terrible cramps.

Geoff has worked as a stone-carver at the Minster's stoneyard for over 40 years and was awarded a British Empire Medal by the Crown for his services helping to mend the south transept of the Minster that was so badly ravaged by fire in 1984.

THE TREASURER'S HOUSE
Minster Yard ✆ 01904 624247; National Trust.

Behind the Minster is the 17th-century Treasurer's House, so called because it stands on the site of the medieval mansion used by the Treasurer of York Minster. Now owned by the National Trust, it was used by a bachelor, Frank Green, to house his collection of antique furniture in period settings. His portrait that hangs in the hall shows quite a friendly looking chap although his frequent notices to staff left around the house suggest a rather pedantic figure – his request for workmen to wear slippers in the house would not pass a health and safety assessment now! There's another chance for a view of the Minster from the drawing room but the Great Hall is really the attraction here, with a hidden minstrel's gallery complete with a small leaded-light window from which to glance at passing visitors below.

A CITY OF GATES
The word gate comes from the Scandinavian word *gata*, which actually means street, and many of York's roads are named this way, often describing the occupation of the original residents that would congregate in the same place – **Swinegate** was the old pig market, **Stonegate** was the thoroughfare to bring the stone from the River Ouse to the building site of the Minster, **Coppergate** residents made cups. Many of these gates are, perhaps rather obviously, in the very heart of York where the Viking residents lived. It's these most ancient of streets that provide the character of the city around the Minster, each one similar and yet dissimilar to others, the plethora of independent retailers, restaurants and bars a refreshing change from the cloned High Streets found in many towns today. From **Bootham Bar**, the city's northwest entrance, the narrow **High Petergate** runs up past the Minster's west front, crossing Stonegate to meet with **Low Petergate**.

Opposite the Minster, on the edge of High Petergate, sits a far smaller church named **St Michael-le-Belfrey**. Though in the shadow of the mighty Minster, it is significant to York history – indeed British history

GUY FAWKES IN YORK

Ironically, James VI of Scotland passed through York in 1603 on his way south to become King James I of England. He stayed at The King's Manor, in St Leonard's Place, yards from his potential murderer's place of birth and baptism. As he had a Catholic wife, it was hoped that James I would provide greater security and tolerance for Catholics than they had known since Henry VIII's abolition of Catholicism in England. It was not to be. Guy Fawkes had become a Catholic some years earlier while at St Peter's School, quarter of a mile from Bootham Bar, and was aware of the antagonistic feeling occurring among Catholics within the city before taking part in one of British history's most notorious events. And while many enjoy burning a Guy on top of a roaring fire each November to commemorate the event, it is a practice that, to this day, St Peter's School does not partake in, it being considered unsporting to burn the effigy of a former pupil!

– by being the church where a baby was baptised as Guy Fawkes. He was born yards away (a couple of buildings in High Petergate and Stonegate lay claim to being the birthplace) as a Protestant son of York; his father and grandparents are buried in the Minster.

Of all the streets in York, **Stonegate** is what I feel to be at the very heart of the city. With the River Ouse, the medieval **Guildhall** and the **Mansion House**, home to the Lord Mayor, behind you, Stonegate runs from **St Helen's Square** towards the Minster. It was originally the Via Praetoria that went to the main gates of the Roman fortress long before the Vikings renamed it. There are glimpses of the Minster from time to time, drawing you ever closer towards this giant beast of a building. But ponder a while along Stonegate; its charm lies within the York paving beneath your feet and the fact that no two buildings are the same. The rooflines, the building materials, the paint colours of the window frames and the decorative iron signs advertising small boutiques, tea shops and ancient inns are all different and all add something to the character of the street. It can get busy around Christmas but there's room for all, including the odd busker or two, their independent tunes turning into a cacophony of sound or a melodic harmony depending on their proximity to one another.

Midway along Stonegate, an unusual pub sign runs across the full width of the street, directing you to **Ye Olde Starre Inn**, hidden down a tiny alleyway. It's the oldest pub in York and reputedly has a posse of ghosts to alarm punters. **The Punchbowl**, also in Stonegate, claims to have a good bunch of ghostly goings-on too, but then, given the number of ghost tours and bump-in-the-night walks, hauntings are big business in York so it makes good financial sense to have a ghost or two running about to scare customers.

For a more serene experience, take a peek into Coffee Yard, a tiny alley off Stonegate, where the medieval **Barley Hall** stands. It was re-discovered in the 1980s, hidden behind the façade of a derelict office block being demolished, and has now been restored to the beautiful timber framed home of a 14th-century Lord Mayor. Community involvement is an element of the building's restoration: there's an oral history project still going on to involve anyone who has ever lived or worked in or around Stonegate.

YORK ART GALLERY
St Leonard's Pl • www.yorkartgallery.org.uk

This notable art collection was closed at time of writing for a much-needed major refurbishment that will increase the exhibition space by 60% – a very welcome development that will include a new Centre for British Studio Ceramics. It will reopen during 2015.

THE MUSEUM GARDENS
& THE YORKSHIRE MUSEUM
Shrouded with daffodils in spring and multi-coloured blooms in summer, the Museum Gardens just north of the River Ouse are still my favourite place to relax in York, finding a sun-strewn piece of Benedictine wall to prop oneself up against, the empty arches of the delicately carved windows towering above. The constant traffic crossing **Lendal Bridge** disappears as the birdsong whistling from the window ledges takes over, the occasional clanging of the Minster's bells ringing out the passing time.

The creamy wall – for there is only one full wall left standing – of St Mary's Abbey, blackened by centuries of decay, belonged once to the largest Benedictine monastery in the north of England. Founded in 1055, it became one of the casualties of Henry VIII's Dissolution. Other parts of the Abbey remain scattered around the gardens like discarded rubble, the stumpy foundation stones of once-magnificent pillars appearing to grow from the grass; they are now the back-scratchers for idle bookworms and lunchtime gatherers escaping the bustle of the city streets and offices.

Behind the abbey, just outside a redundant part of the city walls, is **St Olave's Church** in Marygate. Built in 1055, the parish church is the oldest monument dedicated to the patron saint of Norway, King Olaf, who had died in combat 30 years earlier. The church became the foundation for the Benedictine community that built St Mary's Abbey. In a quiet back street, bordered by the Museum Gardens and close to the river, it is a very peaceful and a quite beautiful sanctuary, well away from the hubbub. The six bells are rung every Sunday morning at service in full view of the congregation and visitors are welcome to witness the bell-ringing practice, held every Wednesday evening (19.00–21.00).

Elsewhere in the Gardens, the **Yorkshire Museum** has an extensive collection of antiquities from the city and around, including the famous Middleham Jewel, unearthed by metal detectorist Ted Seaton in 1985; the exquisite 15th-century diamond-shaped gold pendant inlaid with a single sapphire and engraved with a Latin charm against epilepsy was bought for the tidy sum of £2.5million. The museum was recently renovated with the new displays focusing on the city's Roman heritage.

THE RIVER OUSE

Below the Museum Gardens is the **River Ouse**, whose usually mild-mannered waters entertain visitors on river cruises or dawn-breaking university rowers most days. Sometimes, when the weather has been cruel in the distant Dales forcing the water ever higher, the river forgets its manners, turning into a savage torrent that bullies its way into the front rooms of neighbouring houses and upturning bar stools in the ever-patient **Kings Arms**. Every time it happens, the landlord marks the flood's height on the wall.

When it's not deep under water, the Kings Arms is a great place from which to view aspects of the **Jorvik Viking Festival** (⁀ www. yorkfestivals.com), an event every February where longboats sail down the river in homage to the time when Viking raiders used to head out to the North Sea to trade around the world. Other events take place around the city including battle re-enactments and saga-telling.

A river cruise provides yet another perspective on York. It is one of the best ways from which to view the medieval Guildhall that backs on to the Ouse close to Lendal Bridge. **YorkBoat** (✆ 01904 628324 ⁀ www.yorkboat.co.uk) plies the river in a variety of red-and-white cruisers, departing either from Lendal Bridge, close to the Museum

THE YORK MYSTERY PLAYS

I had a crush on God – or the performer who played him, at least, in York's famous Mystery Plays, when I got involved with a production some 20 years ago. Earlier, these plays launched the professional career of a young Dame Judi Dench. A daughter of York her first theatrical outings, both facing the stage and on it, were in the city. She performed as the Virgin Mary in the 1957 production of the York Mystery Plays, one of the first revivals since the original pageants were banned in 1568, courtesy of religious in-fighting under Elizabeth I.

Originating in the 14th century, the York Mystery Cycle was a collection of community plays put on by the various guilds in the town, each one responsible for a particular Christian story, from the Creation to the Last Judgement. Held around the festival of Corpus Christi (late-May to mid-June), they were a way of educating the largely illiterate townsfolk while providing eagerly anticipated entertainment. Each play was performed on pageant wagons that processed around the city streets, a spectacle that lasted from sunrise to well beyond the midsummer sunset.

The mobile pageantry disappeared for the 1950s revival; the plays were performed instead on a fixed stage in the Museum Gardens until the 1990s. Though not conforming to the original idea of mobile performances, it was a spectacular setting and one that I remember well, having become involved with a production like so many other residents before and after, performing alongside university students and schoolchildren.

The York Mystery Plays continue to be performed regularly with 2014 seeing the next one. The cycle is currently every two years but this may change so check with Visit York nearer the time. But the plays have been returned to their rightful place – on the city streets. The community is still involved: the modern Guilds of York are once again in charge of the productions and pageant wagons as they were in medieval times.

Gardens, or Kings Staith, just outside the Kings Arms. The York City Cruise, with on-board commentary, gives a good introduction to York from the river. YorkBoat run lunch and dinner cruises too if you wish to combine a meal with a river cruise but one of the most atmospheric of trips is to take the Floodlit Evening Cruise to Bishopthorpe Palace, when the lights of York play games on the water and buildings such as the Guildhall take on another dimension.

You don't need to be afloat to use the river as an exploration tool though. Both riverbanks act as **footpaths** and/or **cyclepaths** up and downstream, right out of the city. If your way is blocked on one bank, just cross one of the many bridges and continue on your way. York's other river, the Foss, allows you to do the same for five miles north to the village of Strensall.

If you are walking along the Ouse and heading upstream towards Clifton Ings and beyond, keep your eyes peeled because you may be lucky enough to see one of Britain's rarest animals. The tansy beetle is found on riverside vegetation here and nowhere else in the country. Look out for these iridescent bronze and green insects feeding on tansy leaves in summer.

MERCANTILE YORK: TRADE, DEBT & INDUSTRY

Not surprisingly much of the historical trading area of York grew up between the two rivers, the River Foss flowing into the River Ouse a little southeast of Skeldergate Bridge. Viking traders brought goods in

THE SALMON OF YORK

Mike Bagshaw

If asked to name an English salmon river, very few people would suggest the River Ouse, which slides its way through York. But it's not a typically polluted city river, fed as it is by the clear Dales rivers of Swale, Ure and Nidd.

Bob Drake was a lad in the 1940s, struggling to live on wartime rations in York. 'We'd look forward to late autumn nights, just after a high tide, because that's when the salmon would run. A net across the river, hidden under the railway bridge at Poppleton for a few hours, would always land a few fish, five or ten – enough for our family and a few friends. I know it was poaching, but the river was teeming in those days, and they were desperate times.'

What makes this abundance all the more remarkable is that these are the fish that got past the commercial netters way downstream below York, at Naburn and Cawood, the limit of the tide, and they took nine tons of salmon every year – that's a lot of fish. Fast forward to the 1970s. The Dales rivers that feed the Ouse were still as clear and clean as ever, pike, perch, roach and bream still swam under the city's bridges, and trout in its tributaries, but the King of Fish was gone, not one salmon to be seen. What went wrong? The answer lay in the fatal combination of the fish's incredible life-cycle, and what was going on in 1950s West and South Yorkshire.

Atlantic Salmon (*Salmo salar*) are famously born in fresh water, migrate to the sea to feast and put on weight, returning a few years later to their home river to mate, spawn and produce the next generation of fish. What complicates the situation in and out of the city via the River Ouse, which flows into the North Sea. Many of the Viking artefacts associated with trading have been found in the **Coppergate** area just east of the riverbank while medieval merchants, with a rapidly increasing wealth, chose to position their headquarters, the **Merchant Adventurers' Hall**, in a prominent position next to the River Foss, with water-level storage rooms for goods to be brought in and out.

By contrast to these wealthy merchants' quarters, **York Castle**, built by William the Conqueror as a defence post, became the debtors' prison in the 1800s followed by the felons' prison in the 1900s. The whole area was, and still is, synonymous with law and justice – the Crown Court is still found opposite **York Castle Museum**, where the various prisons were until their closure in 1934. One of York's most infamous 'traders', if he can be called that for his 'trade' was somewhat one-sided, was Dick Turpin, or John Palmer as he liked to call himself in Yorkshire to escape his crimes further south.

Yorkshire, and which almost resulted in the salmon's extinction here, is the dominance of the Humber estuary. All of Yorkshire's major rivers join forces as the Ouse, and flow into the sea together in the Humber. The salmon could not survive the level of pollution in the water in the rivers Don and Aire which entered here from industrial Sheffield and Leeds, and either died as young fish on their way out to sea, or as adults on their way back.

If the salmon's story had ended there it would have been a tragedy, but in the past ten years or so rumours of a possible comeback have been confirmed; some are now making it back up the Humber and returning to their old haunts. 'This is a completely natural recolonisation,' explained John Shannon of the Environment Agency. 'We've not done any stocking of the Dales rivers at all. What we have worked hard at is

habitat restoration, and in particular water quality lower down, and the fish have done the rest themselves.'

The future looks good for Yorkshire salmon, and consequently all the other living parts of the river ecosystem, especially the fish-eaters. Not many people see them, because they're very shy and nocturnal, but otters are back in York as well – possibly because gourmet fish are back on the menu.

If you want to stand a good chance of seeing a Dales salmon, you need to be in the right place at the right time. They tend to run upstream in late autumn, November is the peak time, and when the rivers are full and fast. Weirs and small falls, where the salmon have to leap out of the water, are the best places. Try watching from the weir and fish-pass at Naburn near York or Westwick weir at Ripon.

YORK CASTLE MUSEUM

Eye of York ✆ 01904 687687 ✆ www.yorkcastlemuseum.org.uk.

York Castle Museum was one of my favourite places to visit as a child, the old sweet shop selling sugar mice along the cobbled Victorian street being a truly memorable experience. It's brought the social history up to date since then, with room scenes depicting many different eras to the present day but Kirkgate, the Victorian street, stands out for many visitors. Next door are the very cells that locked up Dick Turpin and other notorious criminals as well as those who got into severe financial debt, a lockable offence in the 1800s.

CLIFFORD'S TOWER

Tower St ✆ 01904 646940; English Heritage.

Originating from the castle built by William the Conqueror in 1070, Clifford's Tower remains a symbol of the Normans' triumphant defeat over the Vikings, although one of York's darkest hours was here one March night in 1190 when the city's Jewish community took shelter from a murderous mob, but many took their own lives or were taken and massacred. The tower sits in a perfect defensive position, snugly between the rivers Ouse and Foss. Despite the magnificent display of daffodils in spring helping you to forget your calf-pulling ascent, the mound is no easier to climb now than it was in 1070, with the exception of a moat to cross and the arrow slits in the circular tower thankfully remaining redundant for anything other than a pigeon's resting place.

DICK TURPIN

Originating from Essex where he was known for a string of offences, including petty crime, robbery and murder, Dick Turpin made a swift exit from the southeast of England with the law hot on his heels. The rogue made his way to Yorkshire where he became involved in horse-trading, or rather horse-stealing before selling the beasts back to their rightful owners. He changed his name to avoid capture but his plan fell apart when he was caught and thrown in to gaol, housed in the old York Castle. Tried in court, he was sentenced to death and taken to the gallows on the Knavesmire to the south of York, rather ironically where the racecourse is today. His hanging has made its way into legend, with the prisoner cavorting with his executioner and the crowd before jumping to his death. His grave is in the churchyard of St George's, just next to the County Court and close to where he was imprisoned.

There are some great views of the city from the top, but that's about all there is now, the tower open to the elements following an unfortunate incident that blew the roof off in the 17th century when gunpowder was stored there.

FAIRFAX HOUSE

Castlegate ✆ 01904 65554 🖰 www.fairfaxhouse.co.uk.

To the north of Clifford's Tower, in Castlegate, Fairfax House is considered to be one of the finest examples of an 18th-century townhouse in Britain. Its façade is imposing in a very classical, ordered way, the symmetry just so, the Georgian windows perfectly aligned. You can imagine how this would have been the talk of the town among society, the windows filled with light and chatter during social evenings and carriages arriving to chauffeur away young ladies and gents.

Inside, the rooms have been restored perfectly to the fashion of the day with brightly painted walls and elegant furnishings, including the Noel Terry collection of 17th- and 18th-century clocks, and cabinets full of secret compartments that, in their day, must have held the hidden secrets and affairs of many a society scandal.

FRIENDS' MEETING HOUSE

On the corner of Castlegate and tiny Friargate is the Friends' Meeting House, the main place of worship in York for the Society of Friends, otherwise known as Quakers. It's a very plain, simple building and deliberately so, owing to the beliefs of the practising Friends. There are no amazing stained glass windows, no elaborate choir screens or decorative stonework but the result is a very restful building where the sun bounces off the cream coloured walls and fills the building with light.

JORVIK VIKING CENTRE

Coppergate Shopping Centre ✆ 01904 615505 🖰 www.jorvik-viking-centre.co.uk.

Between 1979 and 1981, the Coppergate area of town was scoured for clues in one of the largest archaeological digs ever in Britain, revealing a complex of 10th-century Viking buildings and some 40,000 finds. The result was the creation of the Jorvik Viking Centre, one of York's most visited attractions, beneath the 1980s shopping centre erected on the site. Not always obvious to the thousands of queuing visitors

QUAKERS AND CHOCOLATE

The Quakers have a long tradition in York that goes back way before the Rowntree family, but it is the Rowntrees who put Quakerism, or Quaker values, on the map in the city. Although perhaps more renowned for Kit Kat and Smarties, they played a vital philanthropic role within the city that included creating a garden village for their factory workers in New Earswick and providing land for the two Quaker schools in the city – the Mount School for girls and Bootham School (where Joseph Rowntree, the founder of the chocolate factory, went to school). They also created Rowntree Park on the south bank of the River Ouse in memory of those who lost their lives during World War I. A Rowntree Walk through the city has been created, highlighting places relating to the Rowntree family, including the building where the cocoa business began before it moved to the current Haxby Road site (now owned by Nestlé) and the Friends' Meeting House in Friargate. It provides a break from the Roman and Viking history that abounds in the city and gives you the chance to look at a completely different side to York from the more recent past.

A trail leaflet is available from the York Visitor Information Centre in Museum Street or you can download a copy from the Rowntree Society website: www.rowntreesociety.org.uk.

about to descend to this phenomenally successful display (pre-book to avoid the wait) is that they are going to see the genuine Viking archaeology of York in its original position, The site includes timbers preserved in the wet ground, which are only now underground because over them lie the deep deposits created by medieval and later rebuildings of the city. Reconstructions, sound tracks and even authentic aromas from fish markets and cesspits, all highly innovative when the Jorvik first opened in 1984, bring the scenes to life. If you are resistant to the idea of the ride which you have to take to see it, bear in mind that this is proper archaeology, meticulously researched and far from just a theme park: the electric 'cars' were the only feasible way to move large numbers of visitors safely around such a compact and fragile site.

Jorvik continues to bring in funds to support the work of the York Archaeological Trust, such as the activities at **DIG** (✆ 01904 615505 www.digyork.com), housed in St Saviour's Church, Saviourgate, where archaeologists explain what they do and children especially enjoy digging in specially prepared pits of clean 'earth' (actually recycled rubber crumbs) for genuine York artefacts.

THE SHAMBLES

I've always loved the sound of the street named The Shambles, York's finest medieval street. Despite the name referring to the butchers' shops that once lined the street, it so aptly depicts the topsy-turvy nature of the top-heavy houses that lean precariously towards one another on either side of the narrow lane. Each house seems close enough that you could quite easily shake hands with neighbours on the opposite side of the street by merely opening a top floor window.

The Shambles derives its charm from its lack of architectural uniformity, a mixture of brick, timber and rendered buildings. The butchers have long gone, the bow-fronted windows of the tiny shops taken up with a succession of tourist paraphernalia. However, of a more sobering thought that might curtail the spending is the shrine to Margaret Clitherow, halfway along the street. She was the wife of a butcher who harboured Catholic priests at a time when it was not the done thing to do. She was found out and her punishment was to be crushed to death.

ALL SAINTS, GOODRAMGATE

Well worth a peep, though it takes a bit of seeking out. This is the loveliest, most atmospheric of York's city churches, with a notable set of box pews and wonderful 15th-century glass. The Grade 1 building is 13th to 15th century, with very little changed since the 1700s. A board records former lord mayors, among them George Hudson, the 'Railway King'. It's all a world away from the busy shopping streets outside.

THE MERCHANT ADVENTURERS' HALL

Fossgate ☎ 01904 654818 ⬦ www.theyorkcompany.co.uk.

It's the ability to lure passing trade, as shown in The Shambles today, that turned York citizens into wealthy merchants 650 years or so ago. These medieval traders built their communal building, the Merchant Adventurers' Hall, to be able to meet socially and transact their business affairs. It's a fantastic building with timbers the size of tree trunks and a totally uneven floor that slides into the centre of the room. From the outside, the hall sits restfully in its own peaceful garden by the River Foss, though this has caused flooding problems in the past as can be seen from the watermarks in the Undercroft, the flood heights steadily rising since they were first recorded in 1831. The coats of arms of 22 of the medieval guilds hang in the Undercroft too, and the accompanying exhibition puts into perspective just how powerful and important they were. The building, including the guild chapel, is still used for regular events both by the current members and by outside organisations, which helps to ensure that it remains a living and breathing part of York.

THE QUILT MUSEUM & GALLERY

Sandwiched between St Saviourgate and Hungate is **The Stonebow** leading to **Peasholme Green**, where one of York's newest museums, the **Quilt Museum and Gallery** (✆ 01904 613242 ᗪ www.quiltmuseum. org.uk), is housed in St Anthony's Hall, on the corner with Aldwark. This half-stone, half-brick building, built in the 15th century, was once a medieval guildhall too so it is apt that it is now home to the Quilters' Guild of the British Isles. The structure is worth visiting to see the Great Hall alone, its timber roof juxtaposed nicely against the giant quilts and textiles that hang from the walls. But, like the Merchant Adventurers' Hall, this too is a living building and visitors can take part in events organised by the Quilters' Guild, with craft workshops, gallery demonstrations, talks and activities on the programme. The hall also houses the guild library with a collection of 3,000 quilting books and a shop selling quilting and craft equipment too. Outside, the recently created York Conservation Trust garden, partly surrounded by the city walls, is open to the public and provides a lovely area to sit.

"Its timber roof is juxtaposed nicely against the giant quilts and textiles that hang from the walls."

ACROSS THE OUSE

Wander along The Stonebow past the hideous concrete monstrosity known as The Stonebow Building, and you come to the market square bordered by Pavement and Parliament Street. It's where all the major banks congregate if you're short on ready cash, but it's also where regular food markets take place and any other festivities that can happen in a temporary marquee; it's the home for many of the events during the annual York Food Festival (ᗪ www.yorkfoodfestival.com).

Continue along High Ousegate and you'll cross over **Ouse Bridge**, the oldest of the bridges in York, to Micklegate.

MICKLEGATE

I find Micklegate one of the nicest – and longest – streets in York. The first few hundred yards, closest to the bridge, are a bit messy, with shops that seem to frequently change hands and the Park Inn Hotel, another of York's buildings that might not be classed as the city planning department's finest hour.

As you begin to climb the steady slope past this small area in desperate need of a facelift and crossing George Hudson Street, Micklegate becomes a quiet gem. There are no distinguishing tourist attractions along the street, making it appear blissfully uncrowded, but it has some striking Georgian townhouses, built by the wealthy merchants who found the street to be a good trading route when it was the main road into the city centre. Among a clutch of good independent shops is **Ken Spelman** (70 Micklegate ✆ 01904 624414 ✆ www.kenspelman.com), a secondhand bookshop that has been there for eternity. It doesn't matter what books are placed in the window display, there is always something that will catch your eye.

On the opposite side of the street to the shops is **Holy Trinity Church**, a conventionally built stone church, set back from the street line, in its own peaceful grassy graveyard. It's all that remains from a once powerful Benedictine monastery destroyed by Henry VIII. However, the monastery would have been there when previous members of the royal family found their heads being strewn along the top of **Micklegate Bar**, following the Battle of Wakefield during the Wars of the Roses. Micklegate Bar was *the* place for several centuries upon which to find the head of a losing army, traitor or dignitary, royal or not.

THE BAR CONVENT

Blossom St ✆ 01904 643238 ✆ www.bar-convent.org.uk.

In a Georgian building on the busy corner of Blossom Street and Nunnery Lane, just beyond Micklegate Bar, the Bar Convent is the oldest living convent in England. It was founded in 1686 at a time when persecution of Catholics was rife and has been a major part of the York community ever since. Originally set up as a school for girls, the convent and the founding order has a fascinating history with links to Guy Fawkes and the gunpowder plot.

The convent still has a sense here and there of school-ness inside with long corridors covered in ageing linoleum, but the architectural secret is a covered chapel, designed by a York architect in the mid 18th century to be completely hidden from view. And indeed it is – you would never know it was there from the street. The **chapel**, which is open to visitors and still in regular use, has a beautiful gilt-decorated dome that is completely concealed by a pitched roof from the outside. The chapel also has eight exits and a priest hole – necessary security measures at the time it was built.

The convent is a great place to visit to get away from the bustle of the city centre. The plant-filled **Winter Garden**, the entrance hall to the convent, has a striking glass roof and mosaic-tiled floor. It's a quiet place for a cup of tea, as is the peaceful back garden that's tended by the few remaining sisters. For here you can sit with your lunch and not notice a sound coming from the busy roads that surround the building. Jo Dodds, who works at the Bar Convent, commented on how restful a place it is. 'You don't have to be religious to come here and get something out of the place,' she says. 'It's a place to sit quietly and be able to relax; it has a very soothing environment.'

THE NATIONAL RAILWAY MUSEUM & YORK STATION

Leeman Rd ✆ 08448 153139 ⌂ www.nrm.org.uk.

York has one of the most famous railway stations in the world – with a walkway through to the free-to-view National Railway Museum, complete with one of the world's most iconic trains, the Flying Scotsman. Even if you are not a train enthusiast, something here will make you catch your breath, whether it's the sheer scale of the great steam engines, appearing all the larger if you see them from the ground rather than from platform height, or the charmingly changing period detail of the Royal Carriages from different eras. The Warehouse, an open store for some three-quarters of a million smaller railway objects such as sign boards, benches, buckets and china, is big enough to lose yourself in – it's like being surrounded with props from *Brief Encounter*.

"With its Victorian arched, glass and iron canopy, the main railway station is also evocative of tearful goodbyes on a black-and-white film set."

With its Victorian arched, glass and iron canopy, the **main railway station** is also evocative of tearful goodbyes on a black-and-white film

UPDATES WEBSITE

You can post your comments and recommendations, and read the latest feedback and updates from other readers online at 🖰 www.bradtupdates.com/northyorkmoors.

set, and is worth a visit even if you are not arriving or departing by train. Short of being underneath the glass roof, the best place to view the station is from the city walls opposite.

On the opposite side of the city walls from the railway station, underneath the arch through which Station Road disappears, is the **former headquarters of the North Eastern Railway Company**. Built in 1906 as a grand status symbol to signify the company's importance, it simply bristles with chimneys and fancy gable ends. The building now has a new use as Cedar Court Grand, York's first five-star hotel and spa.

•

ACCOMMODATION

This recommended accommodation list is by no means exhaustive, as there are of course a huge range of places to stay in the region. Those featured are my personal choice, with no payment having been made by the businesses concerned. I have tried to suit a range of different pockets, from basic camping to outrageous luxury; and styles – some B&B, some self catering, some for larger groups. All however, I feel are 'special' in some way, historically, architecturally or perhaps with a particular 'Slow' take on things.

The hotels, B&Bs and self-catering options featured in this section are indicated by ♠ under the heading for the town or village in which they are located. Campsites are indicated by ⚠. Where a recommended pub listed within a chapter offers accommodation, I have mentioned it in the listing.

1 CLEVELAND & HAMBLETON
Hotel
Black Swan Hotel Helmsley YO62 5BJ ✆ 01439 770466 🖥 www.blackswan-helmsley. co.uk. Three historic houses on the marketplace amalgamated into one high-class hotel. Everything about this place screams sumptuous luxury, from the tea room and select restaurant to displays of antiques and contemporary art about the place, but you pay for it. B&B is available mid-week only (you have to have dinner as well at weekends). Surprisingly for a bustling town centre hotel there is a serene walled garden around the back – the only place in Helmsley to eat outside on warm days. Dogs are allowed in some rooms.

B&B
Laskill Country House Near Hawnby YO62 5NB ✆ 01439 798265 🖥 www. laskillcountryhouse.co.uk. The tiny hamlet of Laskill in Bilsdale is almost entirely a family run holiday village. Mandy is responsible for the house with its sumptuous B&B facilities (one four-poster and two other doubles) and her mum Sue runs The Grange next door with more B&B and seven self-catering cottages sleeping two, four or six people. You could have a quiet,

get-away-from-it-all stay with excellent walks from the door, the ancient Quaker meeting house over the road and fly-fishing on the nearby River Seph; alternatively you could do what I did and take over most of the accommodation for a family event – my wedding, as it happens. Prices are reasonable and dogs are welcome.

Self-catering
Shepherd's Rest Low Easby TS9 6JQ ☎ 01642 711676 🖱 www.shepherdsrestgreatayton.co.uk. A self-catering cottage for four (two en-suite double/twin rooms) in the tiny hamlet of Low Easby near Great Ayton, with excellent hill and woodland walking on the doorstep. The building is a converted 18th-century barn powered sustainably with a ground source heat pump and wood-burning stove. Inside, the cottage is light and airy with a rustic, agricultural feel to the décor. The owners live in the old farmhouse next door. No dogs.

2 ESKDALE
Hotel
La Rosa Hotel East Terrace, Whitby YO21 3HB ☎ 01947 606981 🖱 www.larosa.co.uk. This classic early Victorian hotel once frequented by Lewis Carroll has been given the 'La Rosa' treatment and is furnished almost entirely with curios and antique finds from auctions, flea markets and car boot sales. All eight double rooms are themed, with Stoker for instance full of Dracula memorabilia and Arabesque like a sultan's boudoir. The attic is a self-contained flat for six people called the Crow's Nest and featuring three double bedrooms and a dressing-up box.

B&B
Bank House Farm Glaisdale YO21 2QA ☎ 01947 897297 🖱 www.bankhousefarmhostel.co.uk. Bank House Farm is such a welcoming corner of the beautiful valley of Glaisdale that it's a given you would want to stay here. The only choice is whether to go for the cosy comfort of B&B in the farmhouse (one night only, ideal for bikers or walkers passing through) where Chris and Emma Padmore will look after you personally, or the more independent options of the bunkhouse or campsite. The farm is also a supplier of organic meat (see page 51) so not only will you eat well while you are there but can take quality food away with you. Dog-friendly throughout.

Self-catering
The Boathouse Whitby harbour YO22 4BH ☎ 01947 893201 🖱 www.welovewhitby.com. You could hardly get more central to town than this as The Boathouse is actually 'afloat' in the harbour (by the lifeboat pier) and accessible only by walking along a gangplank straight into the living room. This room also has a dining area that could seat six, a task that would

involve four guests as the building only sleeps two. The one bedroom, with a double bed and en-suite bathroom, is upstairs. The seaward side of the building is surprisingly private and has a sizeable decked area, ideal for watching boats coming and going. A fully fitted kitchen lies below deck.

Campsites

La Rosa Campsite Murkside YO22 5AS ✆ 01947 606981 ◌ www.larosa.co.uk. A wooded hillside between Egton Bridge and Goathland is the location of this truly amazing place, so well hidden that for years I passed it every week without knowing of its existence (a small sign displaying a red rose marks the access track). Describing La Rosa is almost as difficult as finding the place; it is 'sort of' camping and 'sort of' caravanning but in a hotchpotch of themed sheds, vehicles, vans and tents that the creators describe as 'a fantasy-land full of nostalgia, romance and all things kitsch, camp and bohemian.' Low environmental impact is a premium so lighting is candles, heating is from woodburners and the toilets are compost-loos. No dogs. If this all sounds a little too rustic, the nearby Swallow Barn has proper stone walls, electricity and a double bed.

Priory Farm Campsite Grosmont YO22 5QG ✆ 01947 895324 ◌ www.prioryfarmwhitby. wordpress.com. For some folks, myself included, the attraction of camping is all to do with location; extra facilities are a luxurious irrelevance, sometimes even detracting from the experience. Priory Farm is just a field for tents only with toilets and a washing-up point. Its position however, on a bank of the River Esk near its confluence with the Murk Esk, is idyllic and a convenient short walk from the trains, pubs, cafés and shops of Grosmont village.

Runswick Bay Caravan and Camping Park Hinderwell Lane, Runswick Bay TS13 5HR ✆ 01947 840997 ◌ www.runswickbaycaravanandcampingpark.co.uk. Despite its size (32 pitches and separate tent field) this is a sheltered and secluded site, hidden from the road but only three minutes-walk from the beach. Lots of trees add to the sense of privacy, and pitches are flat and well-drained. Prices are very reasonable and dogs on leads are welcome.

3 EASTERN MOORS
B&B

Troutsdale Lodge Near Hackness YO13 0BS ✆ 01723 882209 ◌ www.troutsdalelodge. co.uk. Troutsdale is a wonderful secret valley that many people in nearby Scarborough have never even heard of, and this charming timber-framed building sits on a hillside overlooking the heart of the dale. Originally built in the early 1900s as a shooting lodge it is now a private house, still with a distinctly Edwardian feel, which the owners offer as B&B accommodation in five comfortable rooms. Its location, tucked between the huge forests of Dalby and Wykeham, is magnificent but very isolated (nearest village four miles away). Prices are very reasonable, evening meals are available and dogs are welcome.

Self-catering

Boggle Hole YHA Robin Hood's Bay YO22 4UQ ✆ 0845 371 9504 🖥 www.yha.org.uk. This unusual building is not in Robin Hood's Bay village but on Robin Hood's Bay itself, Boggle Hole being an old smugglers access point to the beach. The building is a big ex-watermill tucked into the steep valley of Mill Beck just before it flows into the sea. It boasts 85 beds, a café, bar and meeting room but by far its best attributes are proximity to the beach, wild cliff coastline and its isolation. Boggle Hole is only accessible on foot, either from a car park a quarter of a mile up the hill or Robin Hood's Bay half a mile along the beach (when the tide is out!). As this is a youth hostel, the rooms are basic and not en suite but they are very cheap and there are lots of smaller twin and family rooms. Ask for a quiet one if there's a school party in.

Oscar Cloughton Station, YO13 OAD ✆ 01723 870896 🖥 www.cloughtonstation.co.uk. Oscar isn't the only place you can stay at Cloughton's old railway station but he is certainly the most unusual. He is a MK1 railway carriage built in Derby in 1962 and moved here in 2004 to be converted into a self-catering cottage for six people (one en-suite double, one twin and one bunk room). Other options on-site are another six person self-catering venue, this time in the Old Goods Shed and B&B in the station itself. No dogs.

The Pigsty Fylingthorpe YO22 4TH ✆ 01628 825925 🖥 www.landmarktrust.org.uk. What a great thing to be able to say ... the place I stayed in on holiday was an absolute pigsty! But that really is what this building was. Squire Barry of nearby Fyling Hall visited the Mediterranean in the 1880s and was very taken by the Classical architecture he saw there. On his return he decided to build his new pigsty in the same style, columns and all. The Landmark Trust has converted it into a self-catering cottage for two with one double room at its usual not-so-affordable price. No dogs.

Worfolk Cottage Staintondale YO13 OEL ✆ 01482 872403. 🖥 www.worfolkcottage. co.uk. Back in the early 18th century a Staintondale Quaker by the name of William Worfolk bequeathed money in his will towards the building of a meeting house locally, so one was constructed with this cottage adjoining. The meeting house is long gone but the cottage still belongs to the Society of Friends and they have renovated it with a respect for the environment informed by their religious beliefs. Worfolk Cottage is officially carbon-neutral due to a combination of ground source heat pump, wind turbine, solar panels and top class insulation. It is now offered as self-catering accommodation for up to 14 people in five bedrooms and at a very reasonable rate.

4 HOWARDIAN HILLS & RYEDALE
Self-catering

Cold Harbour Shed Hovingham YO62 4NF ✆ 01924 502256 🖥 www.theshedcoldharbour. co.uk. Never was a place more unfairly named. Cold Harbour is an old-fashioned term meaning 'comfortless shelter for wayfarers' and this cosy little self-catering barn conversion is certainly not that. With one en-suite double bedroom, kitchen and living room it sleeps just two people but there is no shortage of space, especially outside in the garden and orchard. What makes staying here a particularly special experience are the little thoughtful extras like complimentary wine on arrival, real coffee- and tea-making basics provided, bikes to borrow and fruit and herbs to pick from the garden. All this and reasonable rates – a welcoming shelter for wayfarers after all (except dogs).

Yew Tree Cottage Westow YO60 7NE ℅ 02032 874884 ⌂ www.yewtreecottagewestow. co.uk. You are in for a surprise when you step inside Yew Tree Cottage. From the outside it seems much the same as the other quaint stone cottages on Main Street, but the inside is a statement of contemporary country chic designed by London owners Natasha and Paul. Other nice little touches to make the stay more pleasant are a welcome hamper of bread, butter, milk, eggs and bacon on arrival, and a complimentary bottle of wine. A fine village pub two doors down is also a bit of a bonus. The cottage has two main double bedrooms and a sofa-bed in the third. Prices are quite steep for four people but better if you use the sofa bed and sleep five or six. No dogs.

Campsite
Jollydays Luxury Camping Village Farm, Scraylingham YO41 1JD ℅ 01759 371776 ⌂ www.jollydaysluxurycamping.co.uk. What the Van Outersterp family set up here in 15 acres of woodland in 2008 is camping but probably not as you've ever known it – more like staying in a hotel in the woods except that your walls are made of canvas and you hear owls in the night, not cars. Jollydays have 22 tents ranging in size and opulence from basic bell tents (sleeping four on two sofa-beds with a small stove and heater), to top of the range luxury tents (six-berth, ensuite with four-poster beds!). It's not cheap to stay here, but there is the option of paying in kind with 20 hours' work in the woods, collecting firewood, planting seedlings and such-like, earning a week's free stay in a bell tent. No dogs.

5 WOLDS
B&Bs
Manor Farm Thixendale YO17 9TG ℅ 01377 288315 ⌂ www.manorfarmthixendale.co.uk. A Victorian edifice that was once part of the Sledmere Estate, this is still a working farm run by Charles and Gilda Brader. They grow a variety of arable crops and keep sheep, highland cattle, geese and chickens. Gilda also breeds thoroughbred horses and designs gardens. Somehow they also manage to find time to run a fine B&B service in the farmhouse. Up to four guests can stay in a private self-contained flat comprising two bedrooms (double and twin), a shared bathroom and a sitting room. Only one booking is taken at any time. No dogs.

Wold Cottage Wold Newton YO25 3HL ℅ 01262 470696 ⌂ www.woldcottage.co.uk. Katrina and Derek Gray offer a variety of good accommodation choices at Wold Cottage.

B&B in one of the six en-suite bedrooms would be my choice. Katrina is a bit of a wiz in the kitchen and has won awards for her breakfasts. Prices are a little higher than average. Self-catering is possible too, in one of two converted farm buildings that both sleep four to six. One of the farm's fields is available for touring caravans and tents.

The Wolds Retreat Kilnwick Percy YO42 1UF ✆ 01759 305968 ⌂ www.thewoldsretreat. co.uk. This is a separate building within the grounds of Kilnwick Percy Hall which offers B&B (two doubles ensuite, one twin ensuite and two singles). Prices are reasonable but there is a two night minimum stay. If you wish to stay only one night the alternative is a more basic room in the hall itself which doubles as the Madhyamaka Kadampa Meditation Centre. This Buddhist organisation owns the whole estate so wherever you stay you will benefit from the relaxing sense of peace and tranquility that seems to pervade everywhere.

Self-catering

Skipwith Station North Duffield YO8 5DE ✆ 01757 282288 ⌂ www.skipwithstation.com. Skipwith Station lies outside the boundaries of this book but it is handy for the Pocklington Canal and the city of York and certainly qualifies as a special place to stay. Or should I say special places to stay as there is more than one choice on offer. In memory of the Derwent Valley Railway that ran through here until 1985, owners Lizanne and David Southworth have converted three old railway carriages and a loading and storage bay into self-catering accommodation sleeping from two to six, some of which are dog friendly.

6 YORK

Hotel

Middlethorpe Hall Hotel Bishopthorpe Rd, YO23 2GB ✆ 01904 641241 ⌂ www. middlethorpe.com. The National Trust owns three historic hotels and this is one of them, restored and opened in 1984. It's not just a perfect William and Mary country house but a high quality hotel as well. There are 29 bedrooms, ten in the house and 19 in the courtyard. Twenty acres of garden and parkland have also been restored. You might expect to pay through the nose for this historic opulence and you would be right, but this is a special place.

Self-catering

The Nottingham Trader Ferry Lane, Bishopthorpe YO23 2SB ✆ 01904 705824 ⌂ www. yorkmarine.co.uk. The *Nottingham Trader* was an 85-foot working barge on the River Trent but now in her retirement she has become a houseboat permanently moored on a bank of the River Ouse. The interior has been converted into a comfortable living space for seven people (two doubles and one with bunks and a single) and two dogs. The houseboat is available to hire for weeks or half-weeks and although it's not cheap, the price does include use of a small motor boat for chugging into the centre of York or just messing about on the river.

INDEX

Page numbers in **bold** refer to main entries.